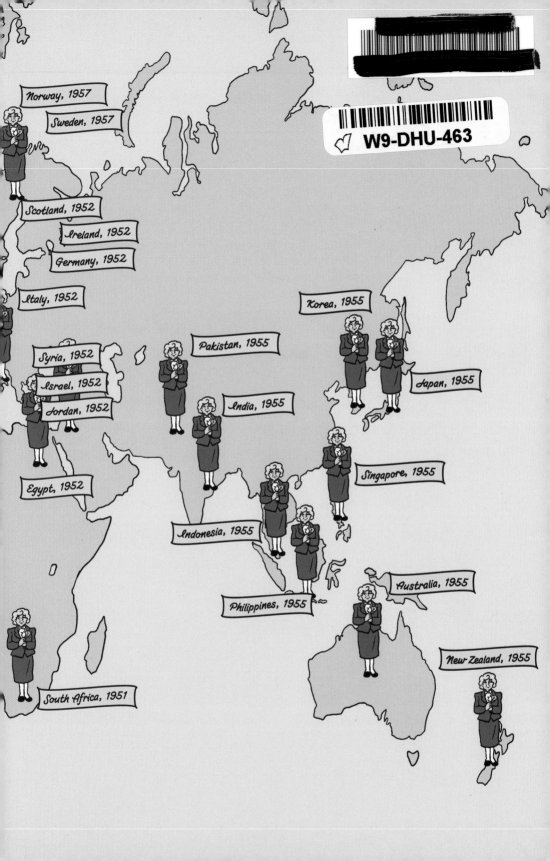

Norway, 1957

Sweden, 1957

Scotland, 1952

Ireland, 1952

Germany, 1952

Italy, 1952

Korea, 1955

Syria, 1952

Israel, 1952

Jordan, 1952

Pakistan, 1955

India, 1955

Japan, 1955

Egypt, 1952

Singapore, 1955

Indonesia, 1955

Philippines, 1955

Australia, 1955

New Zealand, 1955

South Africa, 1951

SHOW ME HISTORY!™

HELEN KELLER

INSPIRATION to EVERYONE!

BY
JAMES BUCKLEY JR.

ILLUSTRATED BY
CAITLIN LIKE

LETTERING & DESIGN BY
SWELL TYPE

COVER ART BY
IAN CHURCHILL

PORTABLE
PRESS

SAN DIEGO, CALIFORNIA

Portable Press
An imprint of Printers Row Publishing Group
9717 Pacific Heights Blvd, San Diego, CA 92121
www.portablepress.com • mail@portablepress.com

Printers Row Publishing Group is a division of Readerlink Distribution Services, LLC. Portable Press is a registered trademark of Readerlink Distribution Services, LLC.

Correspondence regarding the content of this book should be sent to Portable Press, Editorial Department, at the above address. Author and illustrator inquiries should be sent to Oomf, Inc., www.oomf.com.

Portable Press
Publisher: Peter Norton • Associate Publisher: Ana Parker
Art Director: Charles McStravick
Senior Developmental Editor: April Graham Farr
Editor: Angela Garcia
Production Team: Julie Greene, Rusty von Dyl
Consultant: Dan Mansfield

O•MF Produced by Oomf, Inc., www.Oomf.com
Director: Mark Shulman
Producer: James Buckley Jr.

Author: James Buckley Jr.
Illustrator: Caitlin Like
Assistant Editor: Michael Centore
Lettering & design by Swell Type: John Roshell, Forest Dempsey, Sarah Jacobs, Drewes McFarling
Cover illustrator: Ian Churchill

Library of Congress Control Number: 2020949005

ISBN: 978-1-64517-411-0

Printed in China

25 24 23 22 21   1 2 3 4 5

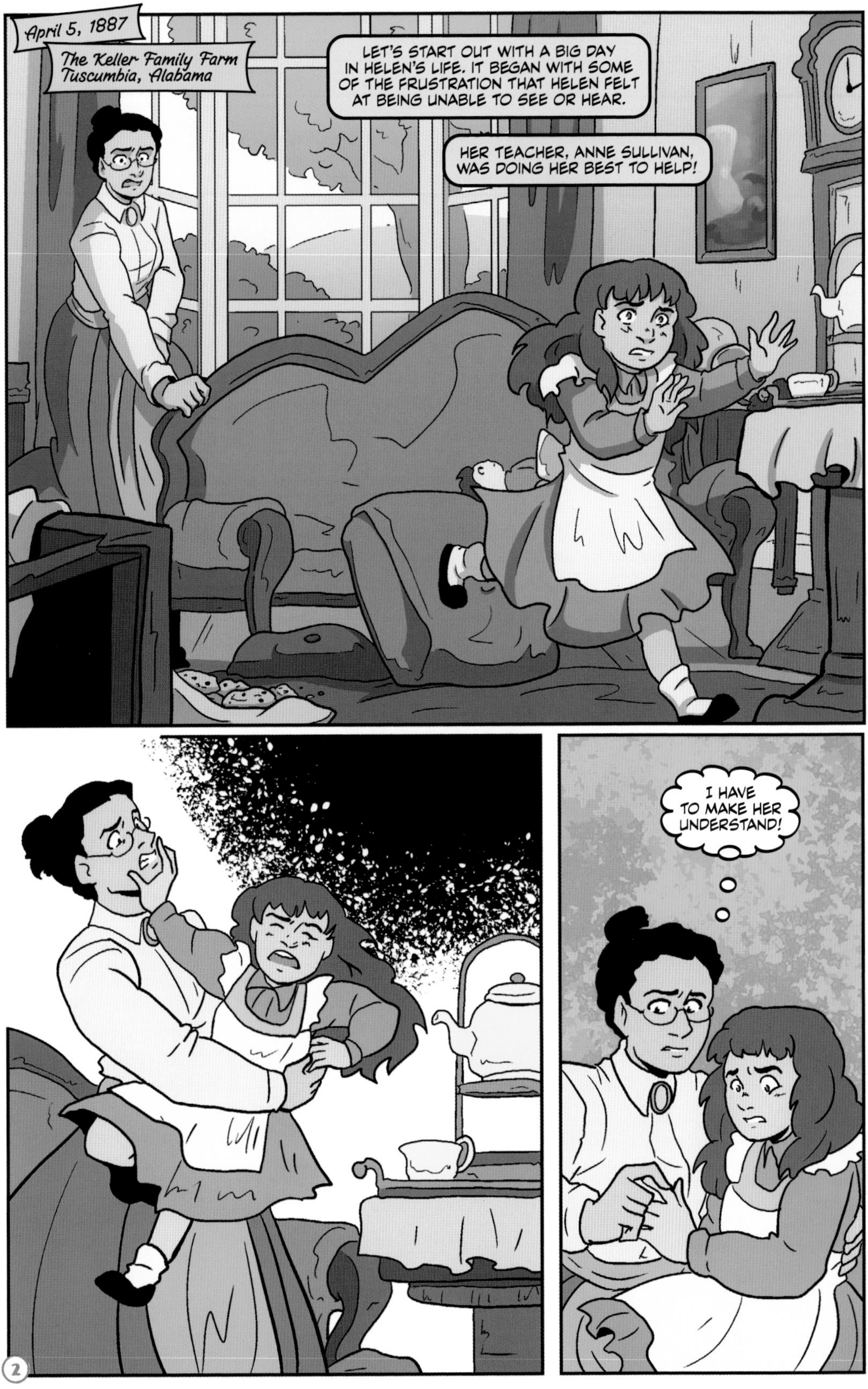
April 5, 1887
The Keller Family Farm Tuscumbia, Alabama
LET'S START OUT WITH A BIG DAY IN HELEN'S LIFE. IT BEGAN WITH SOME OF THE FRUSTRATION THAT HELEN FELT AT BEING UNABLE TO SEE OR HEAR.
HER TEACHER, ANNE SULLIVAN, WAS DOING HER BEST TO HELP!
I HAVE TO MAKE HER UNDERSTAND!

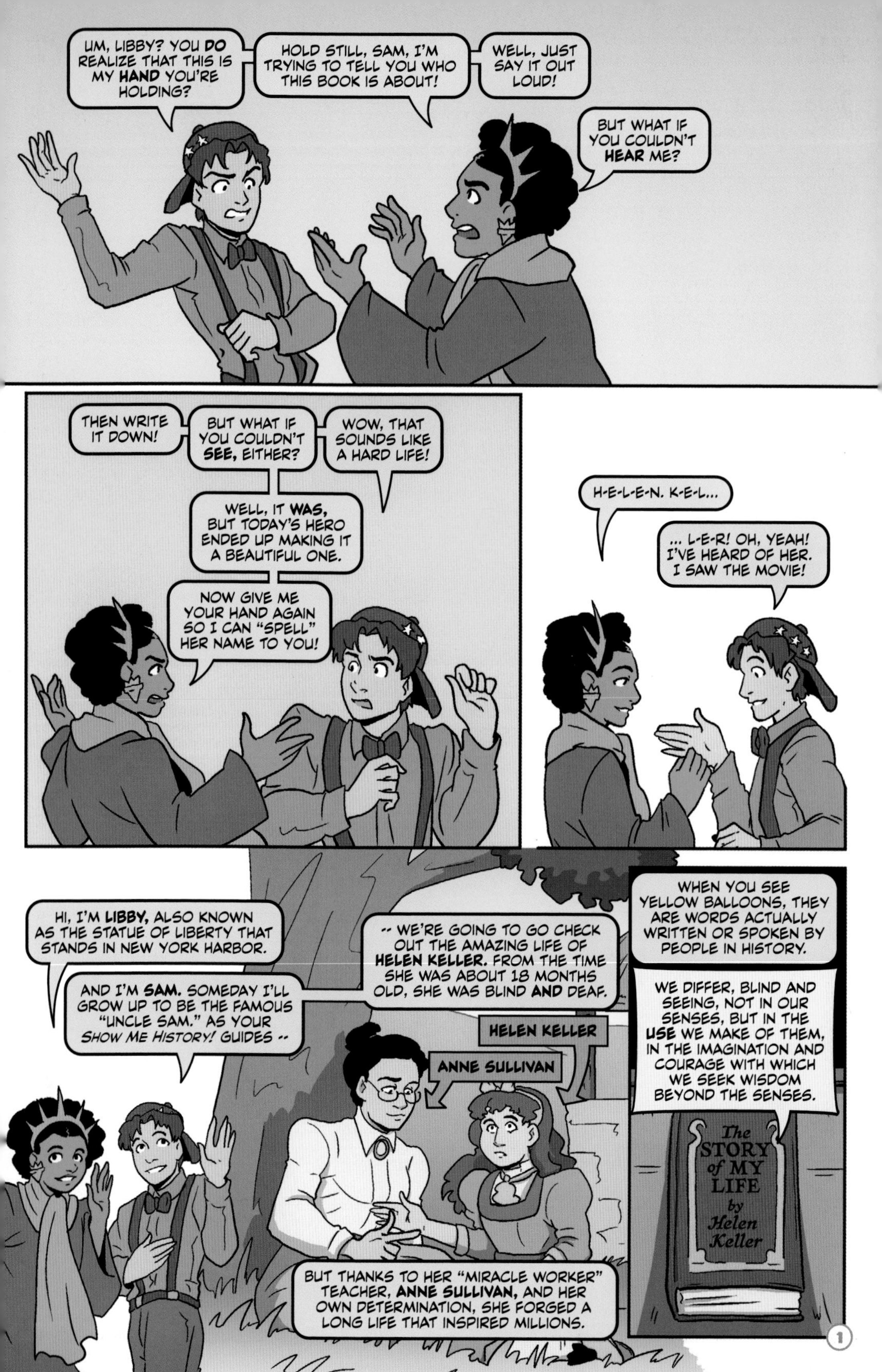

UM, LIBBY? YOU **DO** REALIZE THAT THIS IS MY **HAND** YOU'RE HOLDING?
HOLD STILL, SAM, I'M TRYING TO TELL YOU WHO THIS BOOK IS ABOUT!
WELL, JUST SAY IT OUT LOUD!
BUT WHAT IF YOU COULDN'T **HEAR** ME?
THEN WRITE IT DOWN!
BUT WHAT IF YOU COULDN'T **SEE,** EITHER?
WOW, THAT SOUNDS LIKE A HARD LIFE!
WELL, IT **WAS,** BUT TODAY'S HERO ENDED UP MAKING IT A BEAUTIFUL ONE.
NOW GIVE ME YOUR HAND AGAIN SO I CAN "SPELL" HER NAME TO YOU!
H-E-L-E-N. K-E-L...
... L-E-R! OH, YEAH! I'VE HEARD OF HER. I SAW THE MOVIE!
HI, I'M **LIBBY,** ALSO KNOWN AS THE STATUE OF LIBERTY THAT STANDS IN NEW YORK HARBOR.
AND I'M **SAM.** SOMEDAY I'LL GROW UP TO BE THE FAMOUS "UNCLE SAM." AS YOUR *SHOW ME HISTORY!* GUIDES --
-- WE'RE GOING TO GO CHECK OUT THE AMAZING LIFE OF **HELEN KELLER.** FROM THE TIME SHE WAS ABOUT 18 MONTHS OLD, SHE WAS BLIND **AND** DEAF.
HELEN KELLER
ANNE SULLIVAN
BUT THANKS TO HER "MIRACLE WORKER" TEACHER, **ANNE SULLIVAN,** AND HER OWN DETERMINATION, SHE FORGED A LONG LIFE THAT INSPIRED MILLIONS.
WHEN YOU SEE YELLOW BALLOONS, THEY ARE WORDS ACTUALLY WRITTEN OR SPOKEN BY PEOPLE IN HISTORY.
WE DIFFER, BLIND AND SEEING, NOT IN OUR SENSES, BUT IN THE **USE** WE MAKE OF THEM, IN THE IMAGINATION AND COURAGE WITH WHICH WE SEEK WISDOM BEYOND THE SENSES.
The STORY of MY LIFE by Helen Keller

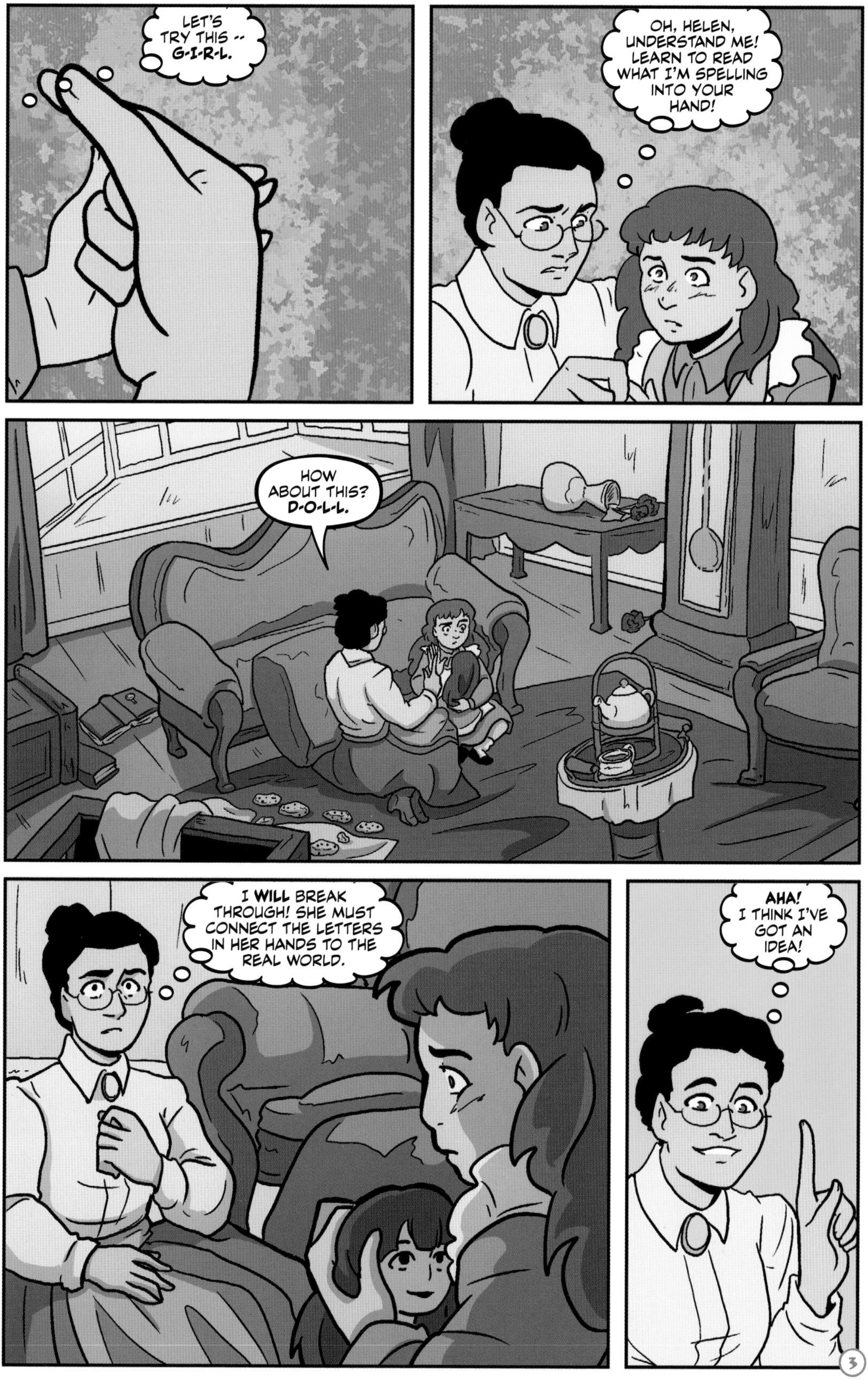
LET'S TRY THIS -- G-I-R-L.
OH, HELEN, UNDERSTAND ME! LEARN TO READ WHAT I'M SPELLING INTO YOUR HAND!
HOW ABOUT THIS? D-O-L-L.
I WILL BREAK THROUGH! SHE MUST CONNECT THE LETTERS IN HER HANDS TO THE REAL WORLD.
AHA! I THINK I'VE GOT AN IDEA!

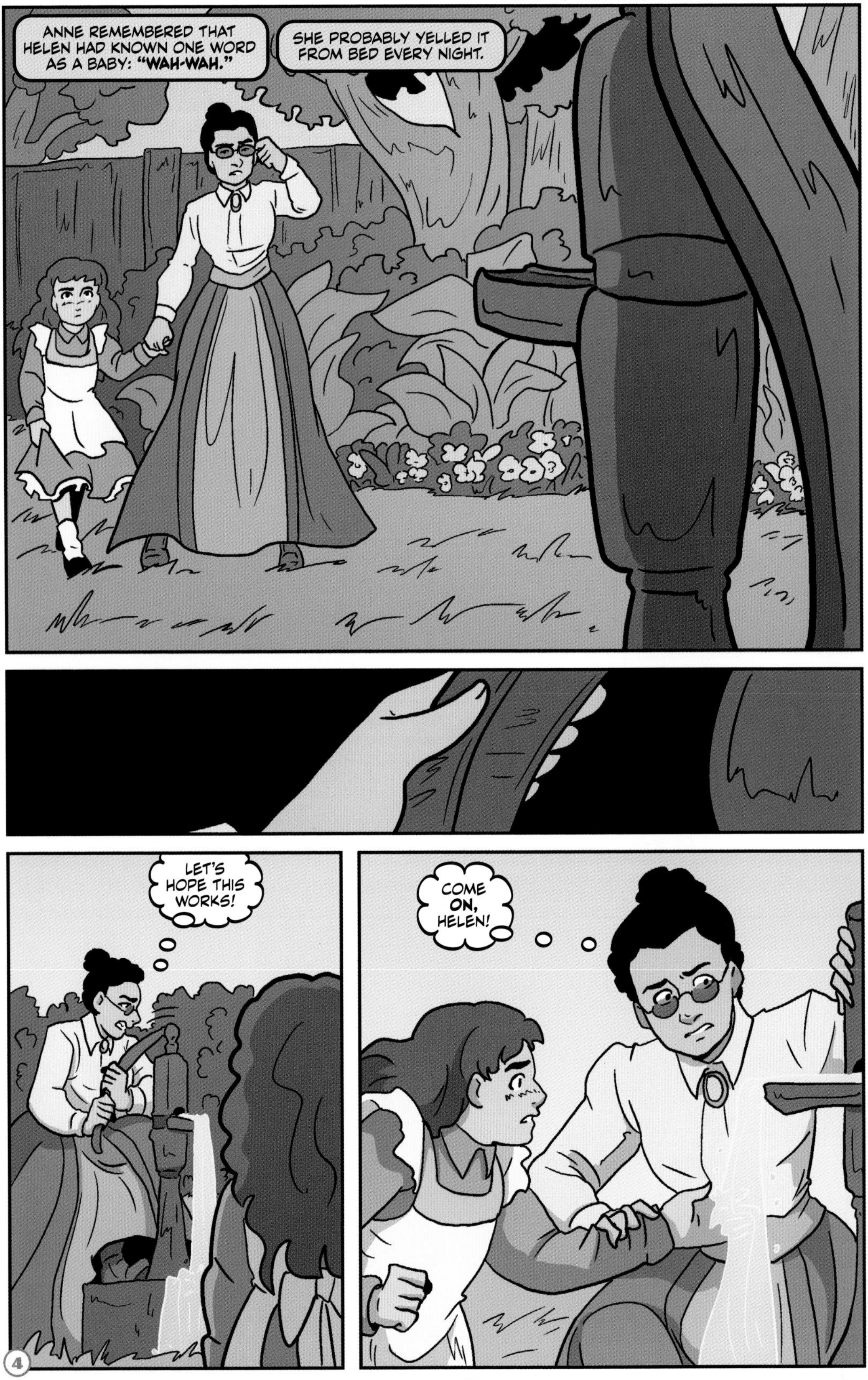
ANNE REMEMBERED THAT HELEN HAD KNOWN ONE WORD AS A BABY: **"WAH-WAH."**
SHE PROBABLY YELLED IT FROM BED EVERY NIGHT.
LET'S HOPE THIS WORKS!
COME **ON,** HELEN!

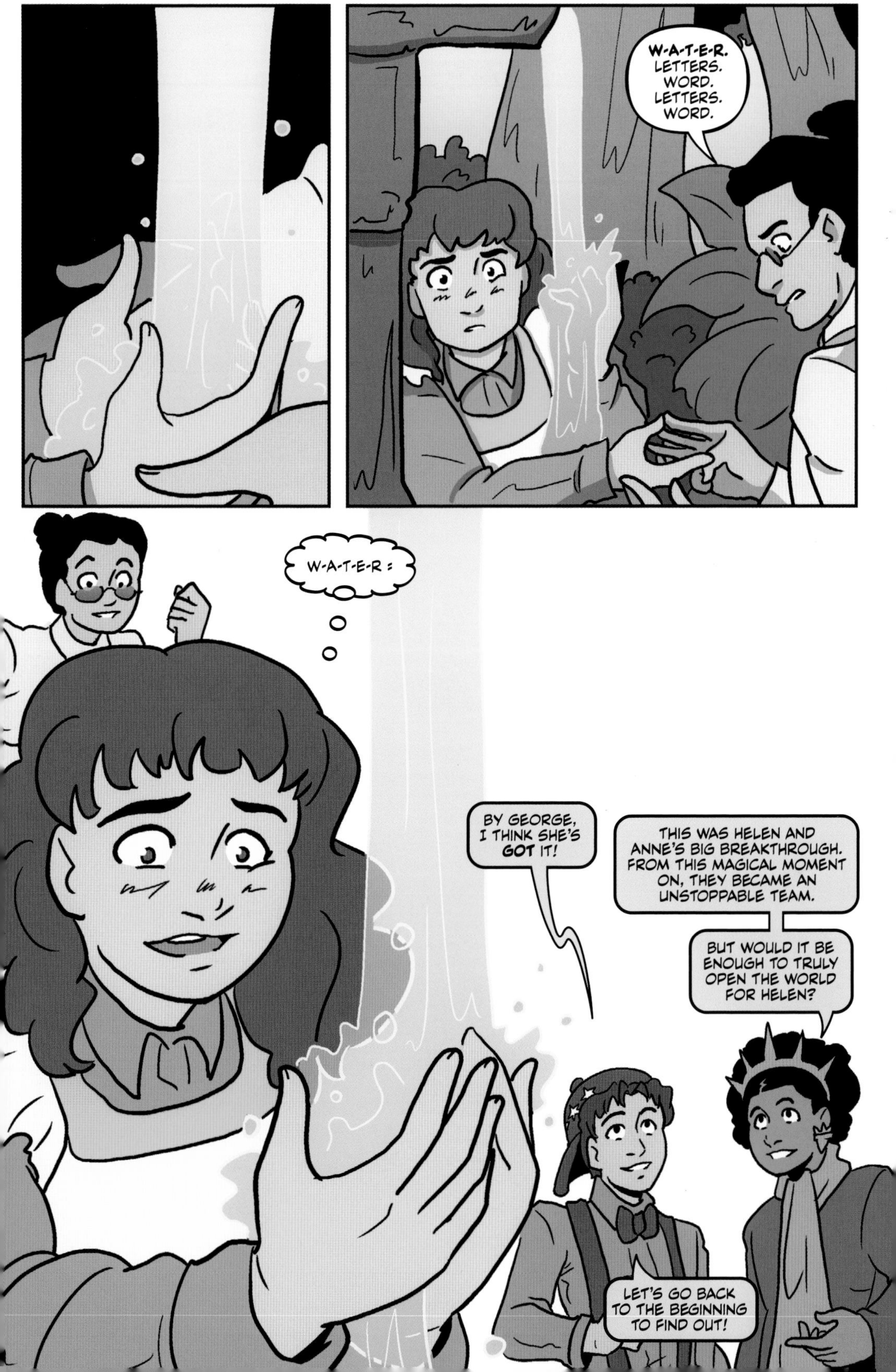
W-A-T-E-R.
LETTERS.
WORD.
LETTERS.
WORD.
W-A-T-E-R =
BY GEORGE, I THINK SHE'S **GOT** IT!
THIS WAS HELEN AND ANNE'S BIG BREAKTHROUGH. FROM THIS MAGICAL MOMENT ON, THEY BECAME AN UNSTOPPABLE TEAM.
BUT WOULD IT BE ENOUGH TO TRULY OPEN THE WORLD FOR HELEN?
LET'S GO BACK TO THE BEGINNING TO FIND OUT!

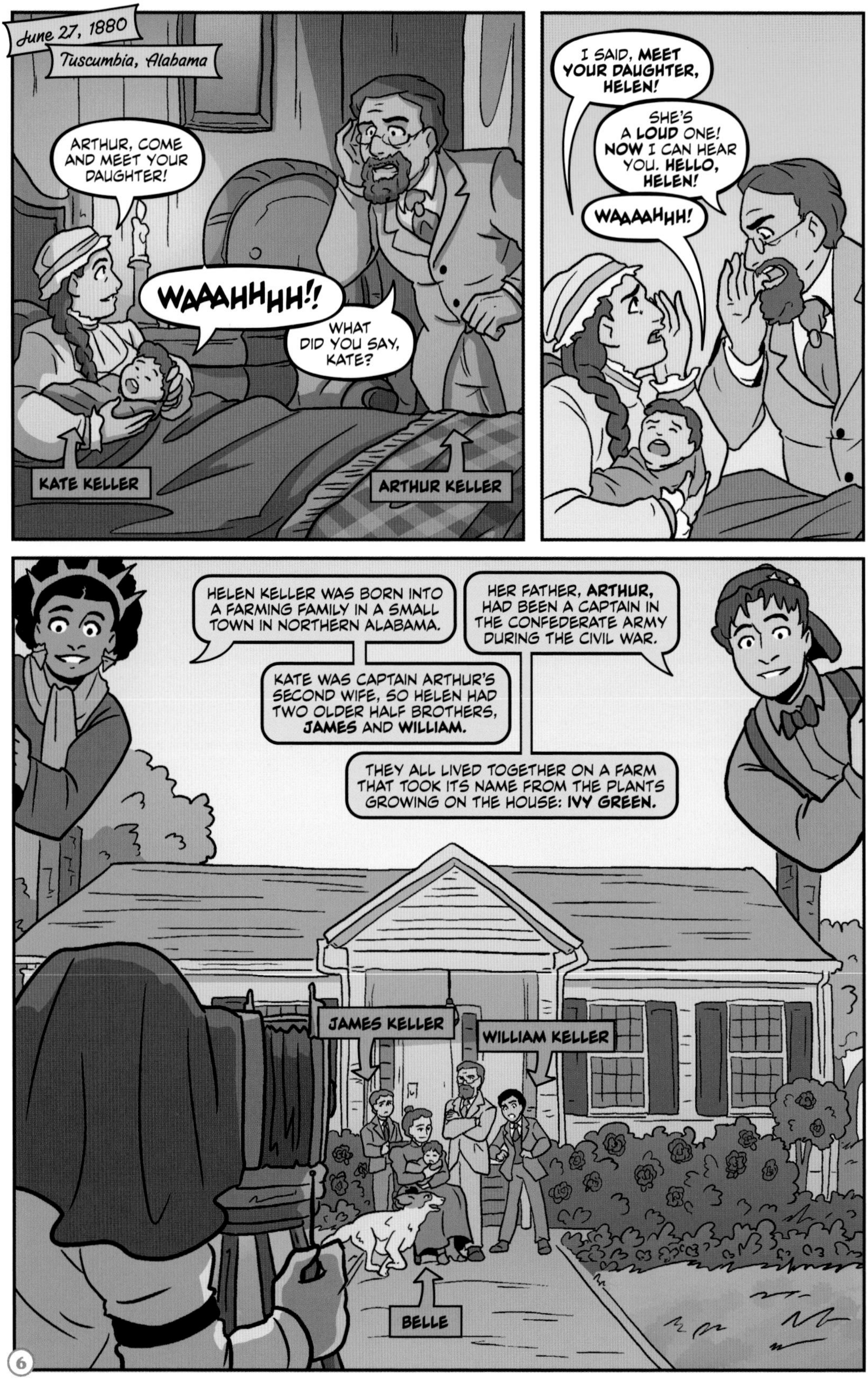

June 27, 1880
Tuscumbia, Alabama
ARTHUR, COME AND MEET YOUR DAUGHTER!
WAAAHHHH!!
WHAT DID YOU SAY, KATE?
KATE KELLER
ARTHUR KELLER
I SAID, MEET YOUR DAUGHTER, HELEN!
SHE'S A LOUD ONE! NOW I CAN HEAR YOU. HELLO, HELEN!
WAAAAHHH!
HELEN KELLER WAS BORN INTO A FARMING FAMILY IN A SMALL TOWN IN NORTHERN ALABAMA.
HER FATHER, ARTHUR, HAD BEEN A CAPTAIN IN THE CONFEDERATE ARMY DURING THE CIVIL WAR.
KATE WAS CAPTAIN ARTHUR'S SECOND WIFE, SO HELEN HAD TWO OLDER HALF BROTHERS, JAMES AND WILLIAM.
THEY ALL LIVED TOGETHER ON A FARM THAT TOOK ITS NAME FROM THE PLANTS GROWING ON THE HOUSE: IVY GREEN.
JAMES KELLER
WILLIAM KELLER
BELLE

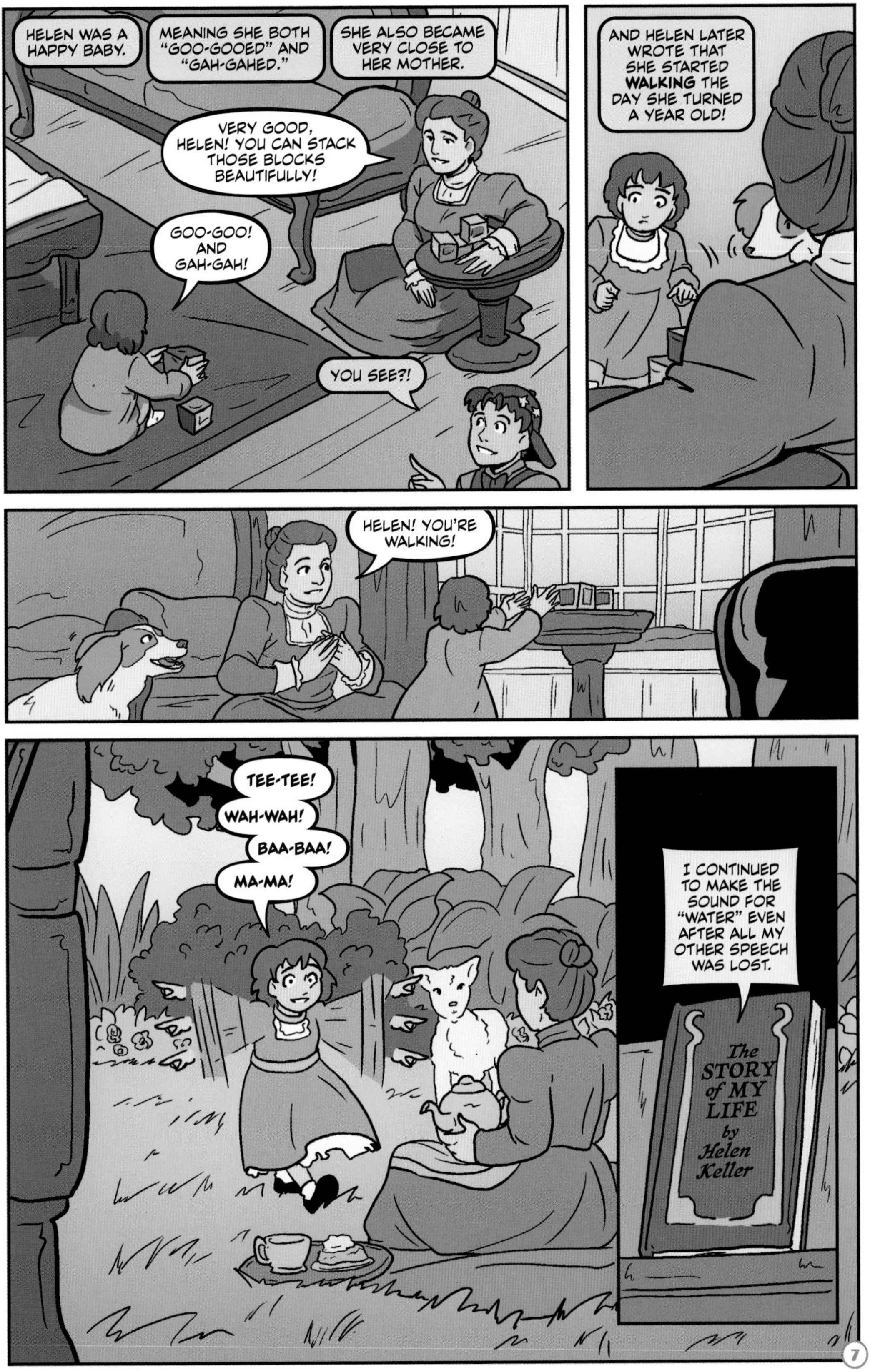
HELEN WAS A HAPPY BABY.
MEANING SHE BOTH "GOO-GOOED" AND "GAH-GAHED."
SHE ALSO BECAME VERY CLOSE TO HER MOTHER.
VERY GOOD, HELEN! YOU CAN STACK THOSE BLOCKS BEAUTIFULLY!
GOO-GOO! AND GAH-GAH!
YOU SEE?!
AND HELEN LATER WROTE THAT SHE STARTED **WALKING** THE DAY SHE TURNED A YEAR OLD!
HELEN! YOU'RE WALKING!
TEE-TEE!
WAH-WAH!
BAA-BAA!
MA-MA!
I CONTINUED TO MAKE THE SOUND FOR "WATER" EVEN AFTER ALL MY OTHER SPEECH WAS LOST.
The STORY of MY LIFE by Helen Keller

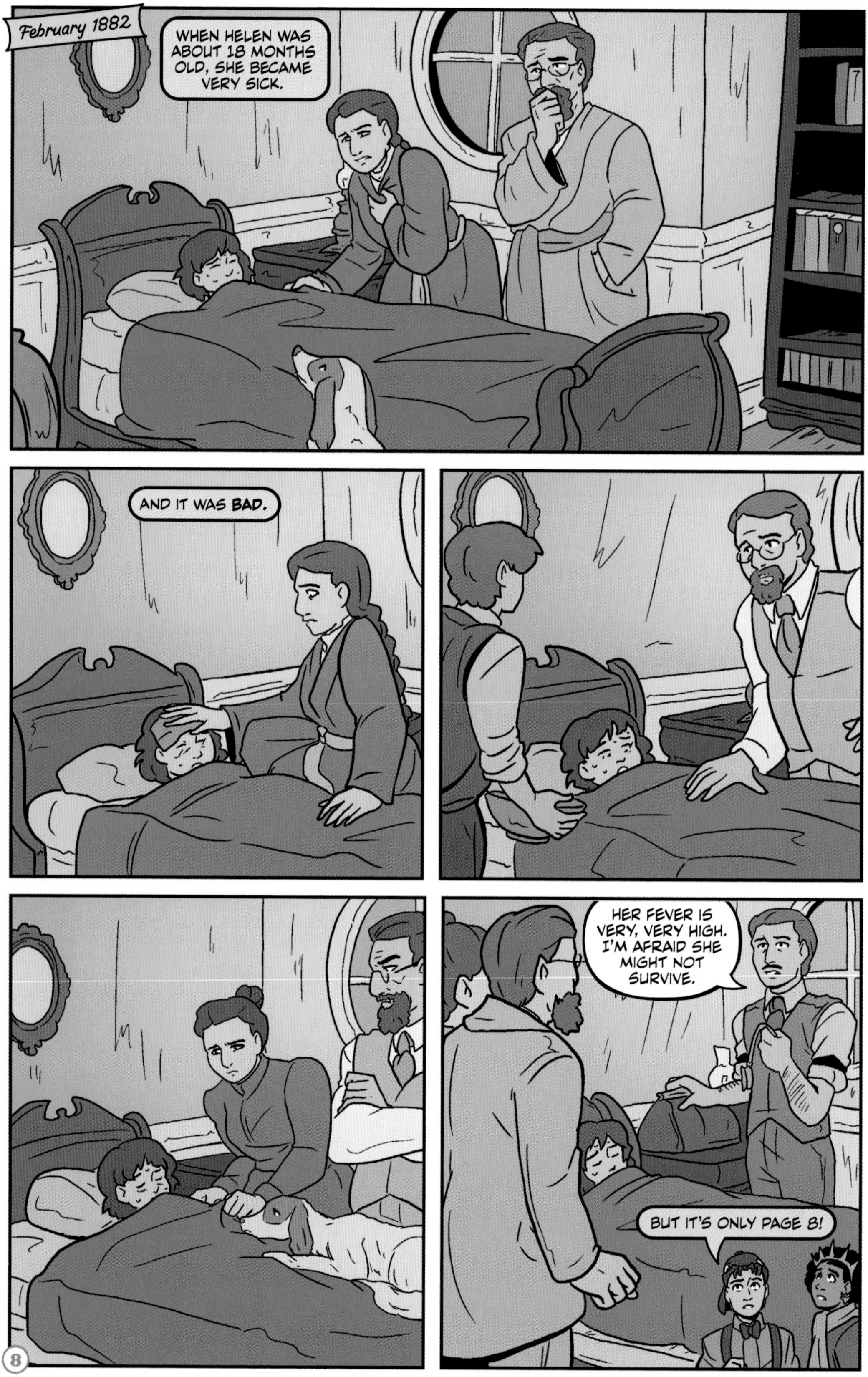
February 1882
WHEN HELEN WAS ABOUT 18 MONTHS OLD, SHE BECAME VERY SICK.
AND IT WAS BAD.
HER FEVER IS VERY, VERY HIGH. I'M AFRAID SHE MIGHT NOT SURVIVE.
BUT IT'S ONLY PAGE 8!

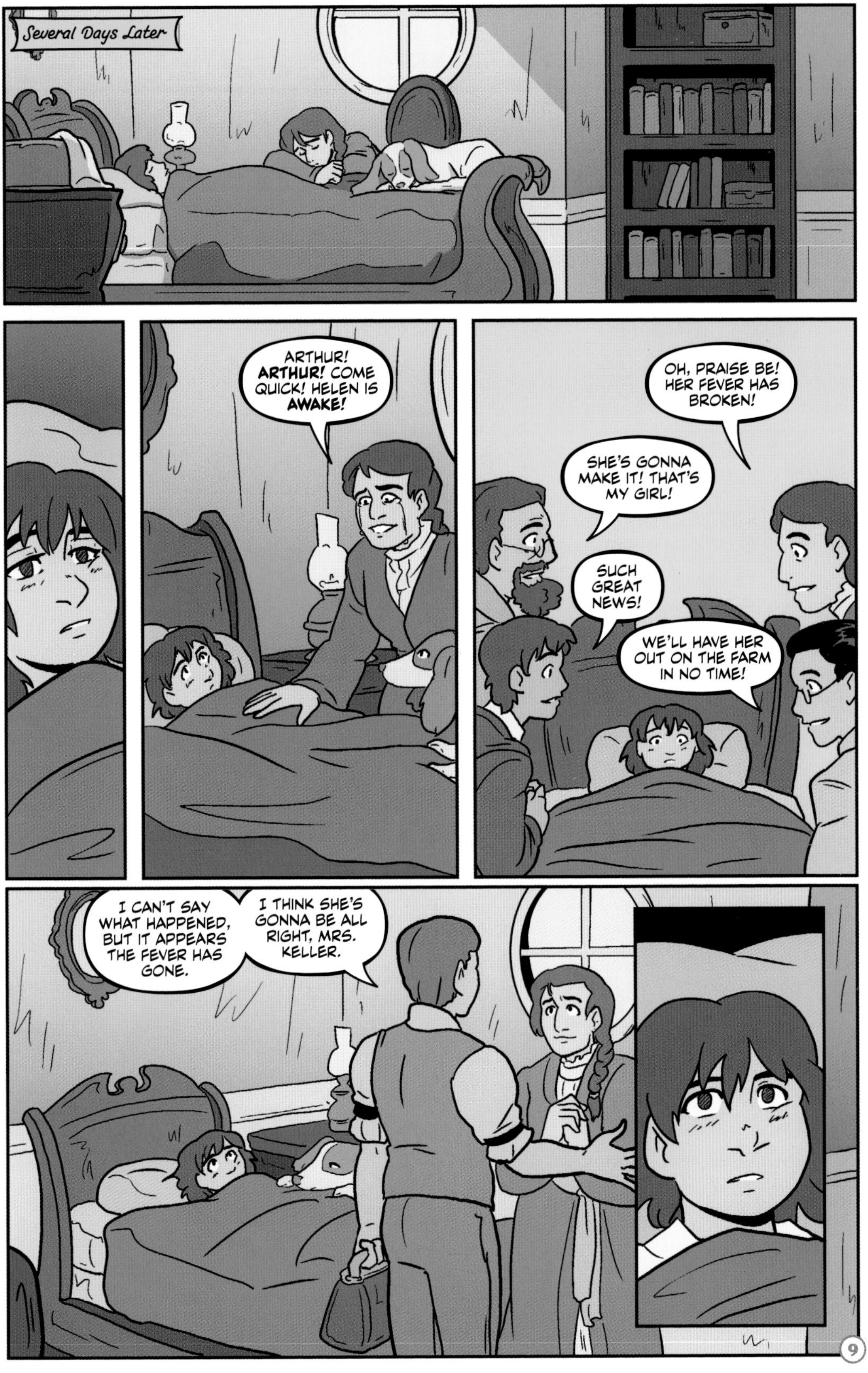
Several Days Later
ARTHUR! ARTHUR! COME QUICK! HELEN IS AWAKE!
OH, PRAISE BE! HER FEVER HAS BROKEN!
SHE'S GONNA MAKE IT! THAT'S MY GIRL!
SUCH GREAT NEWS!
WE'LL HAVE HER OUT ON THE FARM IN NO TIME!
I CAN'T SAY WHAT HAPPENED, BUT IT APPEARS THE FEVER HAS GONE.
I THINK SHE'S GONNA BE ALL RIGHT, MRS. KELLER.

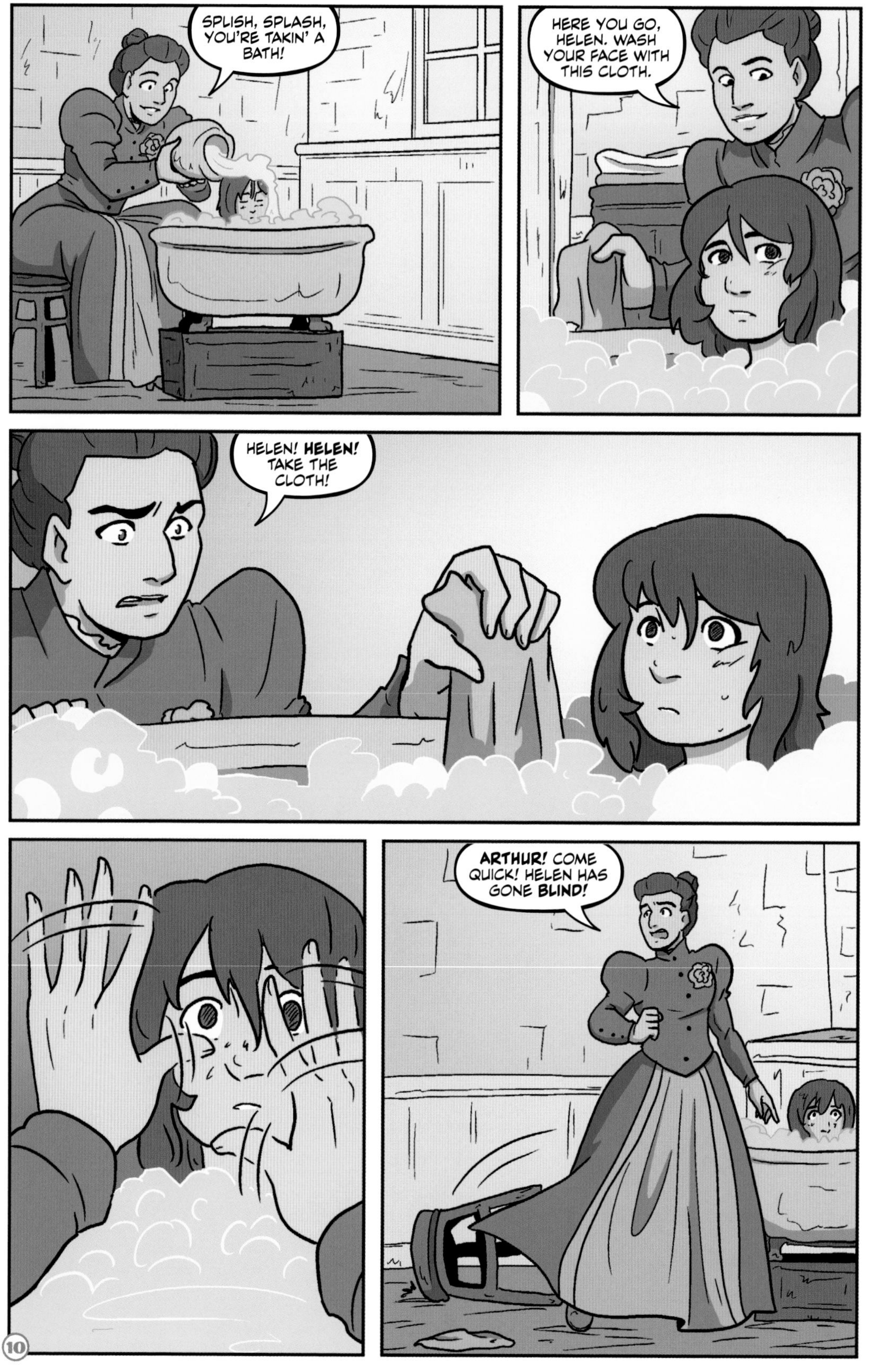
SPLISH, SPLASH, YOU'RE TAKIN' A BATH!
HERE YOU GO, HELEN. WASH YOUR FACE WITH THIS CLOTH.
HELEN! **HELEN!** TAKE THE CLOTH!
ARTHUR! COME QUICK! HELEN HAS GONE **BLIND!**

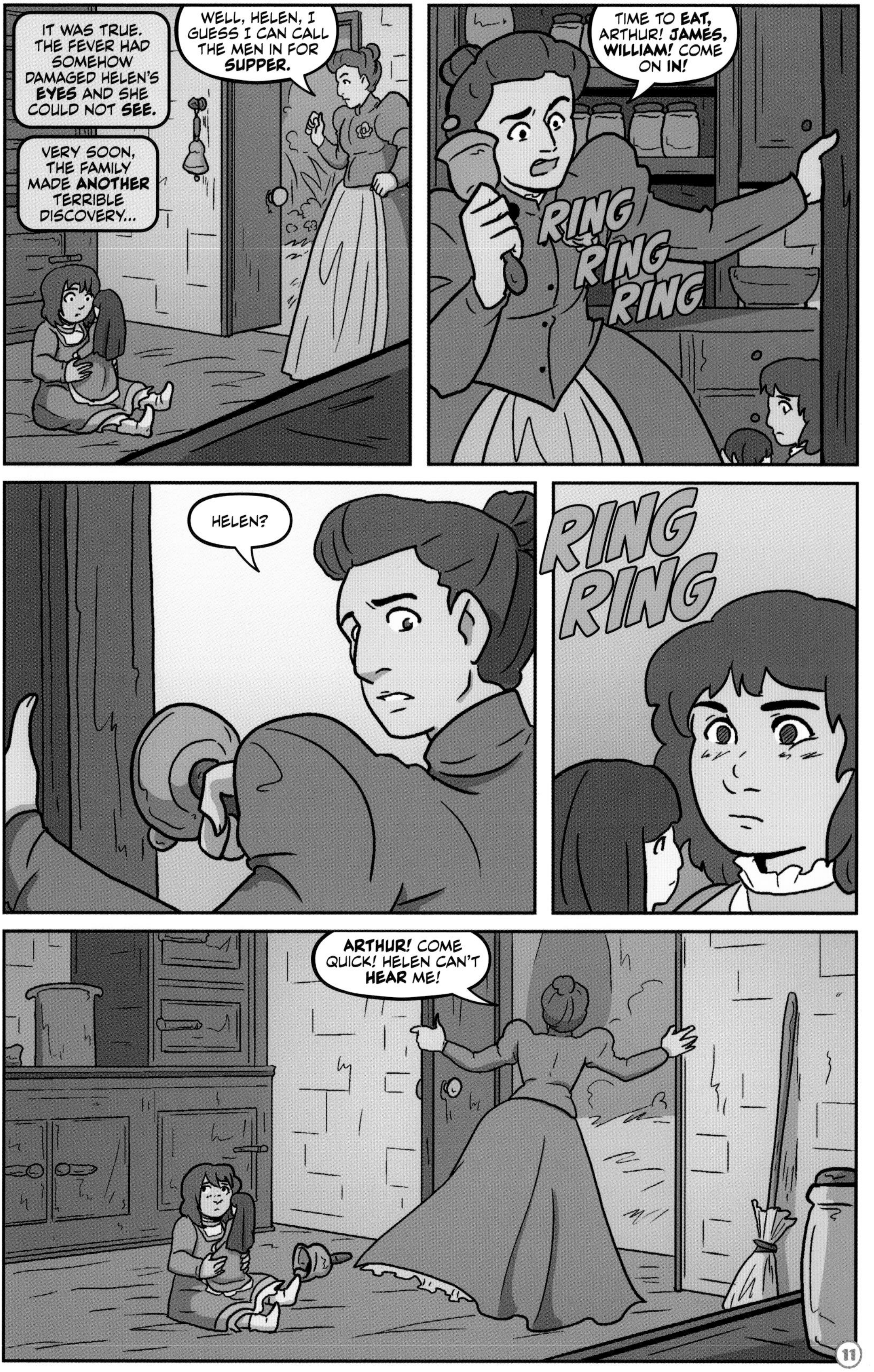
IT WAS TRUE. THE FEVER HAD SOMEHOW DAMAGED HELEN'S EYES AND SHE COULD NOT SEE.
VERY SOON, THE FAMILY MADE ANOTHER TERRIBLE DISCOVERY...
WELL, HELEN, I GUESS I CAN CALL THE MEN IN FOR SUPPER.
TIME TO EAT, ARTHUR! JAMES, WILLIAM! COME ON IN!
RING
RING
RING
HELEN?
RING
RING
ARTHUR! COME QUICK! HELEN CAN'T HEAR ME!

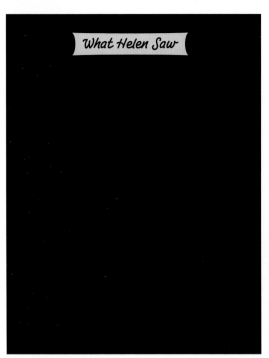

What Helen Saw

What Helen Heard

HELEN'S ILLNESS HAD TAKEN AWAY HER **SIGHT** AND HER **HEARING**.

BUT SHE COULD **TALK**, RIGHT?

SADLY, SAM, YOU CAN'T LEARN TO **TALK** IF YOU CAN'T **HEAR**. AT JUST OVER 18 MONTHS OLD, HELEN WAS BLIND, DEAF, AND BASICALLY MUTE.

SHE HAD A STRANGE NEW LIFE TO ADJUST TO, BUT SHE DID HER **BEST**.

SHE USED A FEW **HAND SIGNALS** TO COMMUNICATE.

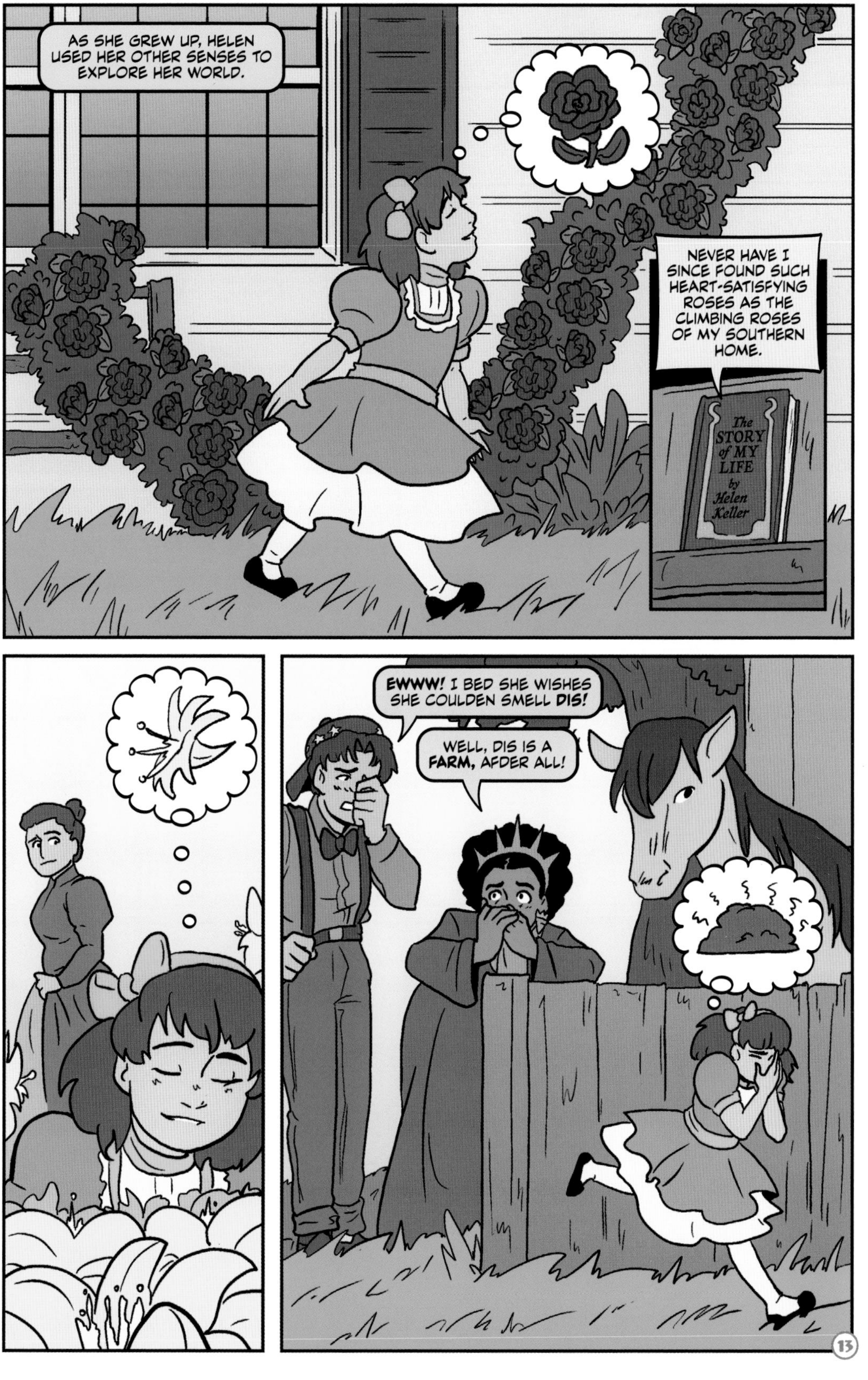
AS SHE GREW UP, HELEN USED HER OTHER SENSES TO EXPLORE HER WORLD.
NEVER HAVE I SINCE FOUND SUCH HEART-SATISFYING ROSES AS THE CLIMBING ROSES OF MY SOUTHERN HOME.
The STORY of MY LIFE by Helen Keller
EWWW! I BED SHE WISHES SHE COULDEN SMELL DIS!
WELL, DIS IS A FARM, AFDER ALL!

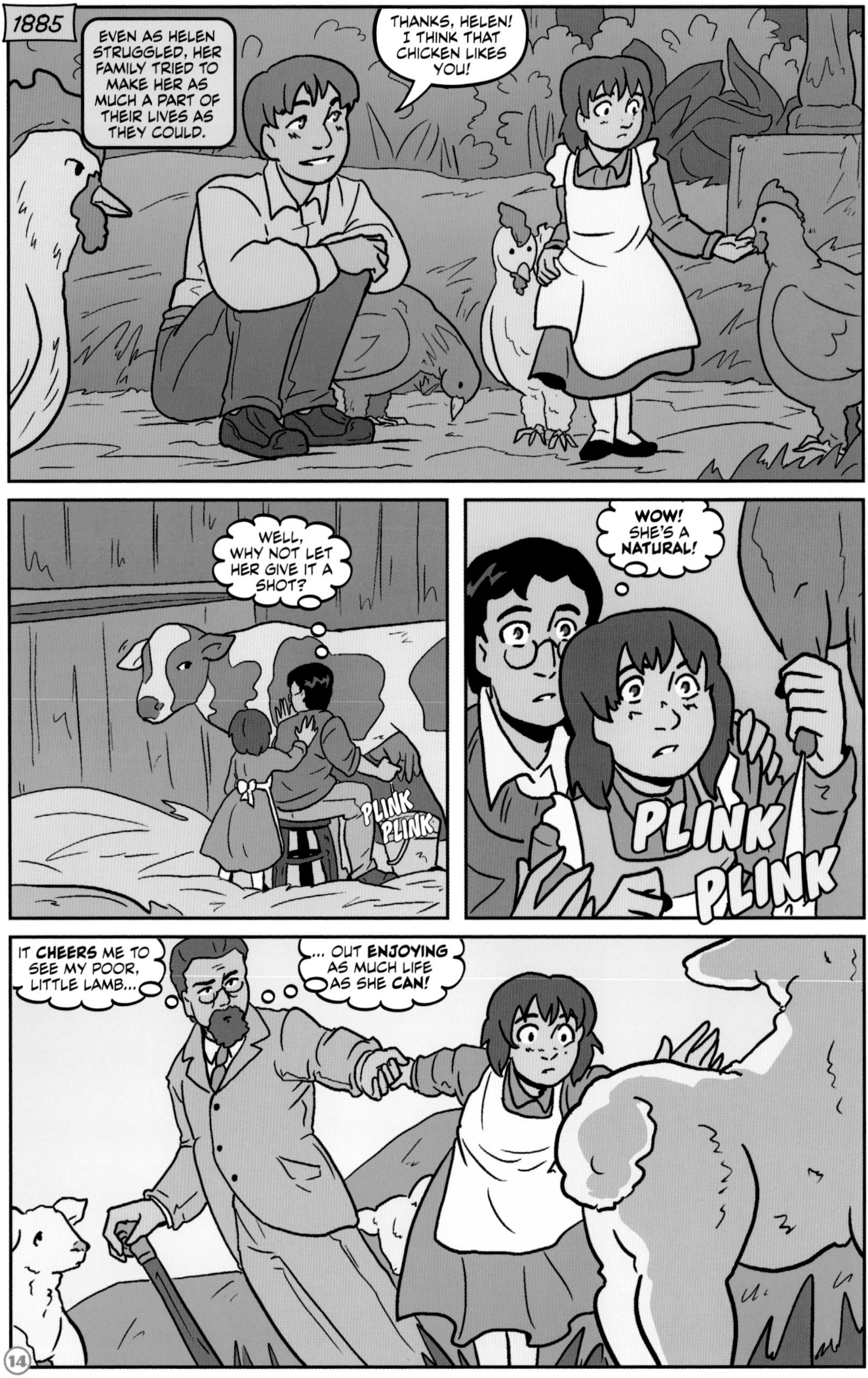
1885
EVEN AS HELEN STRUGGLED, HER FAMILY TRIED TO MAKE HER AS MUCH A PART OF THEIR LIVES AS THEY COULD.
THANKS, HELEN! I THINK THAT CHICKEN LIKES YOU!
WELL, WHY NOT LET HER GIVE IT A SHOT?
PLINK
PLINK
WOW! SHE'S A NATURAL!
PLINK
PLINK
IT CHEERS ME TO SEE MY POOR, LITTLE LAMB...
... OUT ENJOYING AS MUCH LIFE AS SHE CAN!

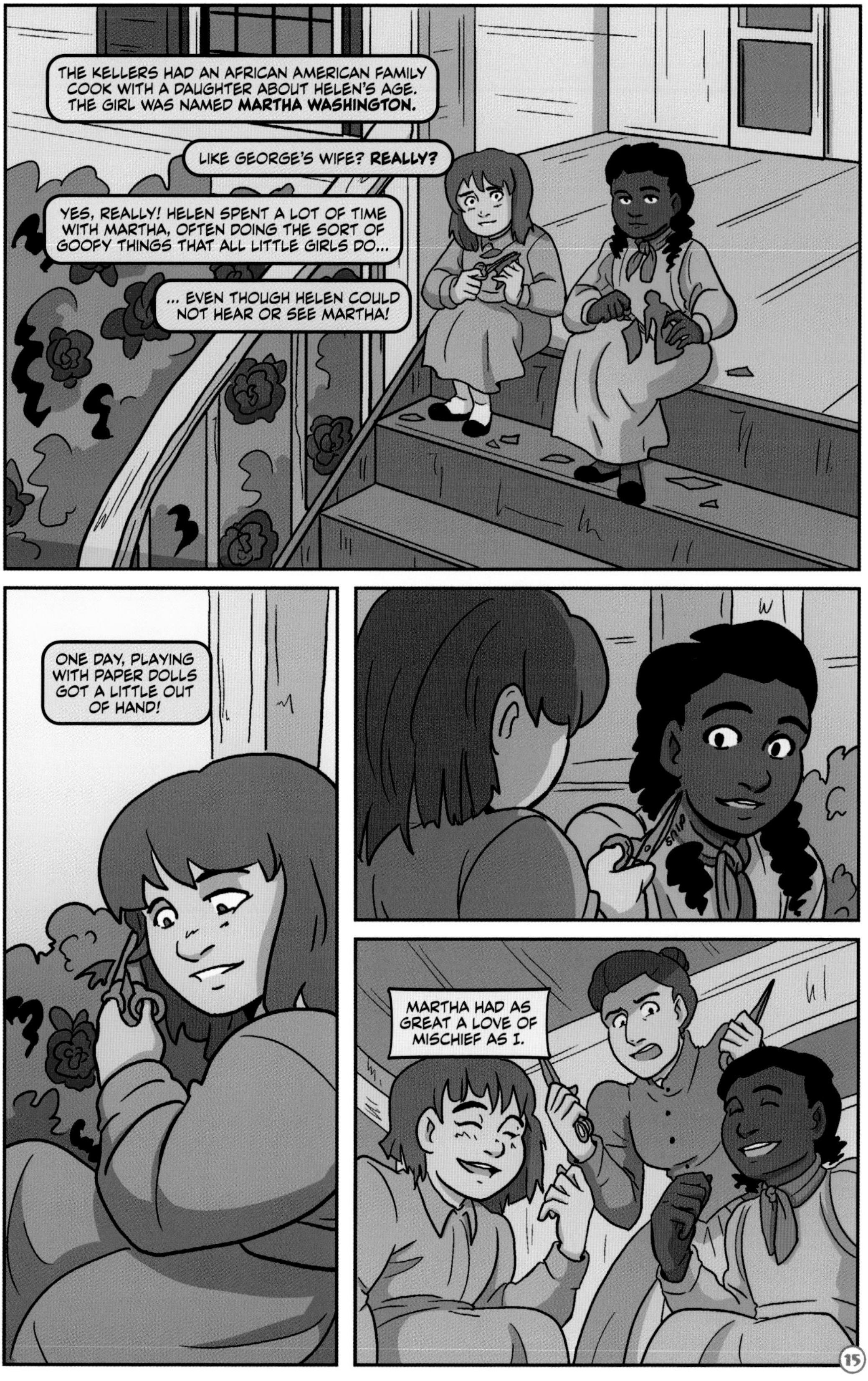
THE KELLERS HAD AN AFRICAN AMERICAN FAMILY COOK WITH A DAUGHTER ABOUT HELEN'S AGE. THE GIRL WAS NAMED **MARTHA WASHINGTON.**
LIKE GEORGE'S WIFE? **REALLY?**
YES, REALLY! HELEN SPENT A LOT OF TIME WITH MARTHA, OFTEN DOING THE SORT OF GOOFY THINGS THAT ALL LITTLE GIRLS DO...
... EVEN THOUGH HELEN COULD NOT HEAR OR SEE MARTHA!
ONE DAY, PLAYING WITH PAPER DOLLS GOT A LITTLE OUT OF HAND!
SNIP
MARTHA HAD AS GREAT A LOVE OF MISCHIEF AS I.

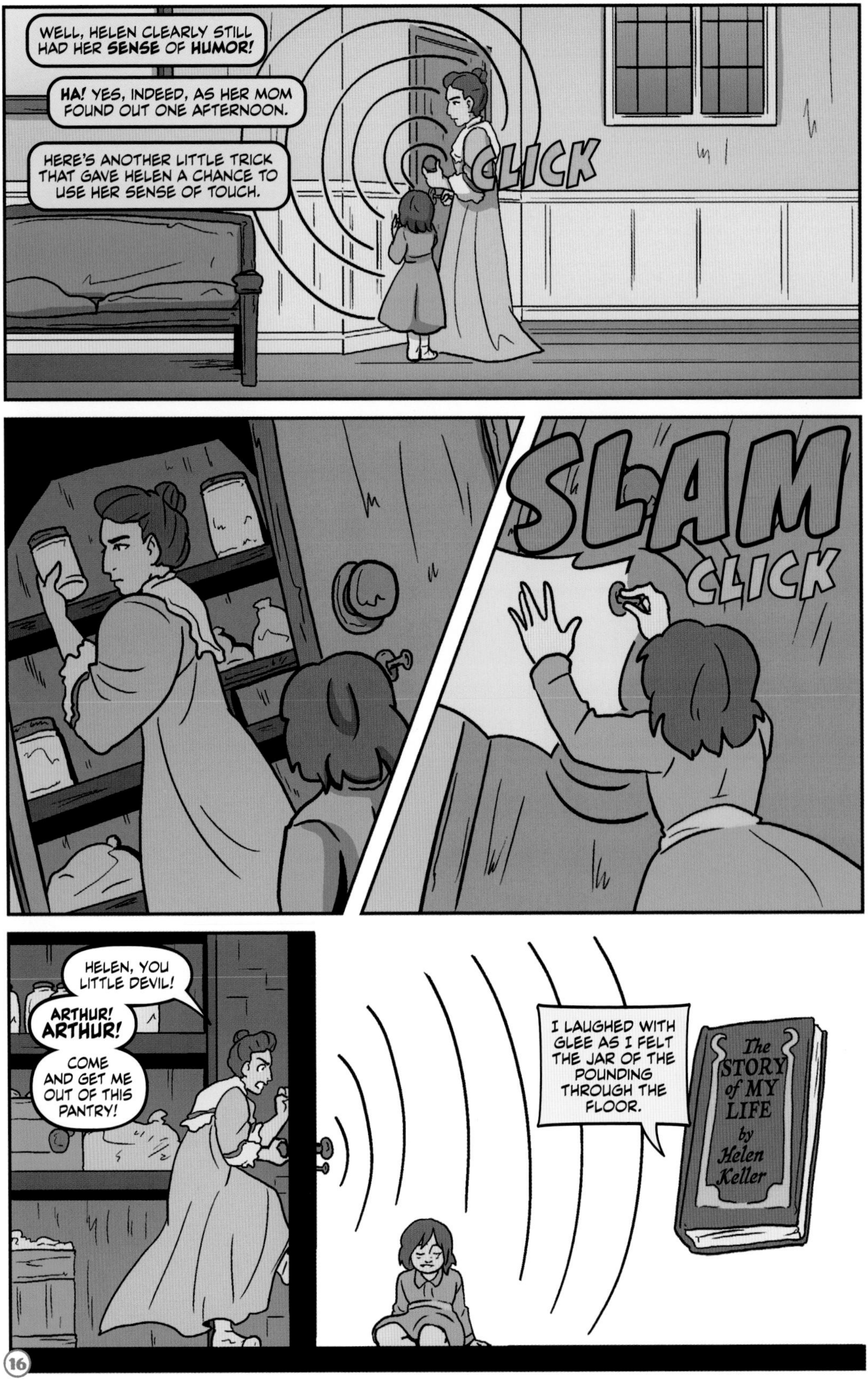
WELL, HELEN CLEARLY STILL HAD HER **SENSE** OF **HUMOR**!
HA! YES, INDEED, AS HER MOM FOUND OUT ONE AFTERNOON.
HERE'S ANOTHER LITTLE TRICK THAT GAVE HELEN A CHANCE TO USE HER SENSE OF TOUCH.
CLICK
SLAM
CLICK
HELEN, YOU LITTLE DEVIL!
ARTHUR! ARTHUR!
COME AND GET ME OUT OF THIS PANTRY!
I LAUGHED WITH GLEE AS I FELT THE JAR OF THE POUNDING THROUGH THE FLOOR.
The STORY of MY LIFE by Helen Keller

HA-HA! THAT'S A GOOD ONE! WAY TO GO, HELEN!

AS MUCH FUN AS SHE TRIED TO HAVE, LIFE WAS ACTUALLY VERY **HARD** FOR HELEN. SHE GOT FRUSTRATED EASILY AND HAD TERRIBLE TEMPER TANTRUMS.

SHE COULDN'T TALK OR HEAR OR SEE. I CAN'T IMAGINE HOW HARD THAT MUST HAVE BEEN!

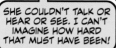

AS HELEN GOT OLDER, HER OUTBURSTS GOT **LONGER** AND **LOUDER**. AND HER FAMILY GOT VERY WORRIED.

I BECAME SO ANGRY AT TIMES THAT I KICKED AND SCREAMED UNTIL I WAS EXHAUSTED.

The STORY of MY LIFE by Helen Keller

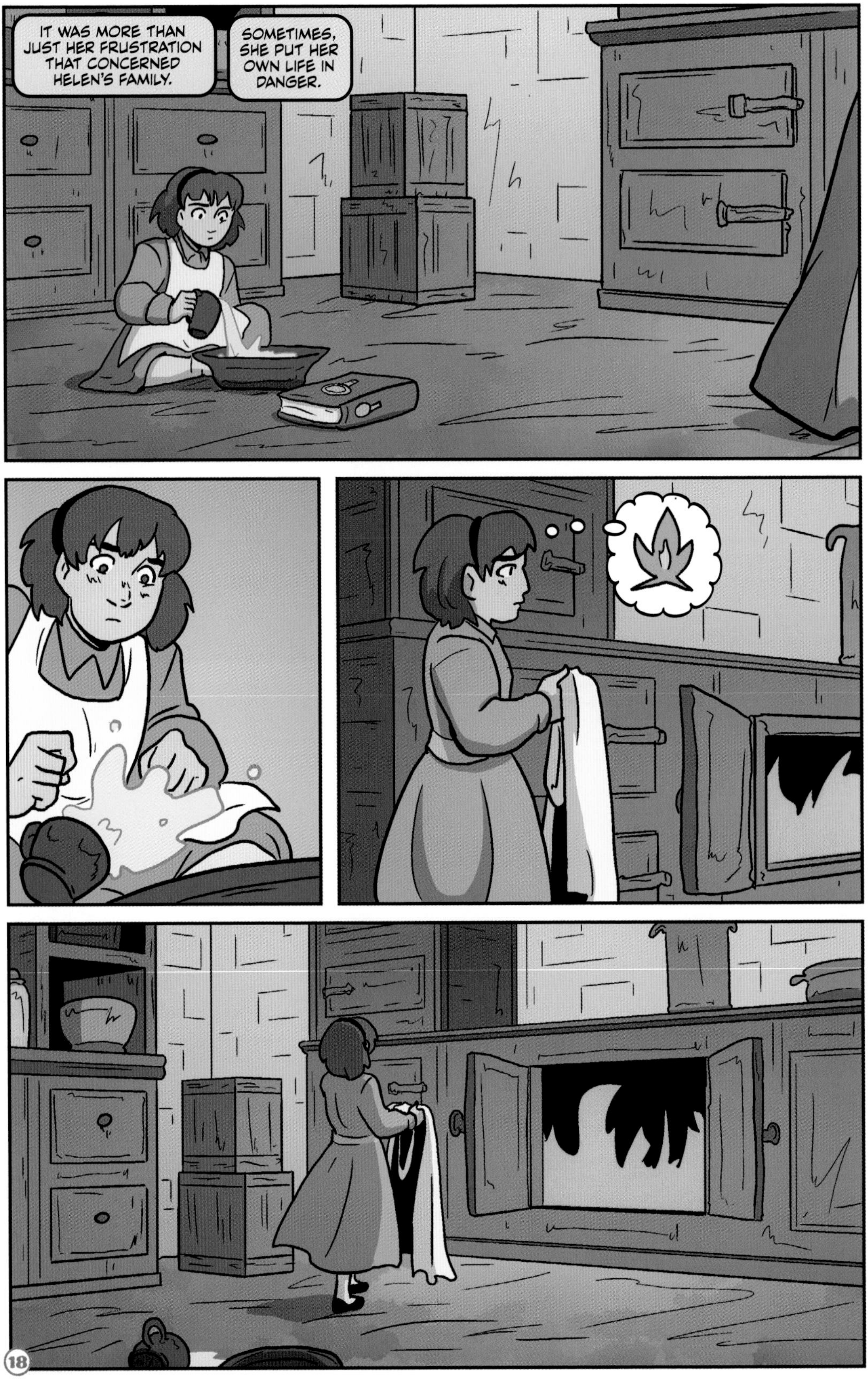
IT WAS MORE THAN JUST HER FRUSTRATION THAT CONCERNED HELEN'S FAMILY.
SOMETIMES, SHE PUT HER OWN LIFE IN DANGER.

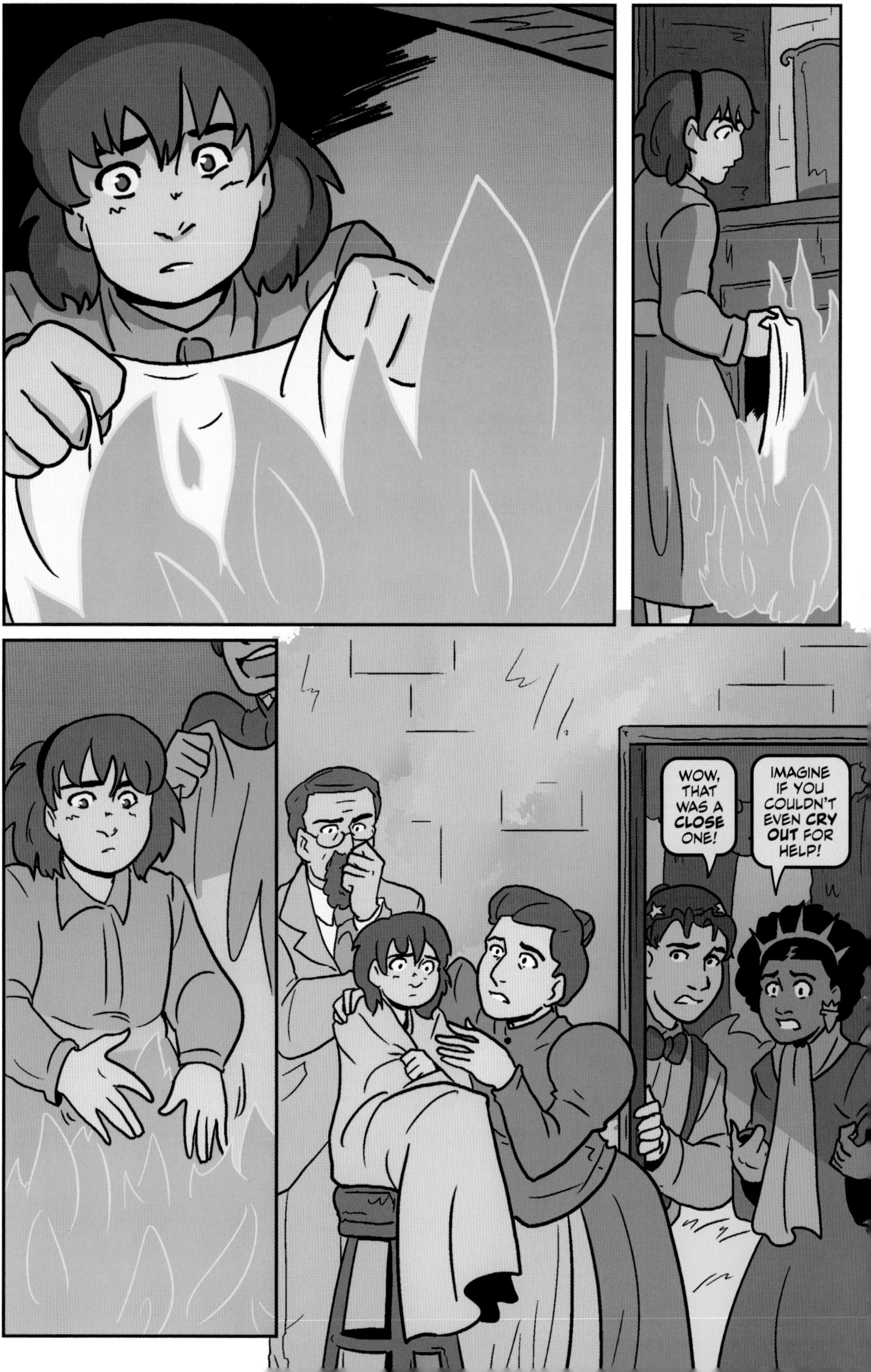
WOW, THAT WAS A CLOSE ONE!
IMAGINE IF YOU COULDN'T EVEN CRY OUT FOR HELP!

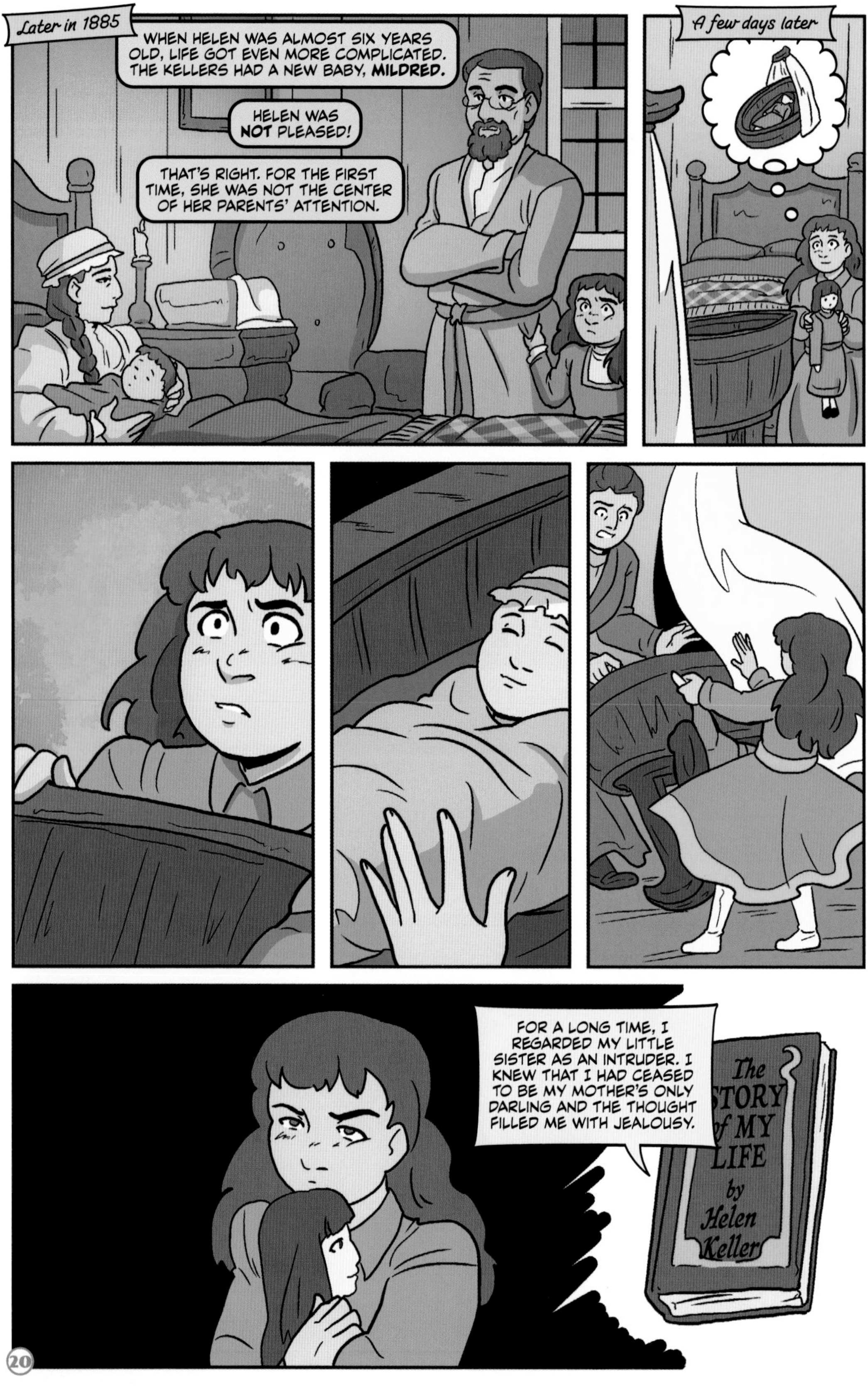
Later in 1885
WHEN HELEN WAS ALMOST SIX YEARS OLD, LIFE GOT EVEN MORE COMPLICATED. THE KELLERS HAD A NEW BABY, MILDRED.
HELEN WAS NOT PLEASED!
THAT'S RIGHT. FOR THE FIRST TIME, SHE WAS NOT THE CENTER OF HER PARENTS' ATTENTION.
A few days later
FOR A LONG TIME, I REGARDED MY LITTLE SISTER AS AN INTRUDER. I KNEW THAT I HAD CEASED TO BE MY MOTHER'S ONLY DARLING AND THE THOUGHT FILLED ME WITH JEALOUSY.
The STORY of MY LIFE by Helen Keller

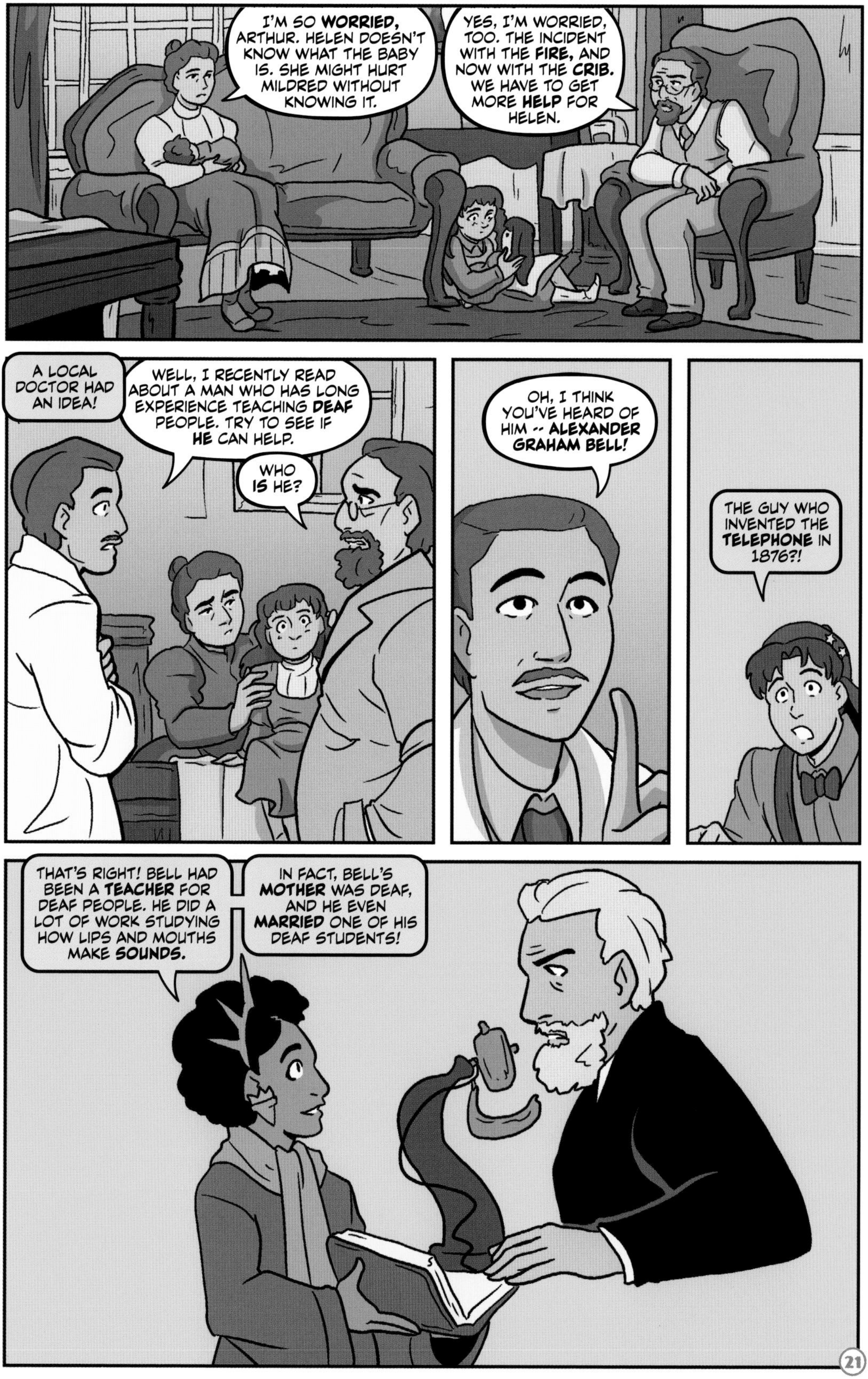
I'M SO WORRIED, ARTHUR. HELEN DOESN'T KNOW WHAT THE BABY IS. SHE MIGHT HURT MILDRED WITHOUT KNOWING IT.
YES, I'M WORRIED, TOO. THE INCIDENT WITH THE FIRE, AND NOW WITH THE CRIB. WE HAVE TO GET MORE HELP FOR HELEN.
A LOCAL DOCTOR HAD AN IDEA!
WELL, I RECENTLY READ ABOUT A MAN WHO HAS LONG EXPERIENCE TEACHING DEAF PEOPLE. TRY TO SEE IF HE CAN HELP.
WHO IS HE?
OH, I THINK YOU'VE HEARD OF HIM -- ALEXANDER GRAHAM BELL!
THE GUY WHO INVENTED THE TELEPHONE IN 1876?!
THAT'S RIGHT! BELL HAD BEEN A TEACHER FOR DEAF PEOPLE. HE DID A LOT OF WORK STUDYING HOW LIPS AND MOUTHS MAKE SOUNDS.
IN FACT, BELL'S MOTHER WAS DEAF, AND HE EVEN MARRIED ONE OF HIS DEAF STUDENTS!

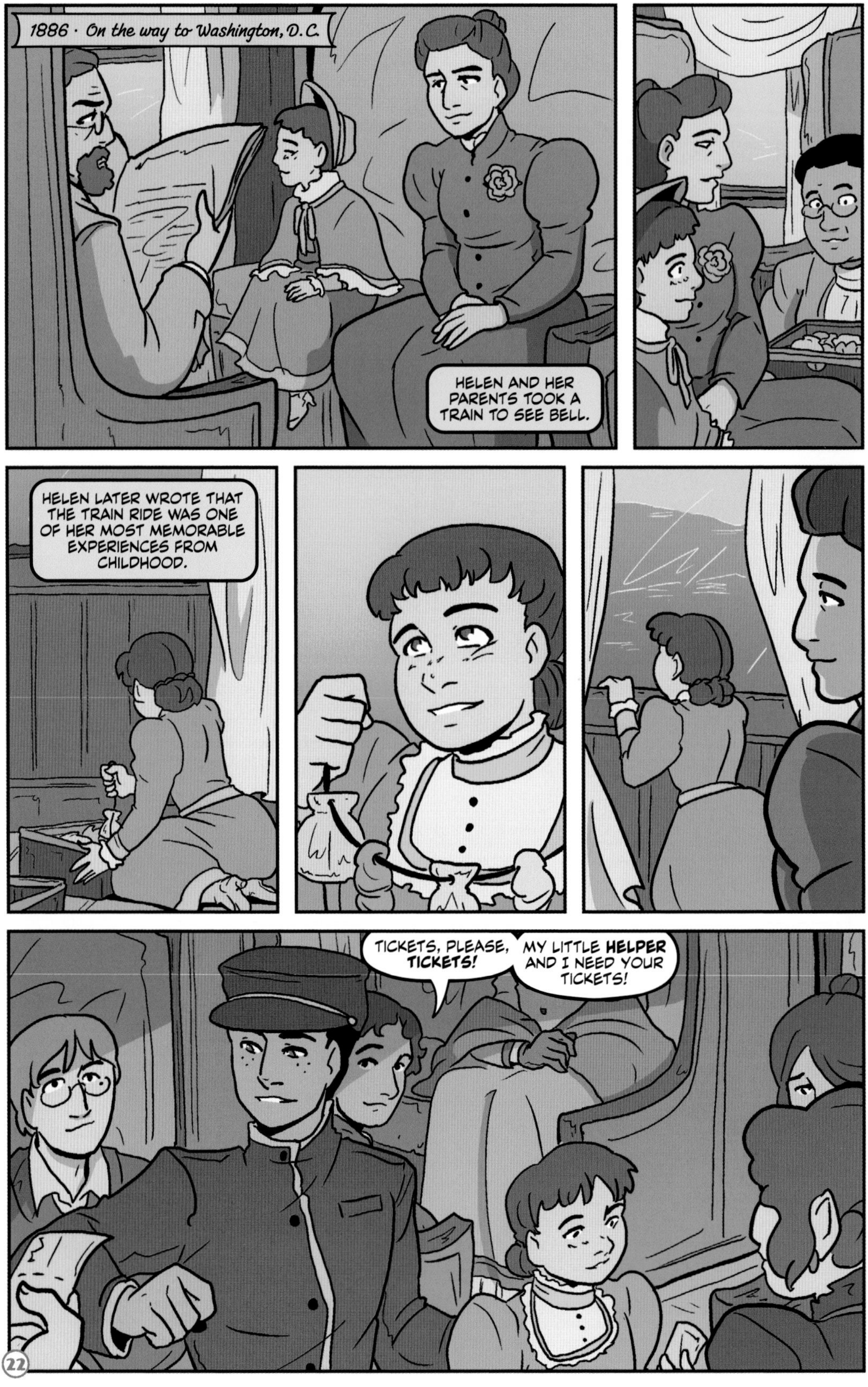
1886 · On the way to Washington, D.C.
HELEN AND HER PARENTS TOOK A TRAIN TO SEE BELL.
HELEN LATER WROTE THAT THE TRAIN RIDE WAS ONE OF HER MOST MEMORABLE EXPERIENCES FROM CHILDHOOD.
TICKETS, PLEASE, TICKETS!
MY LITTLE HELPER AND I NEED YOUR TICKETS!

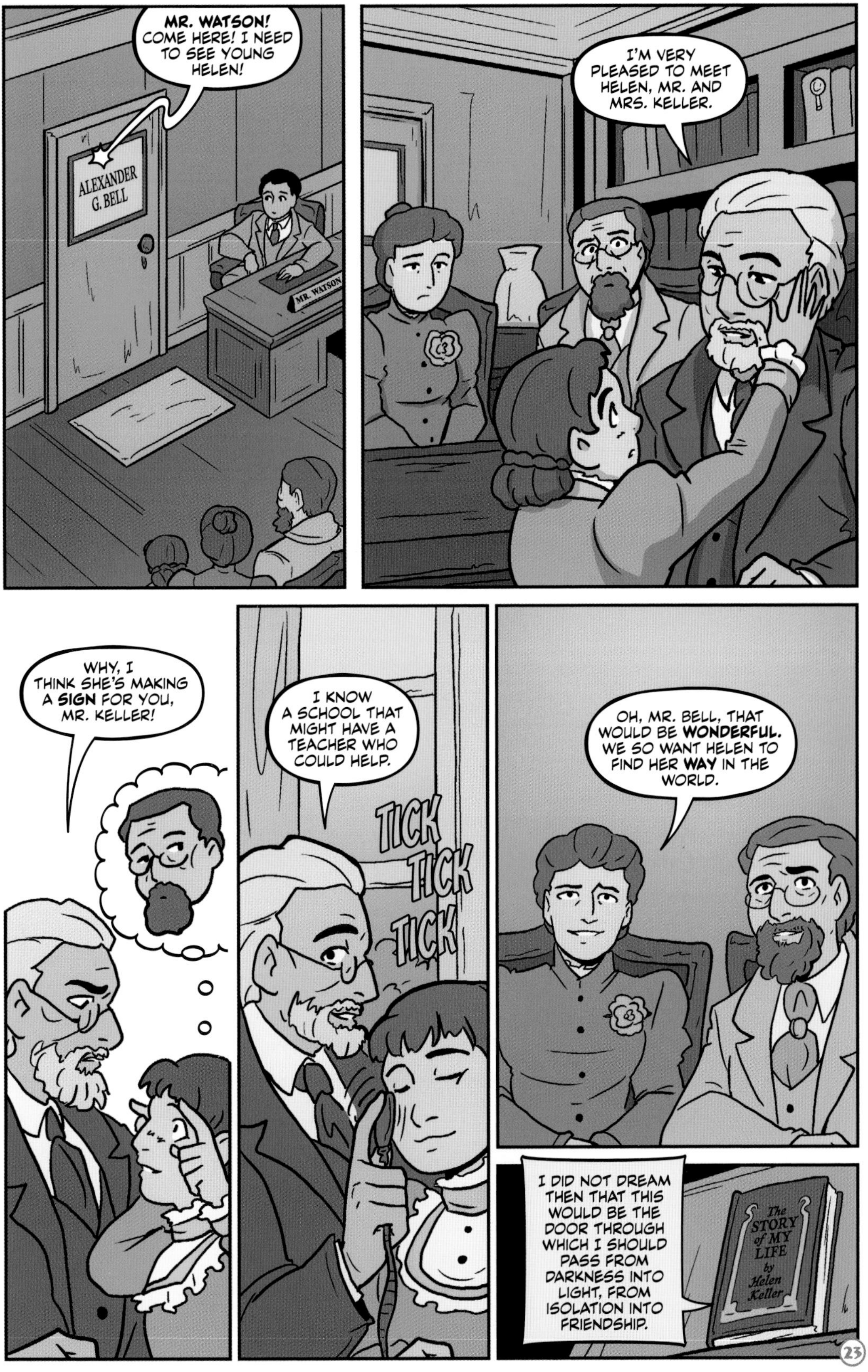
MR. WATSON! COME HERE! I NEED TO SEE YOUNG HELEN!
ALEXANDER G. BELL
MR. WATSON
I'M VERY PLEASED TO MEET HELEN, MR. AND MRS. KELLER.
WHY, I THINK SHE'S MAKING A SIGN FOR YOU, MR. KELLER!
I KNOW A SCHOOL THAT MIGHT HAVE A TEACHER WHO COULD HELP.
TICK TICK TICK
OH, MR. BELL, THAT WOULD BE WONDERFUL. WE SO WANT HELEN TO FIND HER WAY IN THE WORLD.
I DID NOT DREAM THEN THAT THIS WOULD BE THE DOOR THROUGH WHICH I SHOULD PASS FROM DARKNESS INTO LIGHT, FROM ISOLATION INTO FRIENDSHIP.
The STORY of MY LIFE by Helen Keller

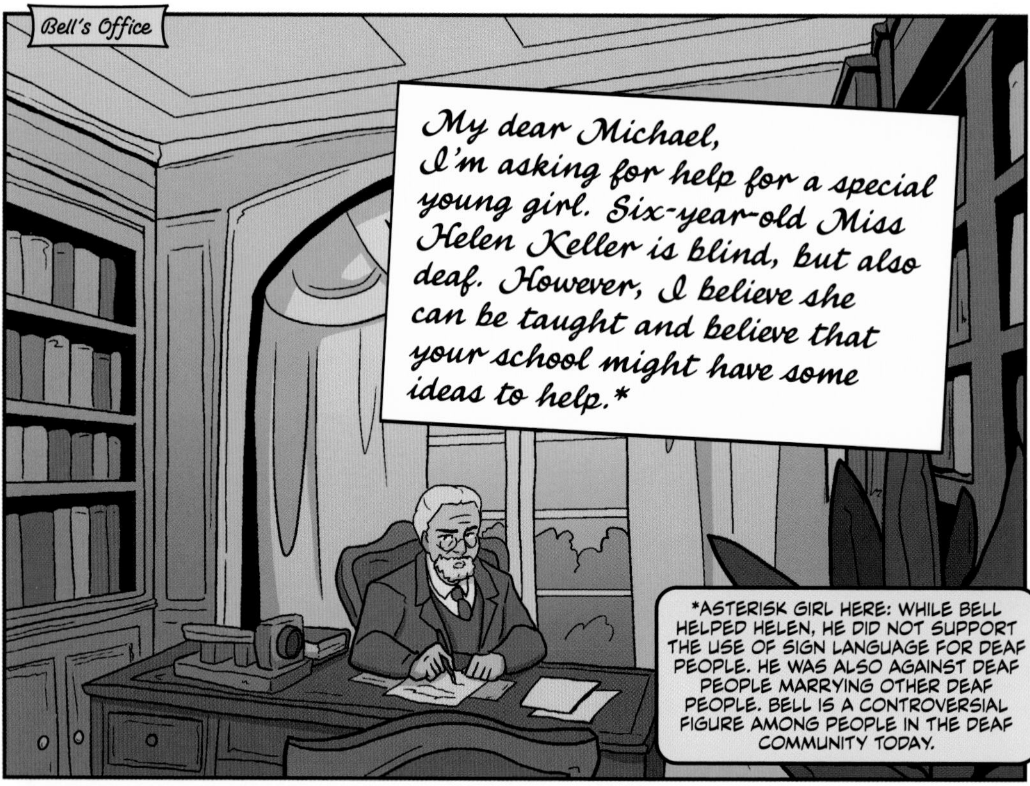
Bell's Office
My dear Michael,
I'm asking for help for a special young girl. Six-year-old Miss Helen Keller is blind, but also deaf. However, I believe she can be taught and believe that your school might have some ideas to help.*
*ASTERISK GIRL HERE: WHILE BELL HELPED HELEN, HE DID NOT SUPPORT THE USE OF SIGN LANGUAGE FOR DEAF PEOPLE. HE WAS ALSO AGAINST DEAF PEOPLE MARRYING OTHER DEAF PEOPLE. BELL IS A CONTROVERSIAL FIGURE AMONG PEOPLE IN THE DEAF COMMUNITY TODAY.

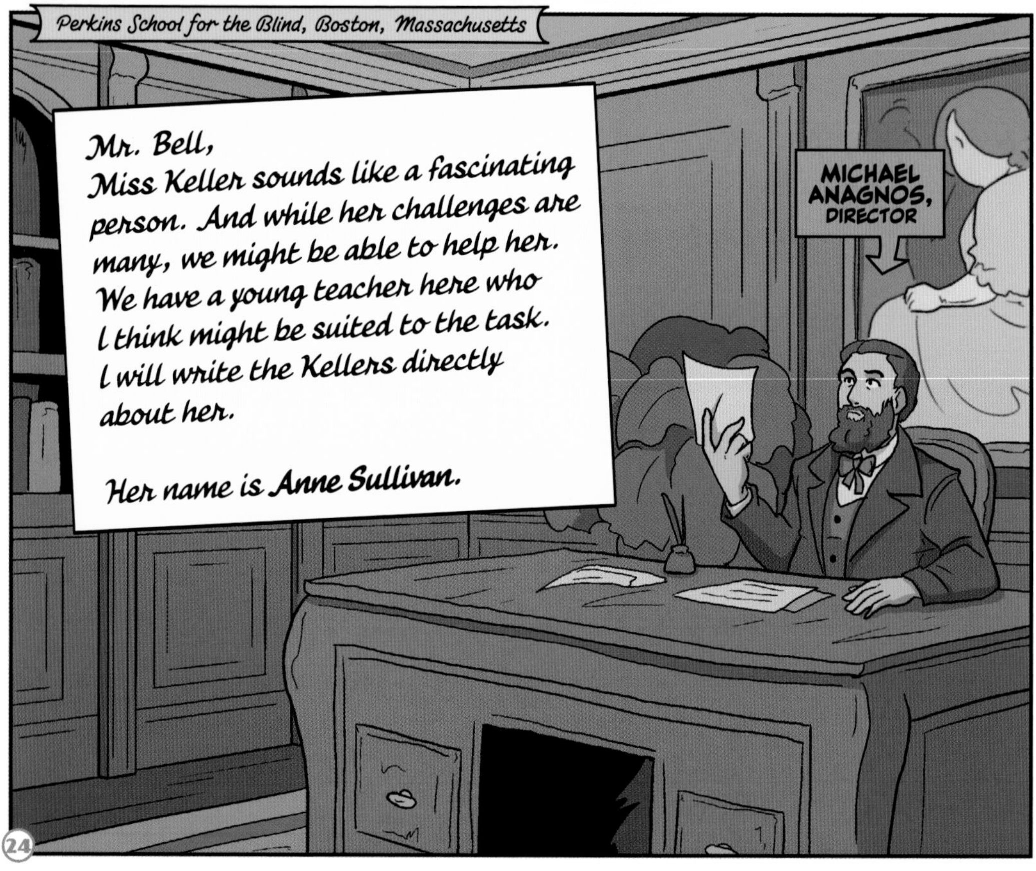
Perkins School for the Blind, Boston, Massachusetts
Mr. Bell,
Miss Keller sounds like a fascinating person. And while her challenges are many, we might be able to help her. We have a young teacher here who I think might be suited to the task. I will write the Kellers directly about her.
Her name is Anne Sullivan.
MICHAEL ANAGNOS, DIRECTOR

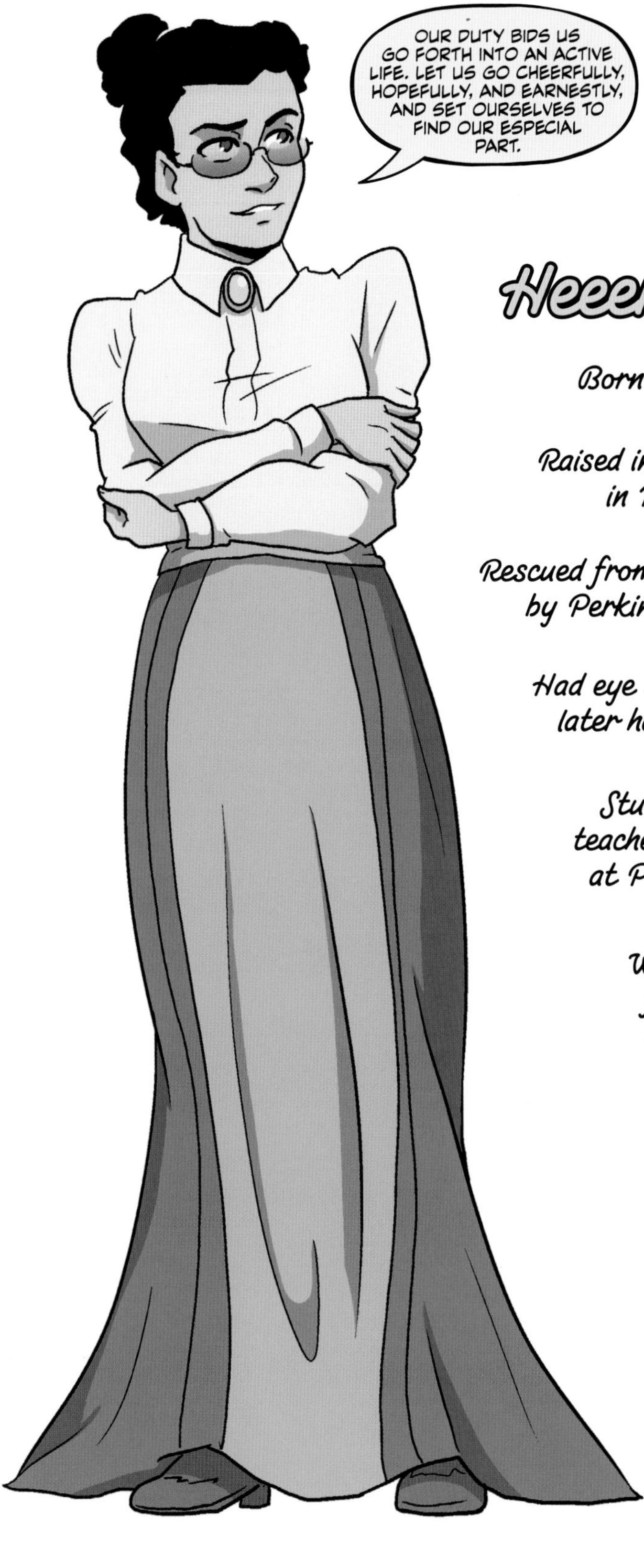
OUR DUTY BIDS US GO FORTH INTO AN ACTIVE LIFE. LET US GO CHEERFULLY, HOPEFULLY, AND EARNESTLY, AND SET OURSELVES TO FIND OUR ESPECIAL PART.

Heeere's Anne!

Born in 1866

Raised in desperate poverty in Massachusetts

Rescued from orphanage by Perkins School

Had eye disease when young, later had surgery to fix it

Studied to be a teacher of the blind at Perkins School

Worked with Helen from 1887 until Sullivan's death in 1936

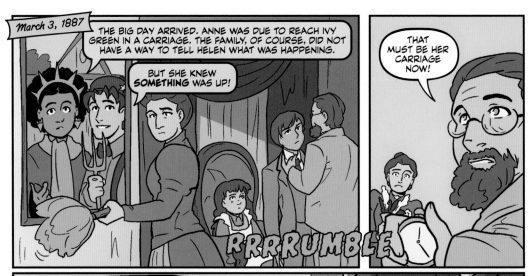

THE BIG DAY ARRIVED. ANNE WAS DUE TO REACH IVY GREEN IN A CARRIAGE. THE FAMILY, OF COURSE, DID NOT HAVE A WAY TO TELL HELEN WHAT WAS HAPPENING.

BUT SHE KNEW **SOMETHING** WAS UP!

THAT MUST BE HER CARRIAGE NOW!

MISS SULLIVAN, WELCOME TO IVY GREEN!

I'M SO PLEASED TO BE HERE, MR. AND MRS. KELLER. I'VE BEEN ON A TRAIN FOR THREE DAYS!

THANK YOU FOR COMING ALL THE WAY FROM MASSACHUSETTS, MISS SULLIVAN. THIS IS **HELEN!**

HELEN, I KNOW YOU CAN'T **HEAR** ME, BUT MY NAME IS ANNE. I'M GOING TO BE YOUR...

26

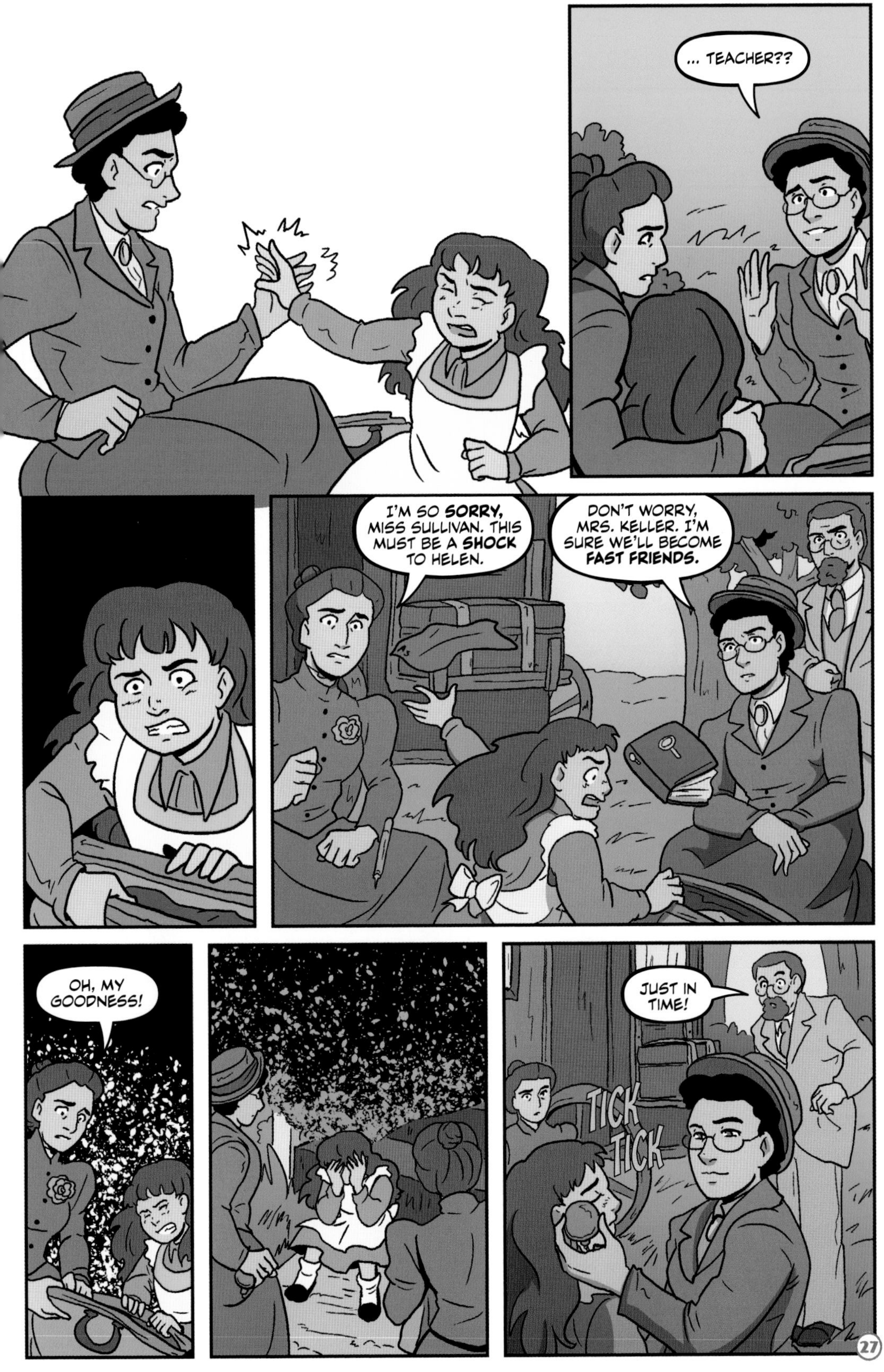
... TEACHER??
I'M SO SORRY, MISS SULLIVAN. THIS MUST BE A SHOCK TO HELEN.
DON'T WORRY, MRS. KELLER. I'M SURE WE'LL BECOME FAST FRIENDS.
OH, MY GOODNESS!
JUST IN TIME!
TICK
TICK

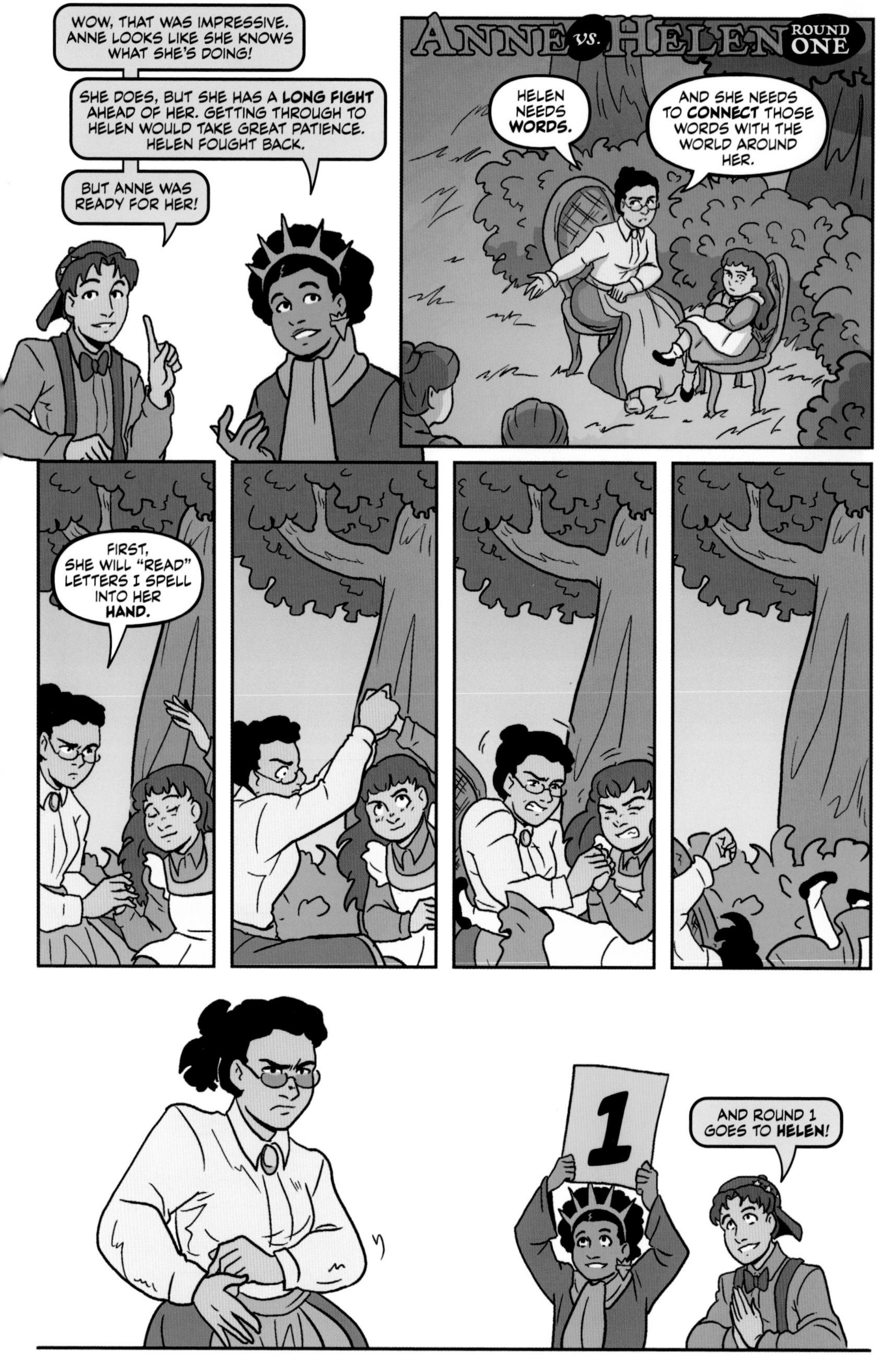
WOW, THAT WAS IMPRESSIVE. ANNE LOOKS LIKE SHE KNOWS WHAT SHE'S DOING!
SHE DOES, BUT SHE HAS A **LONG FIGHT** AHEAD OF HER. GETTING THROUGH TO HELEN WOULD TAKE GREAT PATIENCE. HELEN FOUGHT BACK.
BUT ANNE WAS READY FOR HER!
ANNE vs. HELEN ROUND ONE
HELEN NEEDS **WORDS.**
AND SHE NEEDS TO **CONNECT** THOSE WORDS WITH THE WORLD AROUND HER.
FIRST, SHE WILL "READ" LETTERS I SPELL INTO HER **HAND.**
1
AND ROUND 1 GOES TO **HELEN!**

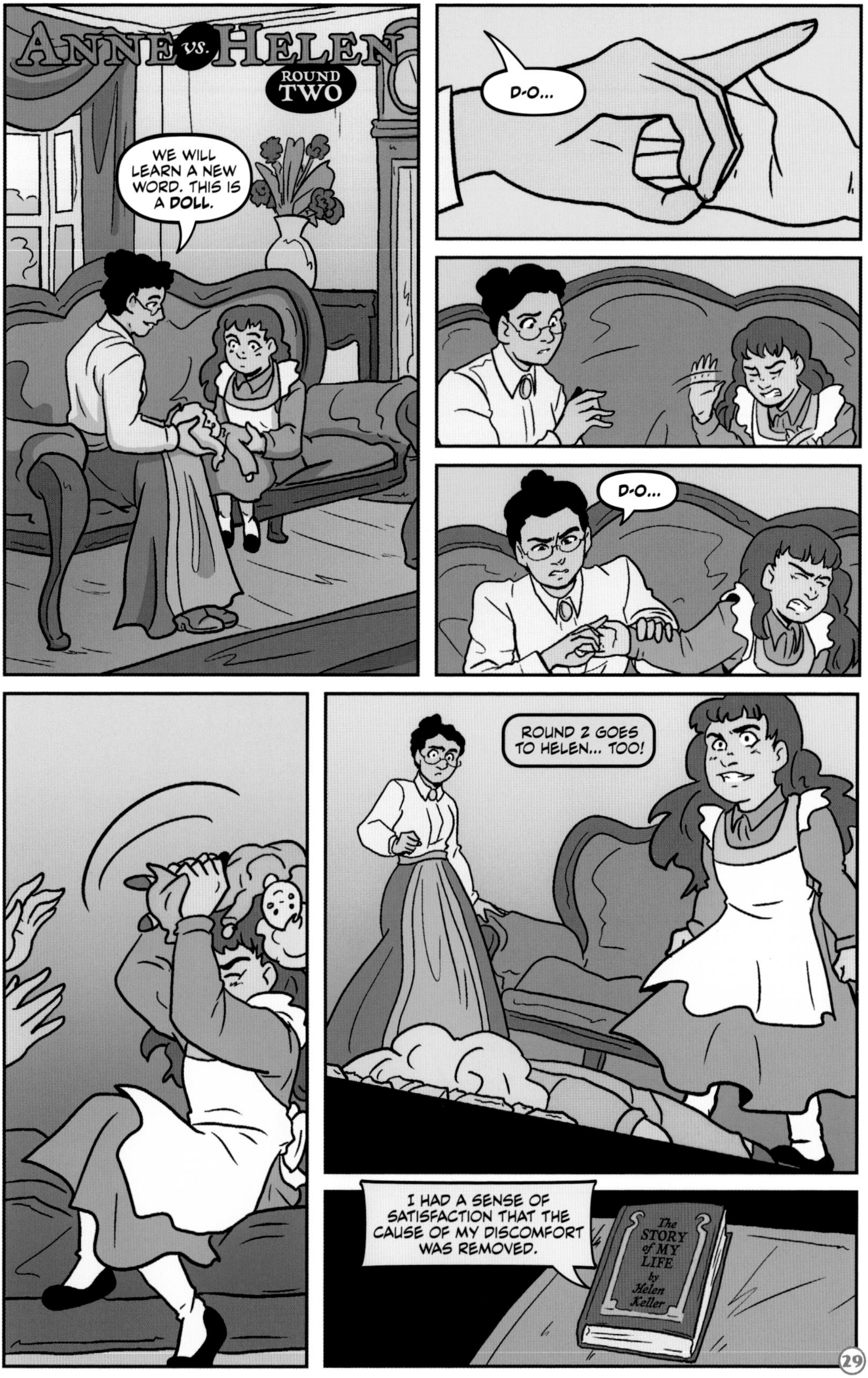
ANNE vs. HELEN
ROUND TWO
WE WILL LEARN A NEW WORD. THIS IS A DOLL.
D-O...
D-O...
ROUND 2 GOES TO HELEN... TOO!
I HAD A SENSE OF SATISFACTION THAT THE CAUSE OF MY DISCOMFORT WAS REMOVED.
The STORY of MY LIFE by Helen Keller

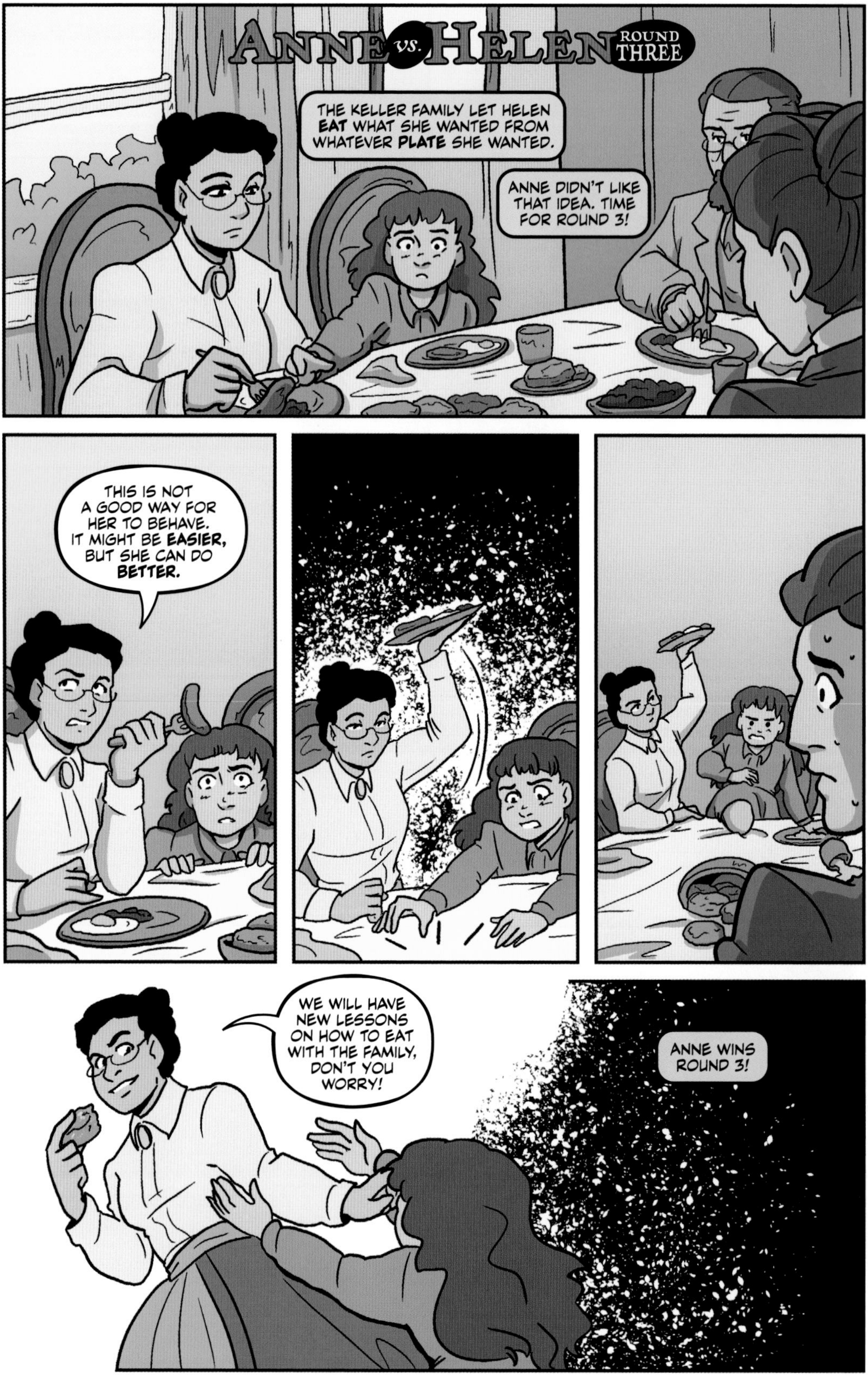
ANNE vs. HELEN ROUND THREE
THE KELLER FAMILY LET HELEN **EAT** WHAT SHE WANTED FROM WHATEVER **PLATE** SHE WANTED.
ANNE DIDN'T LIKE THAT IDEA. TIME FOR ROUND 3!
THIS IS NOT A GOOD WAY FOR HER TO BEHAVE. IT MIGHT BE **EASIER,** BUT SHE CAN DO **BETTER.**
WE WILL HAVE NEW LESSONS ON HOW TO EAT WITH THE FAMILY, DON'T YOU WORRY!
ANNE WINS ROUND 3!

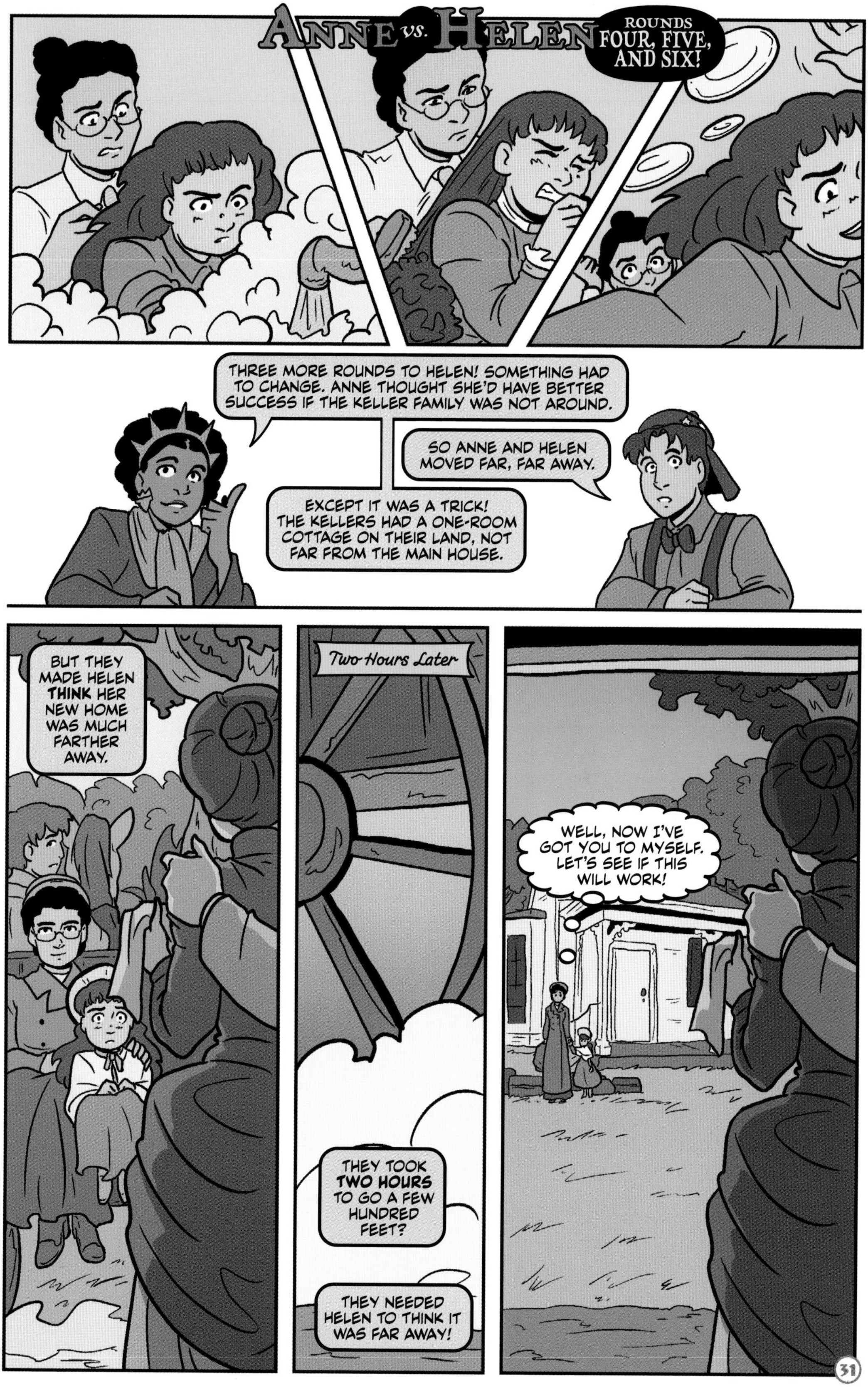
ANNE vs. HELEN
ROUNDS FOUR, FIVE, AND SIX!
THREE MORE ROUNDS TO HELEN! SOMETHING HAD TO CHANGE. ANNE THOUGHT SHE'D HAVE BETTER SUCCESS IF THE KELLER FAMILY WAS NOT AROUND.
SO ANNE AND HELEN MOVED FAR, FAR AWAY.
EXCEPT IT WAS A TRICK! THE KELLERS HAD A ONE-ROOM COTTAGE ON THEIR LAND, NOT FAR FROM THE MAIN HOUSE.
BUT THEY MADE HELEN **THINK** HER NEW HOME WAS MUCH FARTHER AWAY.
Two Hours Later
THEY TOOK **TWO HOURS** TO GO A FEW HUNDRED FEET?
THEY NEEDED HELEN TO THINK IT WAS FAR AWAY!
WELL, NOW I'VE GOT YOU TO MYSELF. LET'S SEE IF THIS WILL WORK!

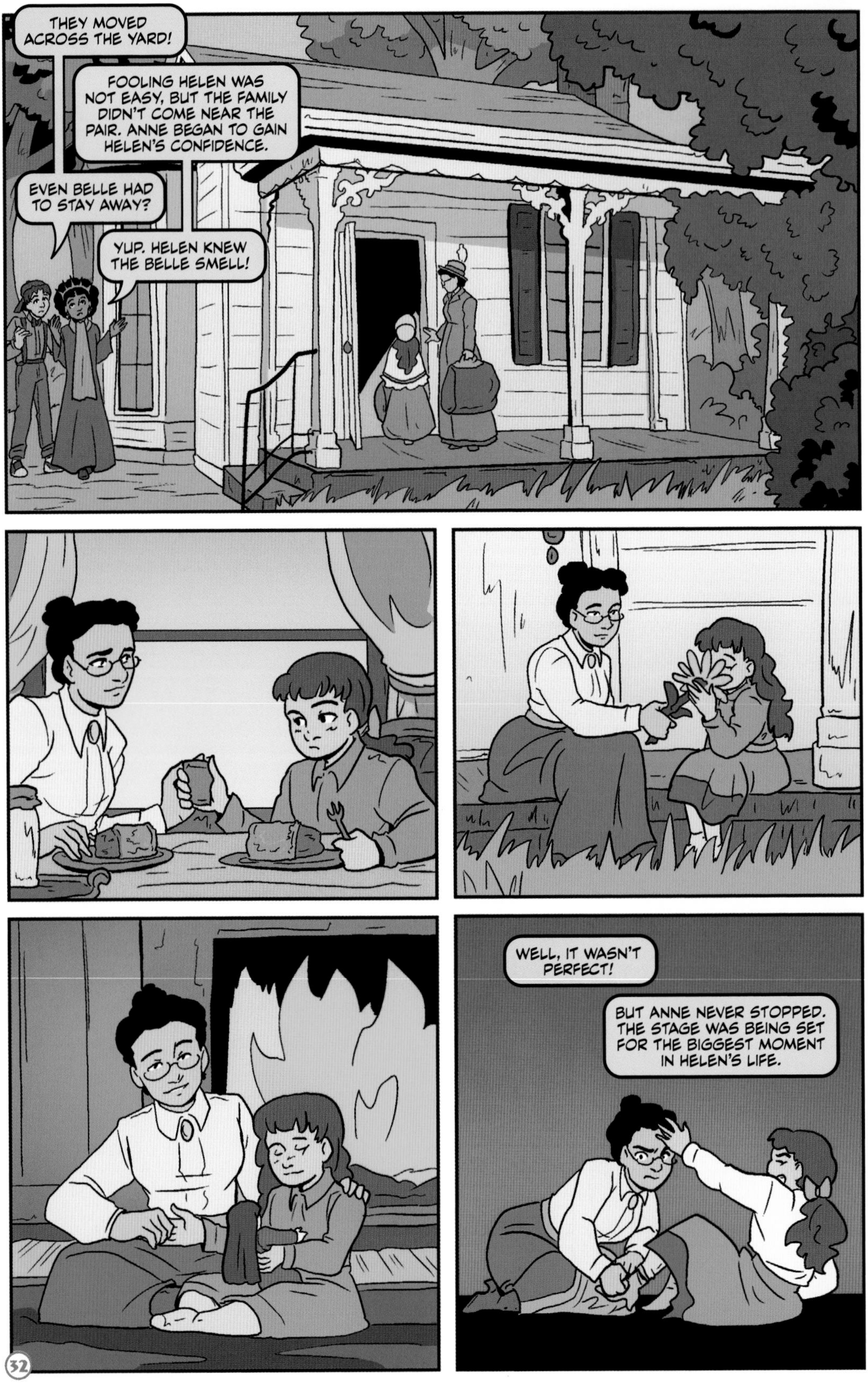
THEY MOVED ACROSS THE YARD!
FOOLING HELEN WAS NOT EASY, BUT THE FAMILY DIDN'T COME NEAR THE PAIR. ANNE BEGAN TO GAIN HELEN'S CONFIDENCE.
EVEN BELLE HAD TO STAY AWAY?
YUP. HELEN KNEW THE BELLE SMELL!
WELL, IT WASN'T PERFECT!
BUT ANNE NEVER STOPPED. THE STAGE WAS BEING SET FOR THE BIGGEST MOMENT IN HELEN'S LIFE.

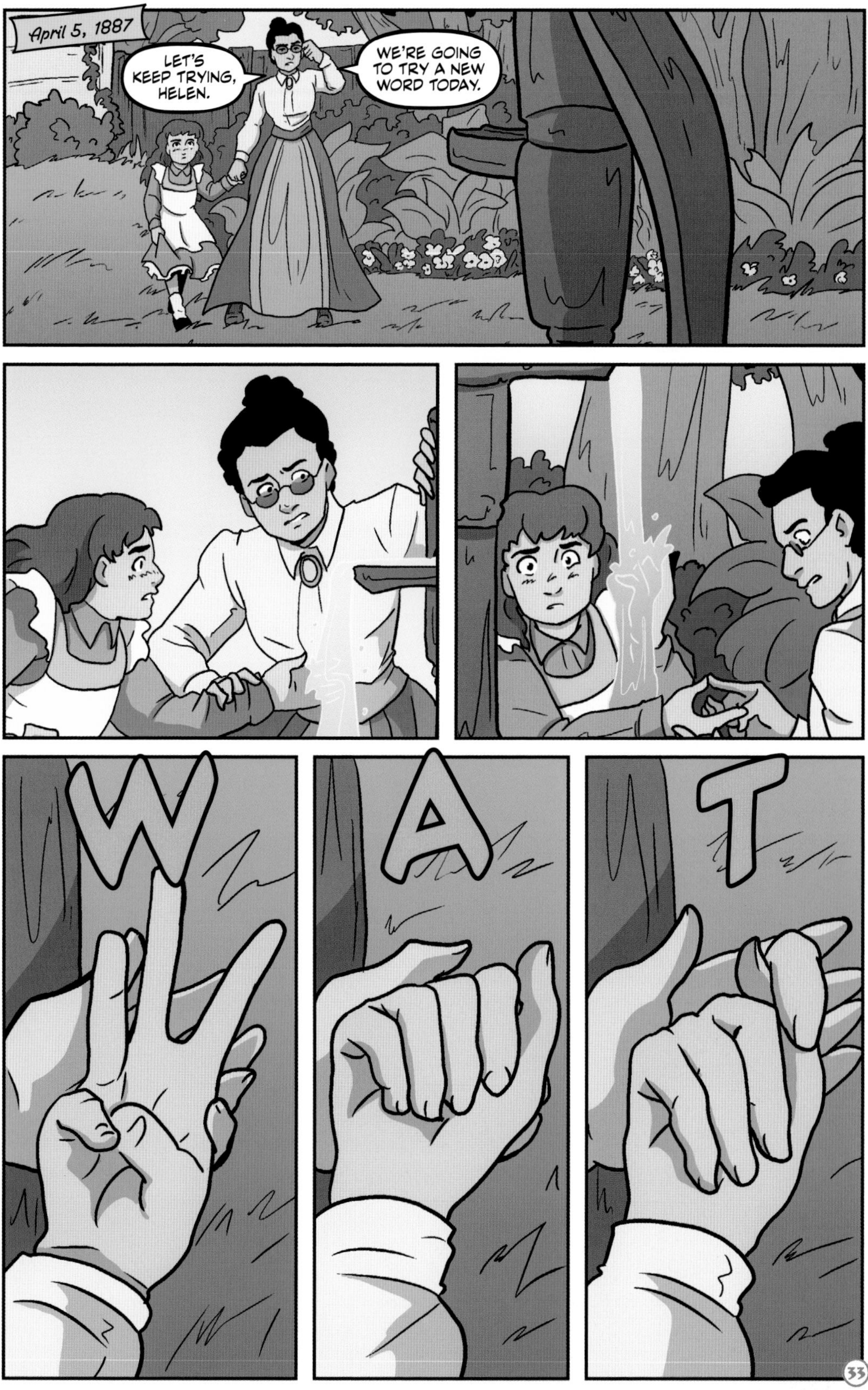
April 5, 1887
LET'S KEEP TRYING, HELEN.
WE'RE GOING TO TRY A NEW WORD TODAY.
W
A
T

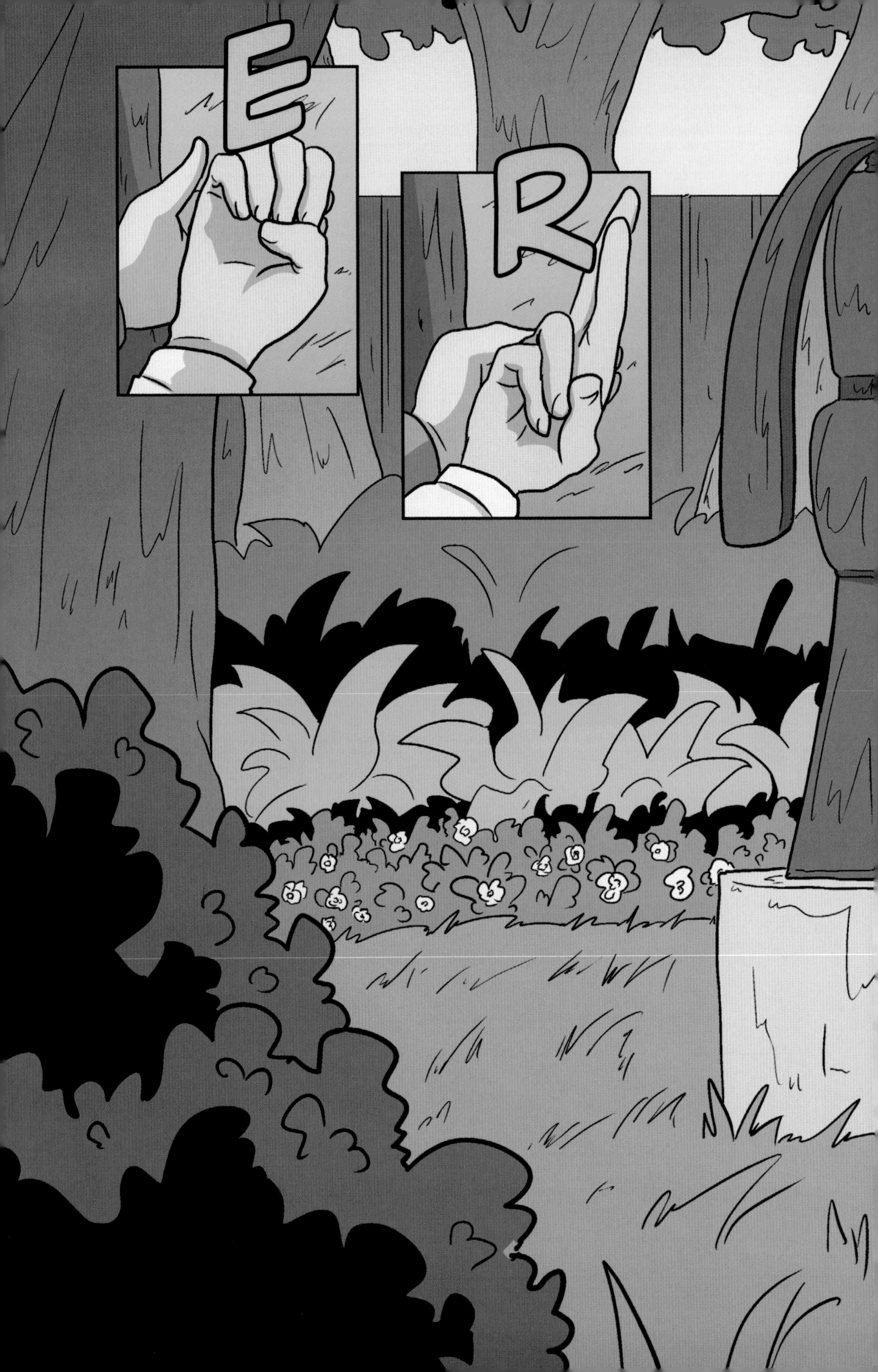
E
R

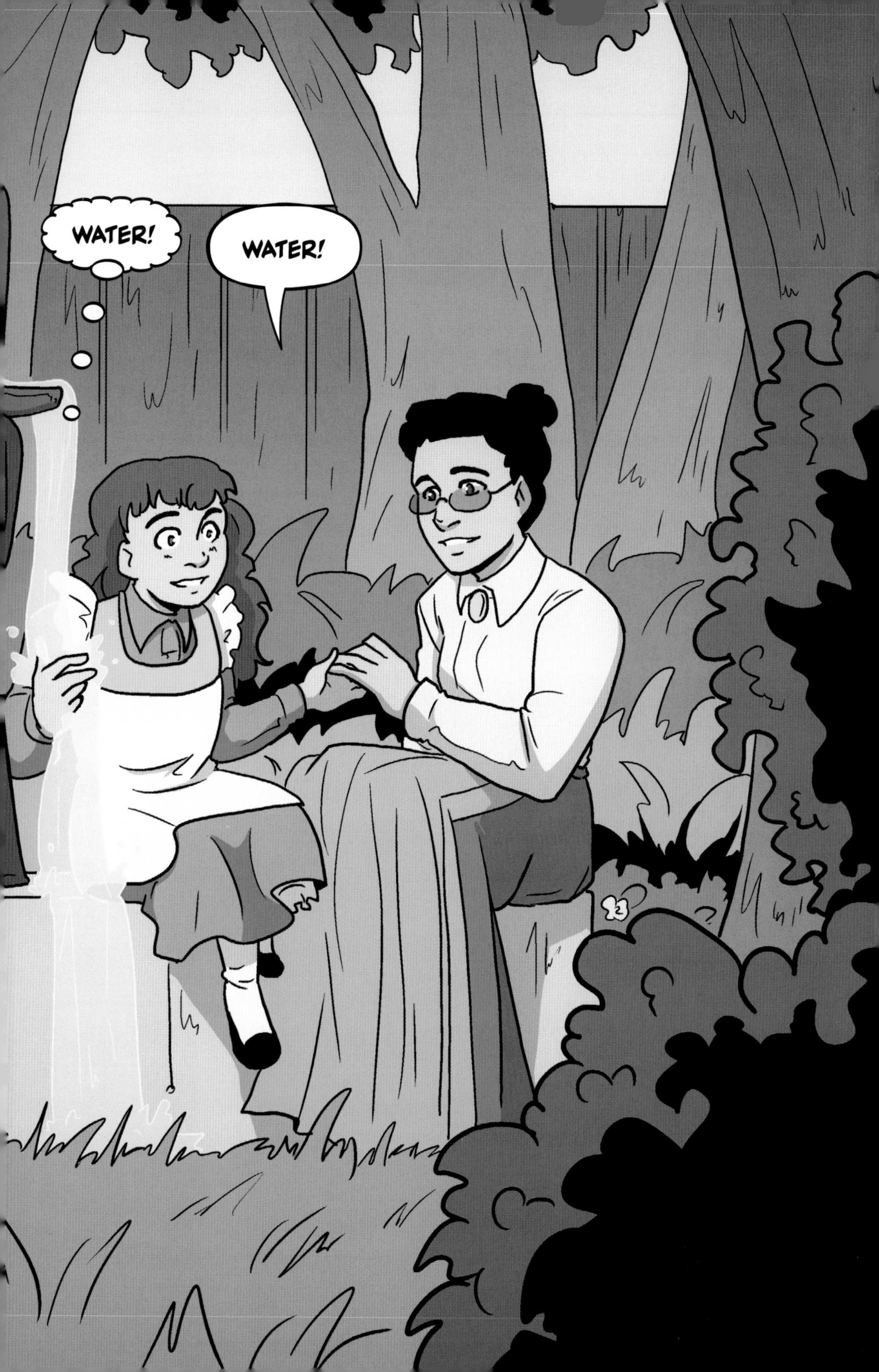
WATER!
WATER!

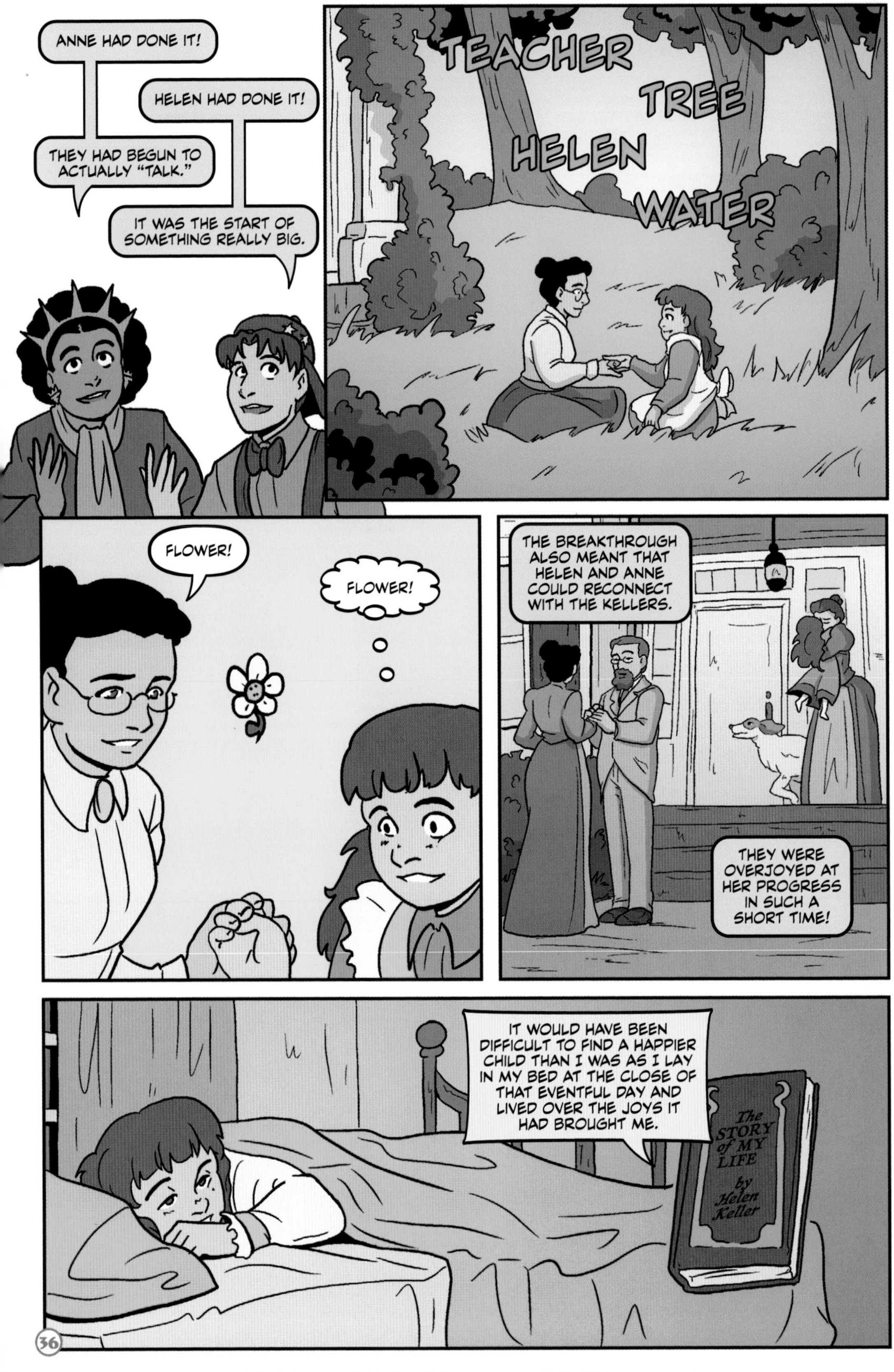

ANNE HAD DONE IT!
HELEN HAD DONE IT!
THEY HAD BEGUN TO ACTUALLY "TALK."
IT WAS THE START OF SOMETHING REALLY BIG.
TEACHER
TREE
HELEN
WATER
FLOWER!
FLOWER!
THE BREAKTHROUGH ALSO MEANT THAT HELEN AND ANNE COULD RECONNECT WITH THE KELLERS.
THEY WERE OVERJOYED AT HER PROGRESS IN SUCH A SHORT TIME!
IT WOULD HAVE BEEN DIFFICULT TO FIND A HAPPIER CHILD THAN I WAS AS I LAY IN MY BED AT THE CLOSE OF THAT EVENTFUL DAY AND LIVED OVER THE JOYS IT HAD BROUGHT ME.
The STORY of MY LIFE by Helen Keller

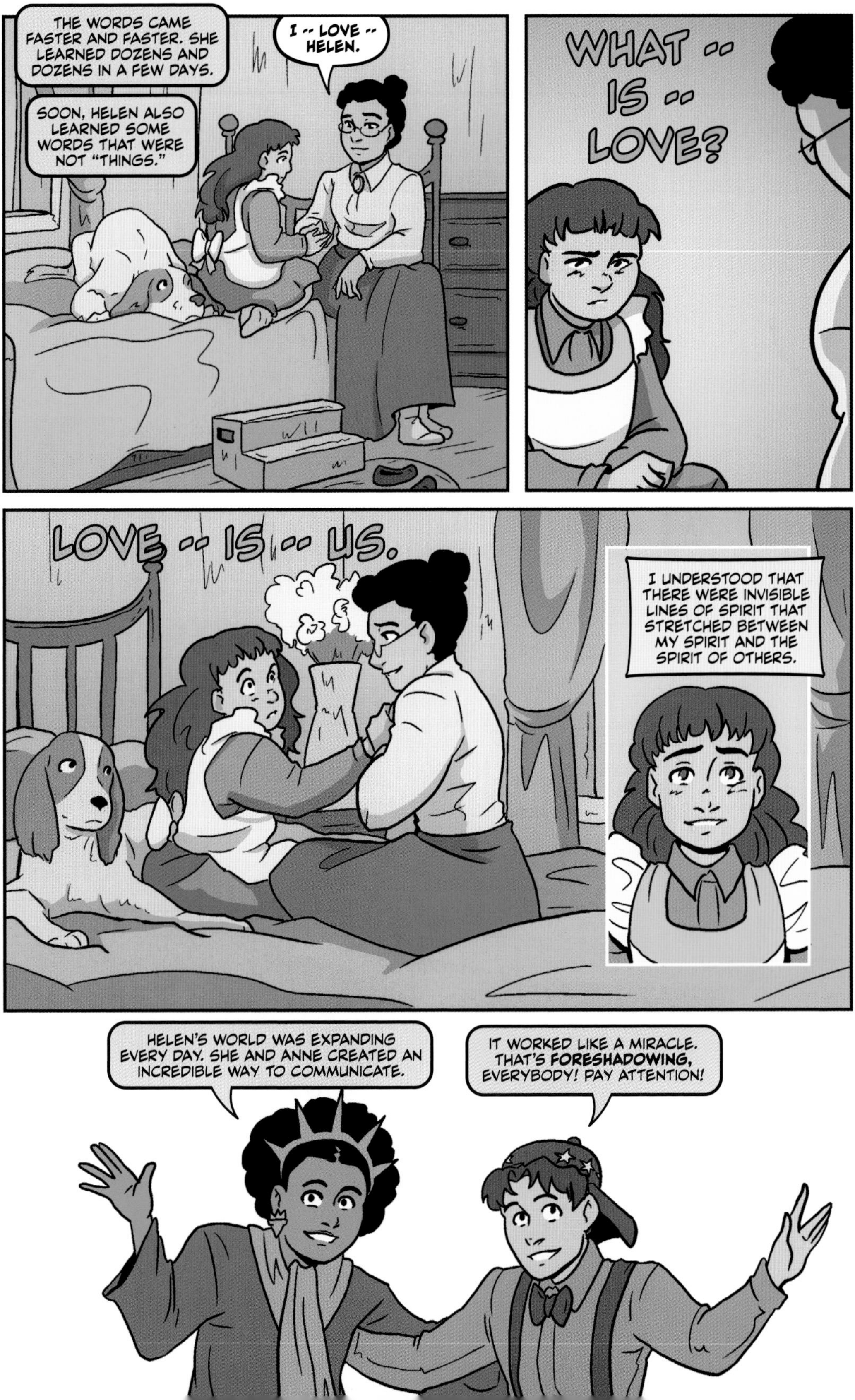
THE WORDS CAME FASTER AND FASTER. SHE LEARNED DOZENS AND DOZENS IN A FEW DAYS.
SOON, HELEN ALSO LEARNED SOME WORDS THAT WERE NOT "THINGS."
I -- LOVE -- HELEN.
WHAT -- IS -- LOVE?
LOVE -- IS -- US.
I UNDERSTOOD THAT THERE WERE INVISIBLE LINES OF SPIRIT THAT STRETCHED BETWEEN MY SPIRIT AND THE SPIRIT OF OTHERS.
HELEN'S WORLD WAS EXPANDING EVERY DAY. SHE AND ANNE CREATED AN INCREDIBLE WAY TO COMMUNICATE.
IT WORKED LIKE A MIRACLE. THAT'S FORESHADOWING, EVERYBODY! PAY ATTENTION!

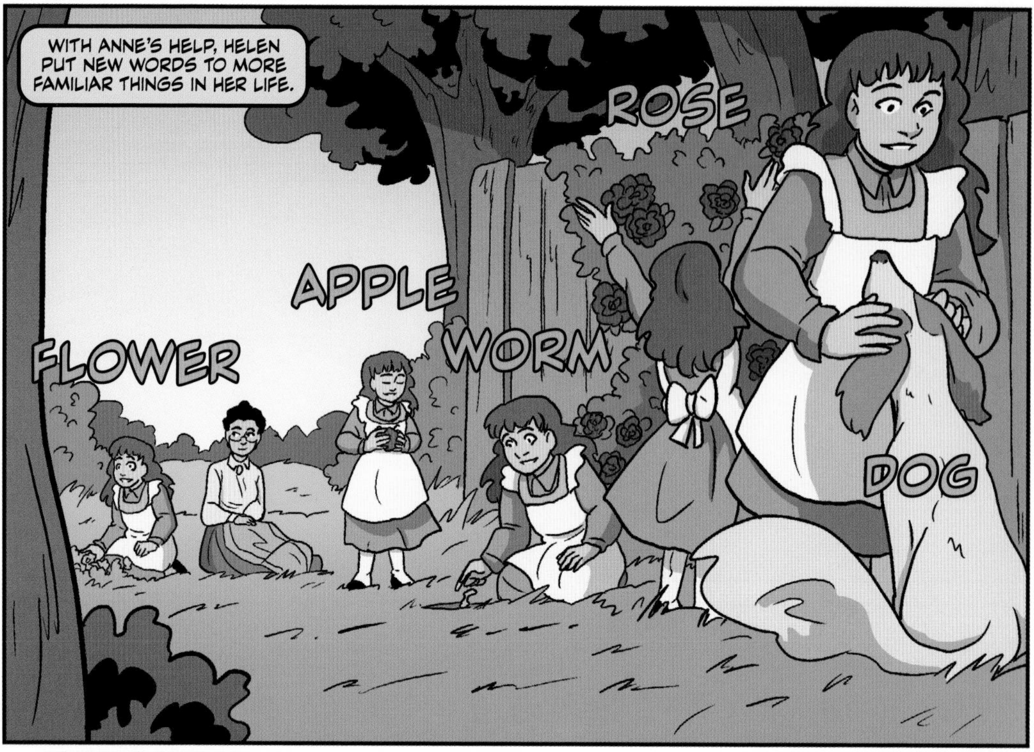
WITH ANNE'S HELP, HELEN PUT NEW WORDS TO MORE FAMILIAR THINGS IN HER LIFE.
FLOWER
APPLE
WORM
ROSE
DOG

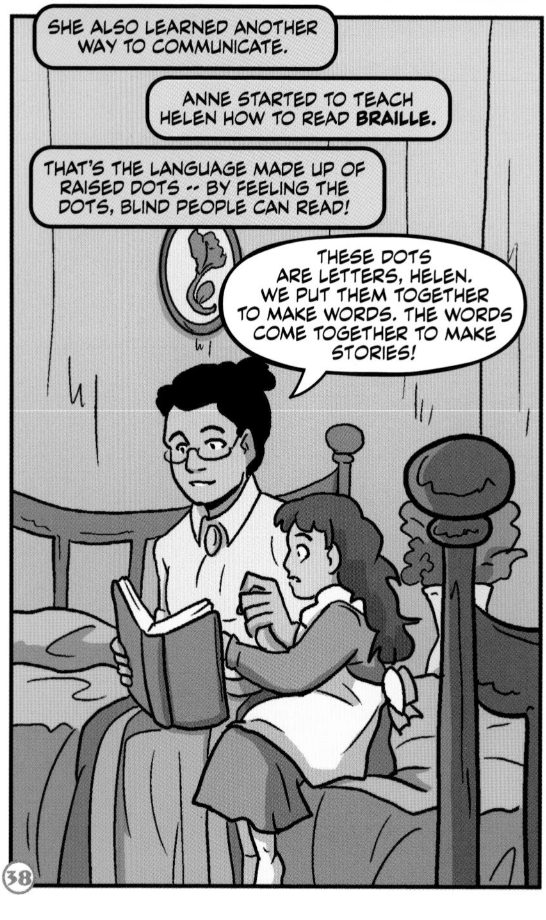
SHE ALSO LEARNED ANOTHER WAY TO COMMUNICATE.
ANNE STARTED TO TEACH HELEN HOW TO READ **BRAILLE.**
THAT'S THE LANGUAGE MADE UP OF RAISED DOTS -- BY FEELING THE DOTS, BLIND PEOPLE CAN READ!
THESE DOTS ARE LETTERS, HELEN. WE PUT THEM TOGETHER TO MAKE WORDS. THE WORDS COME TOGETHER TO MAKE STORIES!

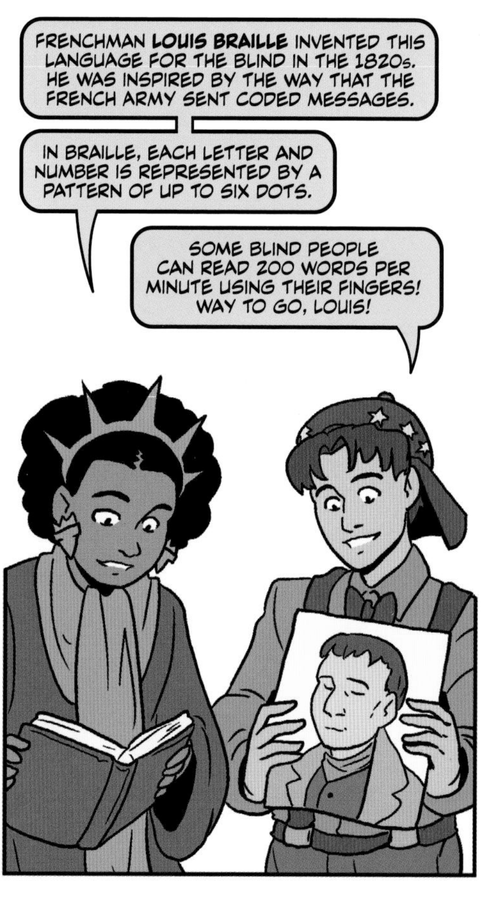
FRENCHMAN **LOUIS BRAILLE** INVENTED THIS LANGUAGE FOR THE BLIND IN THE 1820s. HE WAS INSPIRED BY THE WAY THAT THE FRENCH ARMY SENT CODED MESSAGES.
IN BRAILLE, EACH LETTER AND NUMBER IS REPRESENTED BY A PATTERN OF UP TO SIX DOTS.
SOME BLIND PEOPLE CAN READ 200 WORDS PER MINUTE USING THEIR FINGERS! WAY TO GO, LOUIS!

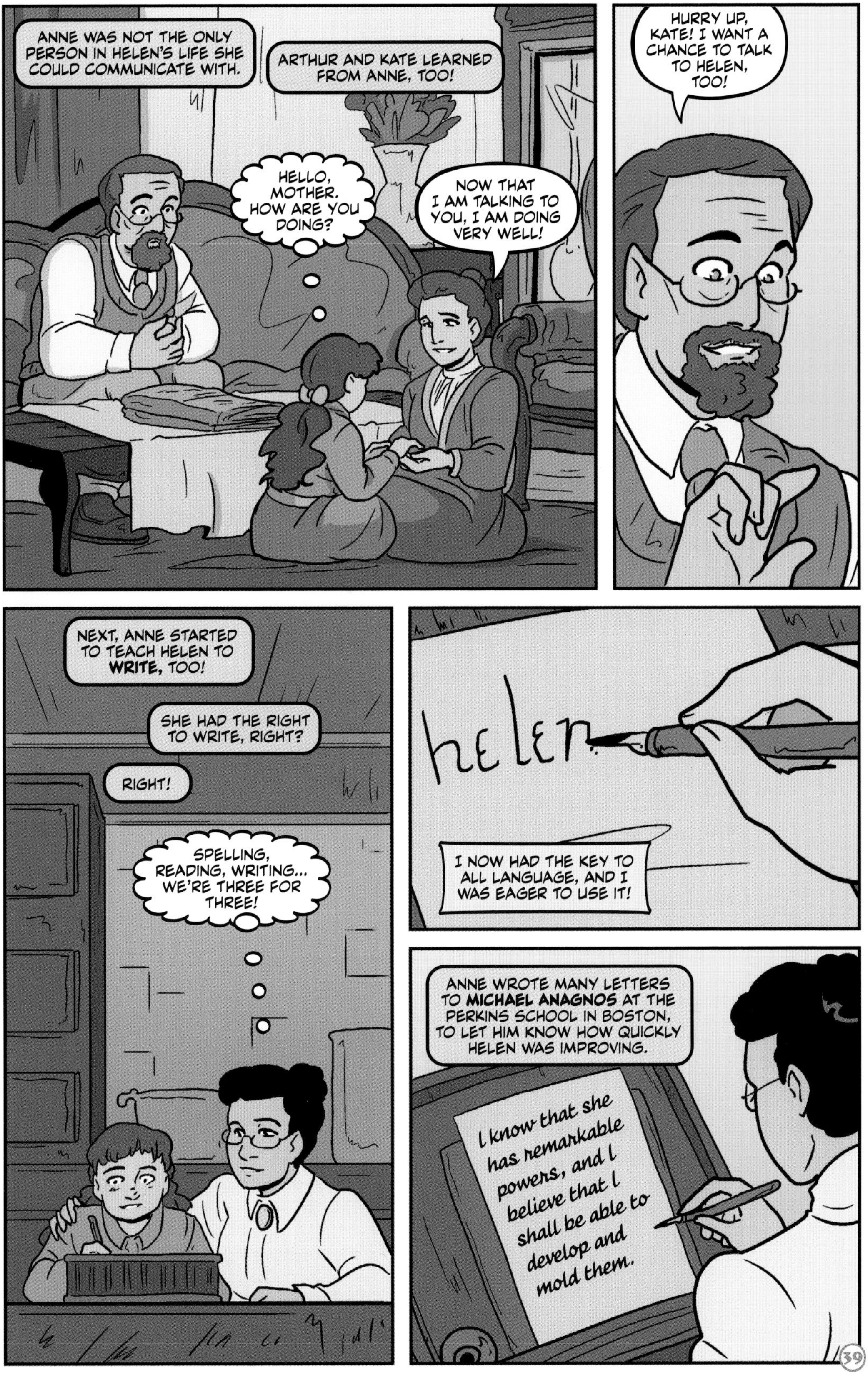
ANNE WAS NOT THE ONLY PERSON IN HELEN'S LIFE SHE COULD COMMUNICATE WITH.
ARTHUR AND KATE LEARNED FROM ANNE, TOO!
HELLO, MOTHER. HOW ARE YOU DOING?
NOW THAT I AM TALKING TO YOU, I AM DOING VERY WELL!
HURRY UP, KATE! I WANT A CHANCE TO TALK TO HELEN, TOO!
NEXT, ANNE STARTED TO TEACH HELEN TO **WRITE**, TOO!
SHE HAD THE RIGHT TO WRITE, RIGHT?
RIGHT!
SPELLING, READING, WRITING... WE'RE THREE FOR THREE!
helen
I NOW HAD THE KEY TO ALL LANGUAGE, AND I WAS EAGER TO USE IT!
ANNE WROTE MANY LETTERS TO **MICHAEL ANAGNOS** AT THE PERKINS SCHOOL IN BOSTON, TO LET HIM KNOW HOW QUICKLY HELEN WAS IMPROVING.
I know that she has remarkable powers, and I believe that I shall be able to develop and mold them.

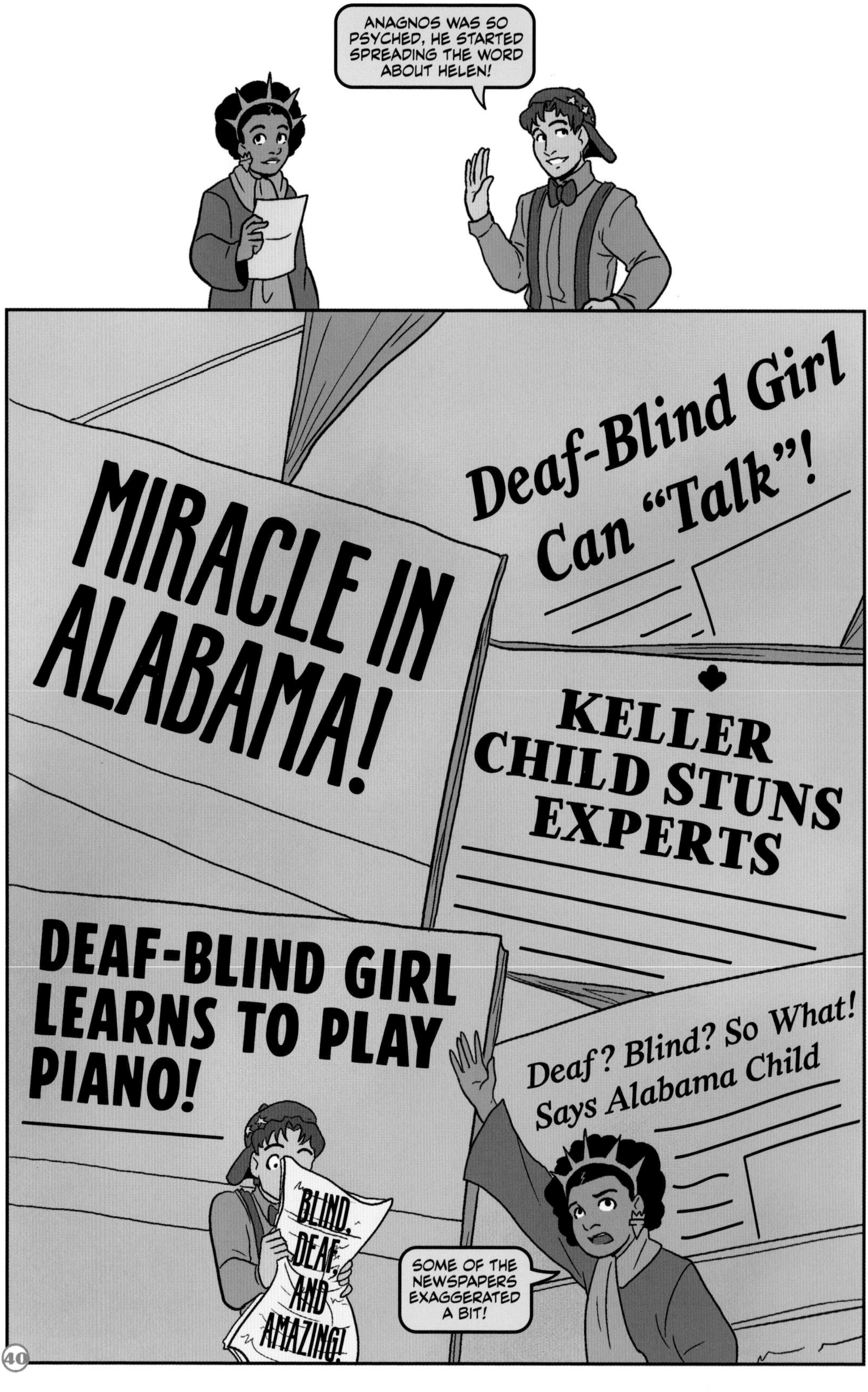

ANAGNOS WAS SO PSYCHED, HE STARTED SPREADING THE WORD ABOUT HELEN!
MIRACLE IN ALABAMA!
Deaf-Blind Girl Can "Talk"!
KELLER CHILD STUNS EXPERTS
DEAF-BLIND GIRL LEARNS TO PLAY PIANO!
Deaf? Blind? So What! Says Alabama Child
BLIND, DEAF AND AMAZING!
SOME OF THE NEWSPAPERS EXAGGERATED A BIT!

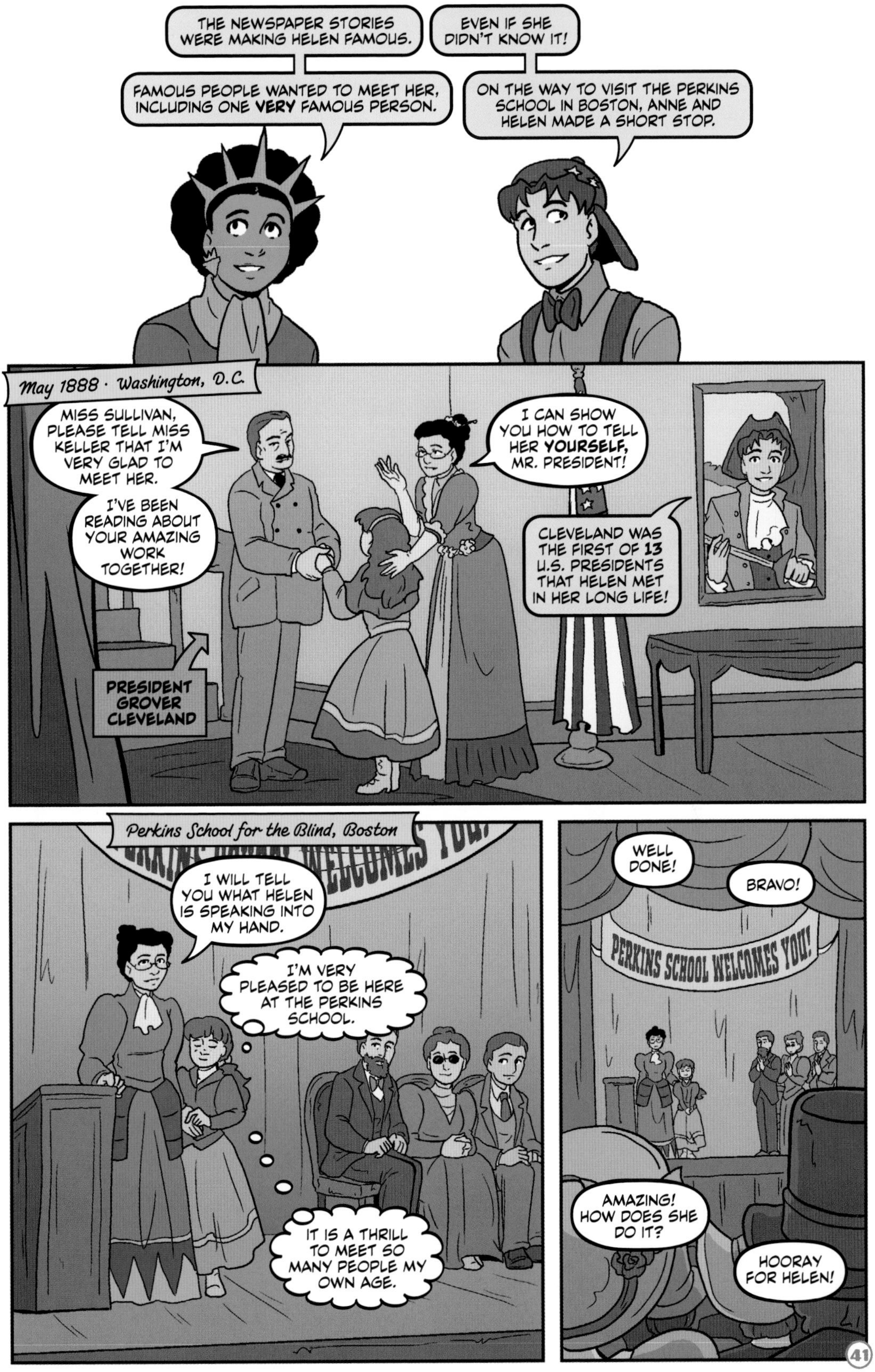

THE NEWSPAPER STORIES WERE MAKING HELEN FAMOUS.
FAMOUS PEOPLE WANTED TO MEET HER, INCLUDING ONE **VERY** FAMOUS PERSON.
EVEN IF SHE DIDN'T KNOW IT!
ON THE WAY TO VISIT THE PERKINS SCHOOL IN BOSTON, ANNE AND HELEN MADE A SHORT STOP.
May 1888 · Washington, D.C.
MISS SULLIVAN, PLEASE TELL MISS KELLER THAT I'M VERY GLAD TO MEET HER.
I'VE BEEN READING ABOUT YOUR AMAZING WORK TOGETHER!
PRESIDENT GROVER CLEVELAND
I CAN SHOW YOU HOW TO TELL HER **YOURSELF,** MR. PRESIDENT!
CLEVELAND WAS THE FIRST OF **13** U.S. PRESIDENTS THAT HELEN MET IN HER LONG LIFE!
Perkins School for the Blind, Boston
I WILL TELL YOU WHAT HELEN IS SPEAKING INTO MY HAND.
I'M VERY PLEASED TO BE HERE AT THE PERKINS SCHOOL.
IT IS A THRILL TO MEET SO MANY PEOPLE MY OWN AGE.
WELL DONE!
BRAVO!
PERKINS SCHOOL WELCOMES YOU!
AMAZING! HOW DOES SHE DO IT?
HOORAY FOR HELEN!

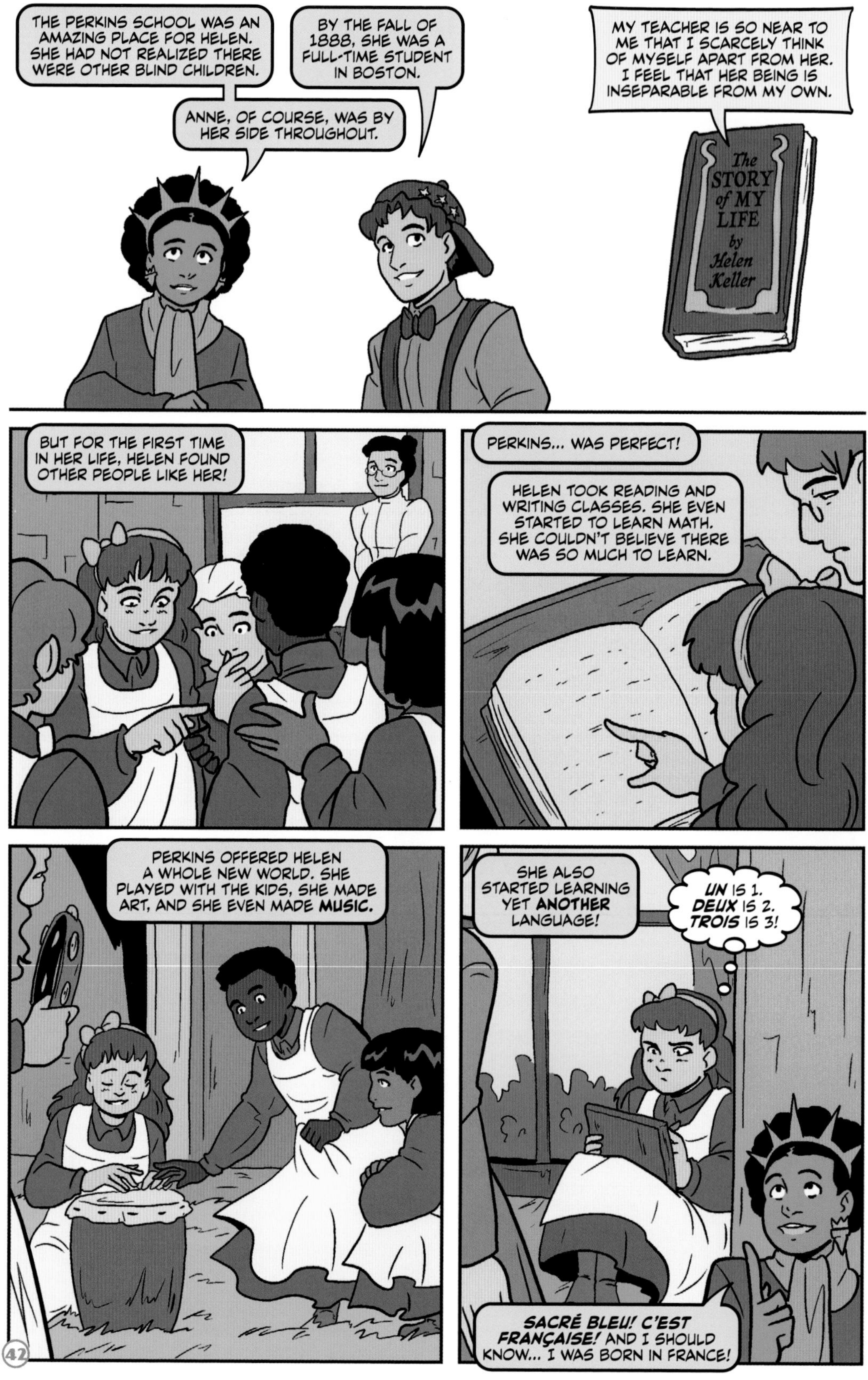
THE PERKINS SCHOOL WAS AN AMAZING PLACE FOR HELEN. SHE HAD NOT REALIZED THERE WERE OTHER BLIND CHILDREN.
BY THE FALL OF 1888, SHE WAS A FULL-TIME STUDENT IN BOSTON.
ANNE, OF COURSE, WAS BY HER SIDE THROUGHOUT.
MY TEACHER IS SO NEAR TO ME THAT I SCARCELY THINK OF MYSELF APART FROM HER. I FEEL THAT HER BEING IS INSEPARABLE FROM MY OWN.
The STORY of MY LIFE by Helen Keller
BUT FOR THE FIRST TIME IN HER LIFE, HELEN FOUND OTHER PEOPLE LIKE HER!
PERKINS... WAS PERFECT!
HELEN TOOK READING AND WRITING CLASSES. SHE EVEN STARTED TO LEARN MATH. SHE COULDN'T BELIEVE THERE WAS SO MUCH TO LEARN.
PERKINS OFFERED HELEN A WHOLE NEW WORLD. SHE PLAYED WITH THE KIDS, SHE MADE ART, AND SHE EVEN MADE **MUSIC.**
SHE ALSO STARTED LEARNING YET **ANOTHER** LANGUAGE!
UN IS 1. ***DEUX*** IS 2. ***TROIS*** IS 3!
SACRÉ BLEU! C'EST FRANÇAISE! AND I SHOULD KNOW... I WAS BORN IN FRANCE!

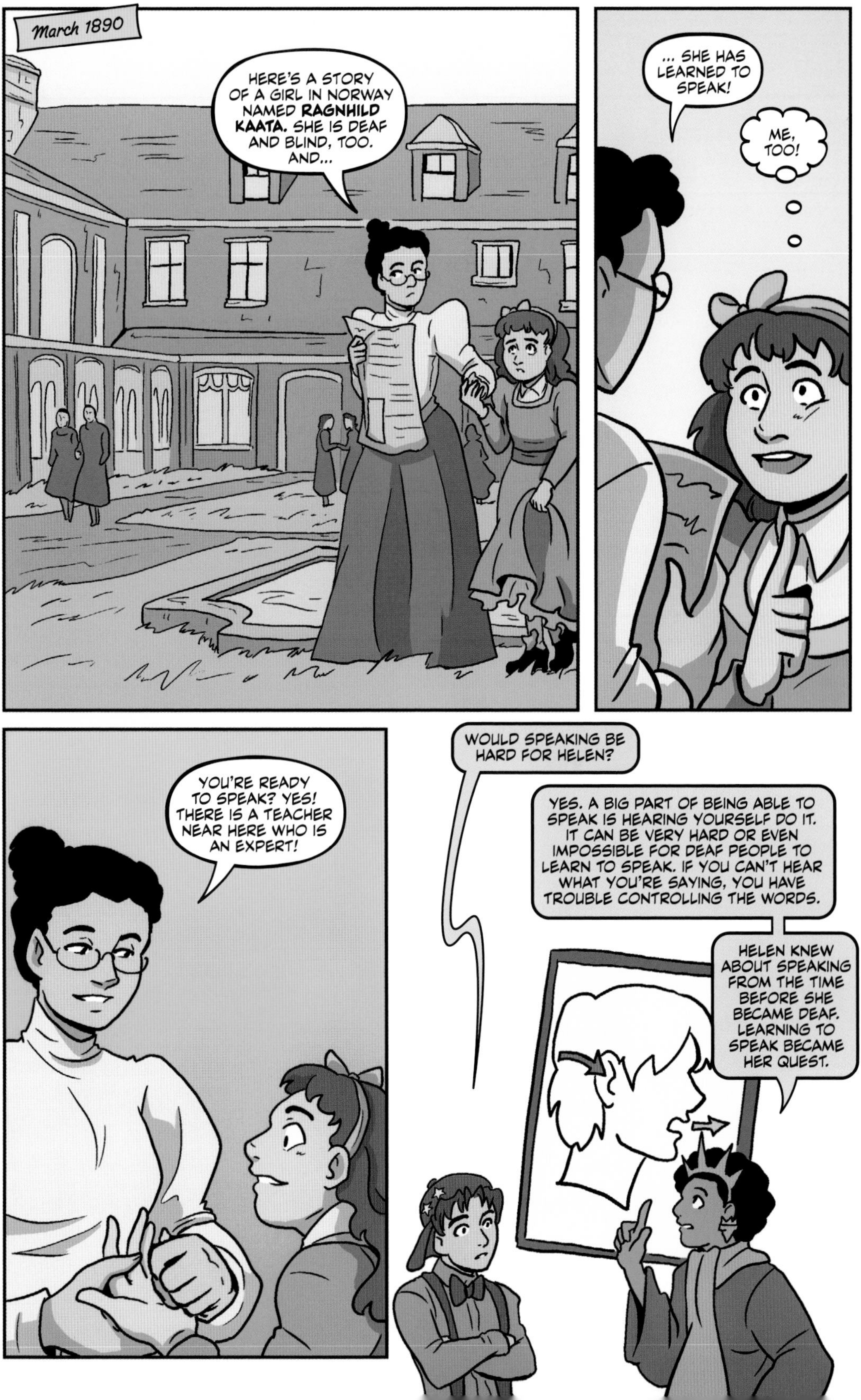
March 1890
HERE'S A STORY OF A GIRL IN NORWAY NAMED **RAGNHILD KAATA.** SHE IS DEAF AND BLIND, TOO. AND...
... SHE HAS LEARNED TO SPEAK!
ME, TOO!
YOU'RE READY TO SPEAK? YES! THERE IS A TEACHER NEAR HERE WHO IS AN EXPERT!
WOULD SPEAKING BE HARD FOR HELEN?
YES. A BIG PART OF BEING ABLE TO SPEAK IS HEARING YOURSELF DO IT. IT CAN BE VERY HARD OR EVEN IMPOSSIBLE FOR DEAF PEOPLE TO LEARN TO SPEAK. IF YOU CAN'T HEAR WHAT YOU'RE SAYING, YOU HAVE TROUBLE CONTROLLING THE WORDS.
HELEN KNEW ABOUT SPEAKING FROM THE TIME BEFORE SHE BECAME DEAF. LEARNING TO SPEAK BECAME HER QUEST.

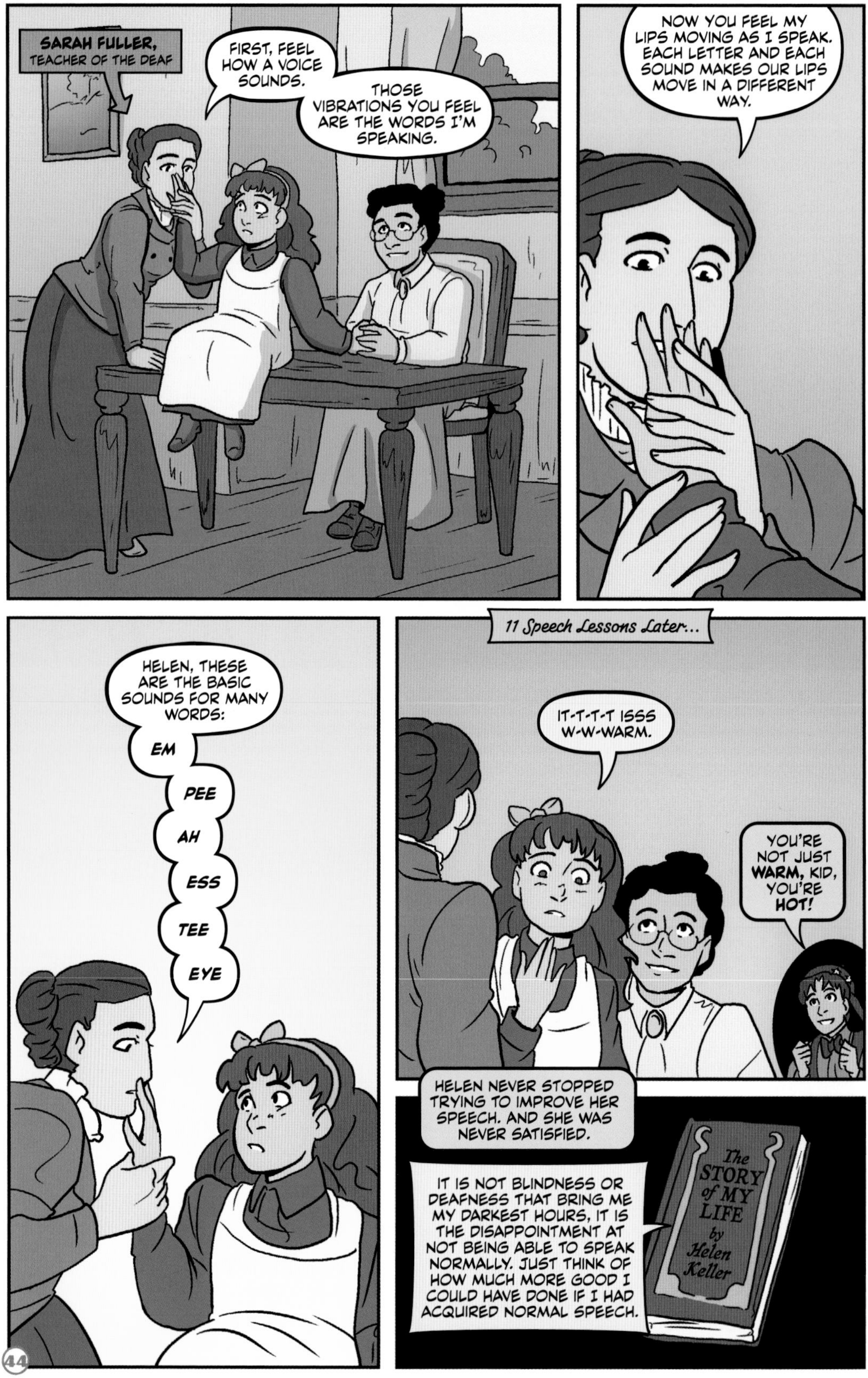
SARAH FULLER, TEACHER OF THE DEAF
FIRST, FEEL HOW A VOICE SOUNDS.
THOSE VIBRATIONS YOU FEEL ARE THE WORDS I'M SPEAKING.
NOW YOU FEEL MY LIPS MOVING AS I SPEAK. EACH LETTER AND EACH SOUND MAKES OUR LIPS MOVE IN A DIFFERENT WAY.
HELEN, THESE ARE THE BASIC SOUNDS FOR MANY WORDS:
EM
PEE
AH
ESS
TEE
EYE
11 Speech Lessons Later...
IT-T-T-T ISSS W-W-WARM.
YOU'RE NOT JUST WARM, KID, YOU'RE HOT!
HELEN NEVER STOPPED TRYING TO IMPROVE HER SPEECH. AND SHE WAS NEVER SATISFIED.
IT IS NOT BLINDNESS OR DEAFNESS THAT BRING ME MY DARKEST HOURS, IT IS THE DISAPPOINTMENT AT NOT BEING ABLE TO SPEAK NORMALLY. JUST THINK OF HOW MUCH MORE GOOD I COULD HAVE DONE IF I HAD ACQUIRED NORMAL SPEECH.
The STORY of MY LIFE by Helen Keller

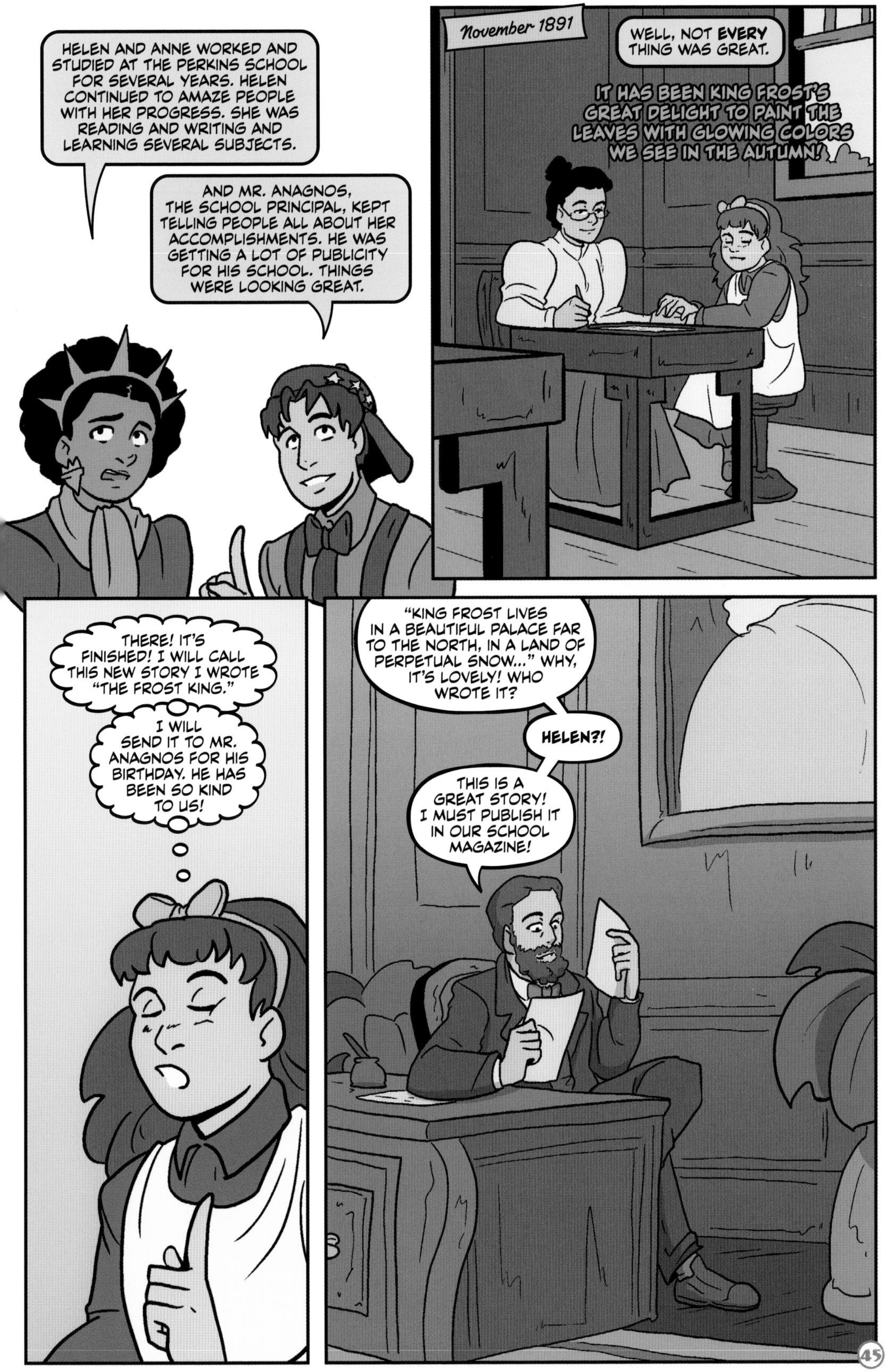
HELEN AND ANNE WORKED AND STUDIED AT THE PERKINS SCHOOL FOR SEVERAL YEARS. HELEN CONTINUED TO AMAZE PEOPLE WITH HER PROGRESS. SHE WAS READING AND WRITING AND LEARNING SEVERAL SUBJECTS.
AND MR. ANAGNOS, THE SCHOOL PRINCIPAL, KEPT TELLING PEOPLE ALL ABOUT HER ACCOMPLISHMENTS. HE WAS GETTING A LOT OF PUBLICITY FOR HIS SCHOOL. THINGS WERE LOOKING GREAT.
November 1891
WELL, NOT **EVERY** THING WAS GREAT.
IT HAS BEEN KING FROST'S GREAT DELIGHT TO PAINT THE LEAVES WITH GLOWING COLORS WE SEE IN THE AUTUMN!
THERE! IT'S FINISHED! I WILL CALL THIS NEW STORY I WROTE "THE FROST KING."
I WILL SEND IT TO MR. ANAGNOS FOR HIS BIRTHDAY. HE HAS BEEN SO KIND TO US!
"KING FROST LIVES IN A BEAUTIFUL PALACE FAR TO THE NORTH, IN A LAND OF PERPETUAL SNOW..." WHY, IT'S LOVELY! WHO WROTE IT?
HELEN?!
THIS IS A GREAT STORY! I MUST PUBLISH IT IN OUR SCHOOL MAGAZINE!

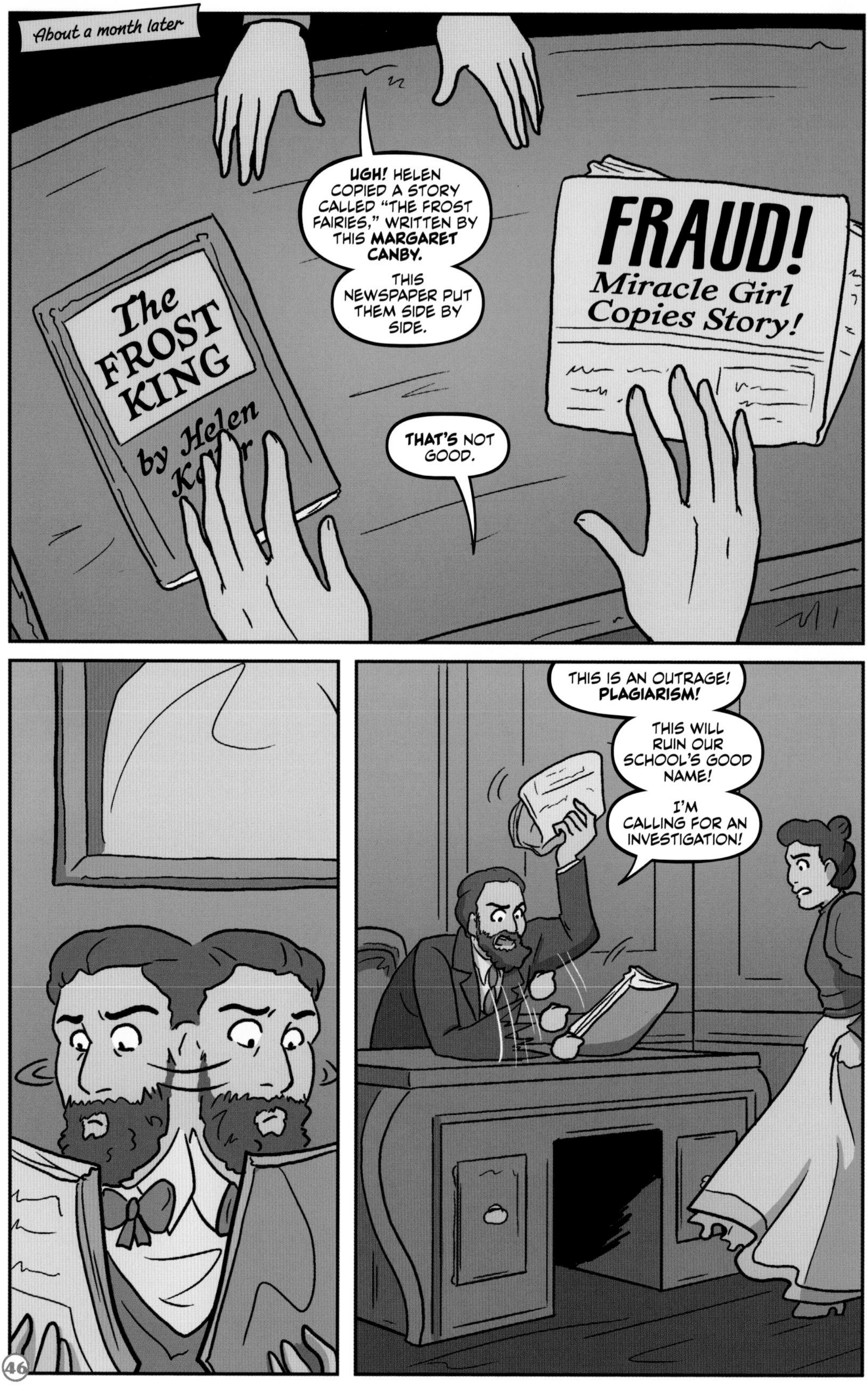
About a month later
UGH! HELEN COPIED A STORY CALLED "THE FROST FAIRIES," WRITTEN BY THIS MARGARET CANBY.
THIS NEWSPAPER PUT THEM SIDE BY SIDE.
The FROST KING by Helen Keller
FRAUD! Miracle Girl Copies Story!
THAT'S NOT GOOD.
THIS IS AN OUTRAGE! PLAGIARISM!
THIS WILL RUIN OUR SCHOOL'S GOOD NAME!
I'M CALLING FOR AN INVESTIGATION!

THIS COPY OF MISS CANBY'S BOOK WAS FOUND IN A HOME YOU ONCE VISITED IN CAPE COD! YOU AND YOUR TEACHER MUST HAVE READ IT THERE.

YOU COPIED IT!

The FROST KING Canby

SHE SAYS, "I DON'T REMEMBER READING IT, SIR."

AND NEITHER DO I.

HOW COULD YOU **NOT?**

WELL, I'M SORRY, BUT THIS IS A DISASTER FOR THE SCHOOL. WE CAN'T HAVE THE APPEARANCE OF PLAGIARISM AT PERKINS.

WE'RE GOING TO HAVE TO ASK YOU TO **LEAVE.**

I CAN'T BELIEVE THIS IS HAPPENING.

SO DID SHE REALLY DO IT?

NO ONE REALLY KNOWS. SHE CERTAINLY DIDN'T DO IT ON PURPOSE.

HELEN'S AMAZING MEMORY MAY HAVE BROUGHT THE STORY BACK WITHOUT HER KNOWING IT!

HE BELIEVED, OR AT LEAST SUSPECTED, THAT MISS SULLIVAN AND I HAD DELIBERATELY STOLEN THE BRIGHT THOUGHTS OF ANOTHER AND IMPOSED THEM ON HIM TO WIN HIS ADMIRATION.

AS I LAY IN MY BED THAT NIGHT, I WEPT AS I HOPE FEW CHILDREN HAVE WEPT.

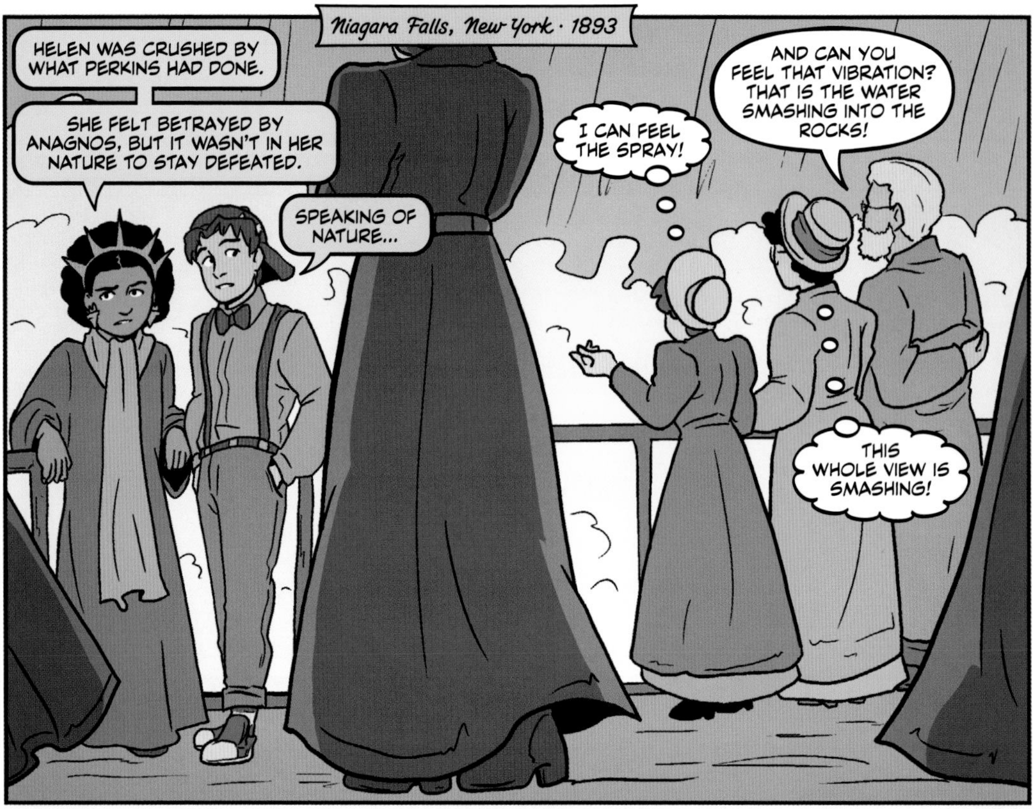
Niagara Falls, New York · 1893
HELEN WAS CRUSHED BY WHAT PERKINS HAD DONE.
SHE FELT BETRAYED BY ANAGNOS, BUT IT WASN'T IN HER NATURE TO STAY DEFEATED.
SPEAKING OF NATURE...
I CAN FEEL THE SPRAY!
AND CAN YOU FEEL THAT VIBRATION? THAT IS THE WATER SMASHING INTO THE ROCKS!
THIS WHOLE VIEW IS SMASHING!

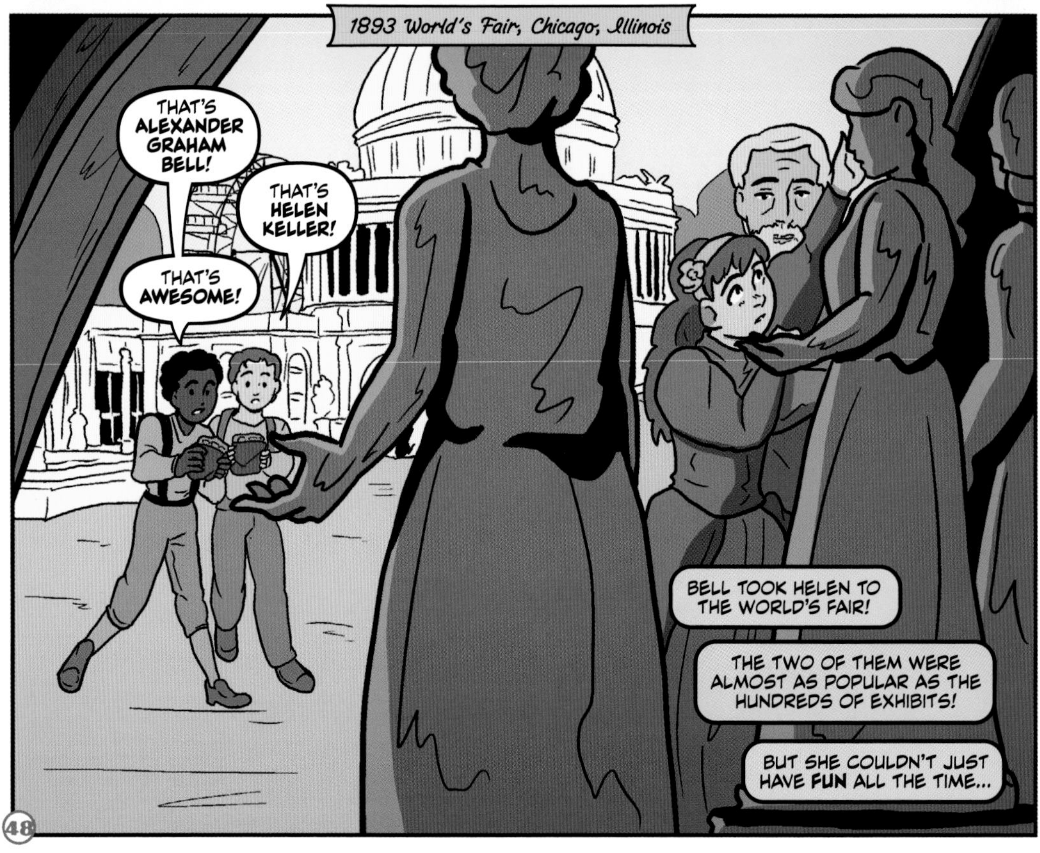
1893 World's Fair, Chicago, Illinois
THAT'S **ALEXANDER GRAHAM BELL!**
THAT'S **HELEN KELLER!**
THAT'S **AWESOME!**
BELL TOOK HELEN TO THE WORLD'S FAIR!
THE TWO OF THEM WERE ALMOST AS POPULAR AS THE HUNDREDS OF EXHIBITS!
BUT SHE COULDN'T JUST HAVE **FUN** ALL THE TIME...

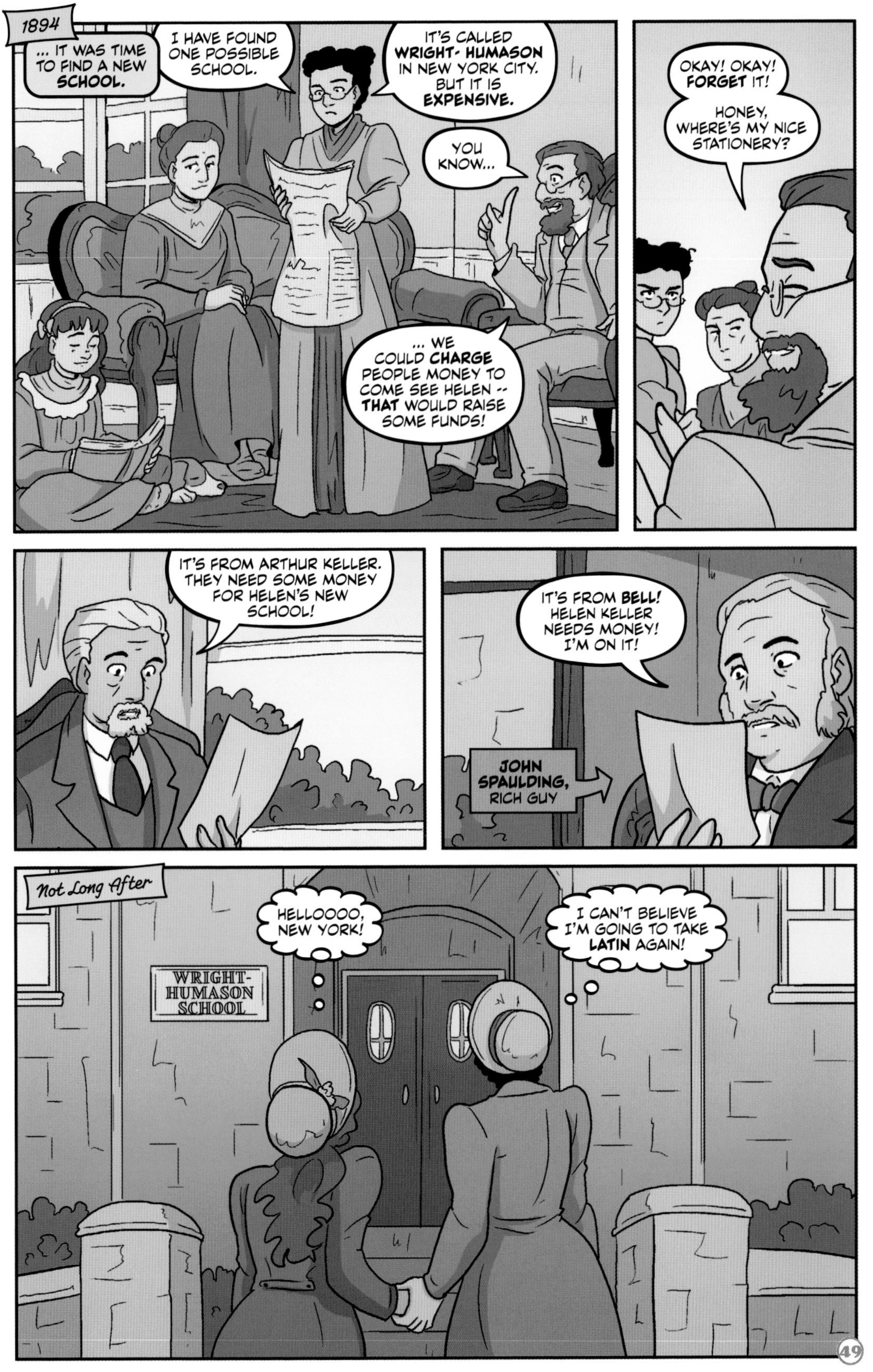
1894
... IT WAS TIME TO FIND A NEW **SCHOOL.**
I HAVE FOUND ONE POSSIBLE SCHOOL.
IT'S CALLED **WRIGHT- HUMASON** IN NEW YORK CITY. BUT IT IS **EXPENSIVE.**
YOU KNOW...
... WE COULD **CHARGE** PEOPLE MONEY TO COME SEE HELEN -- **THAT** WOULD RAISE SOME FUNDS!
OKAY! OKAY! **FORGET** IT!
HONEY, WHERE'S MY NICE STATIONERY?
IT'S FROM ARTHUR KELLER. THEY NEED SOME MONEY FOR HELEN'S NEW SCHOOL!
IT'S FROM **BELL!** HELEN KELLER NEEDS MONEY! I'M ON IT!
JOHN SPAULDING, RICH GUY
Not Long After
HELLOOOO, NEW YORK!
I CAN'T BELIEVE I'M GOING TO TAKE **LATIN** AGAIN!
WRIGHT-HUMASON SCHOOL

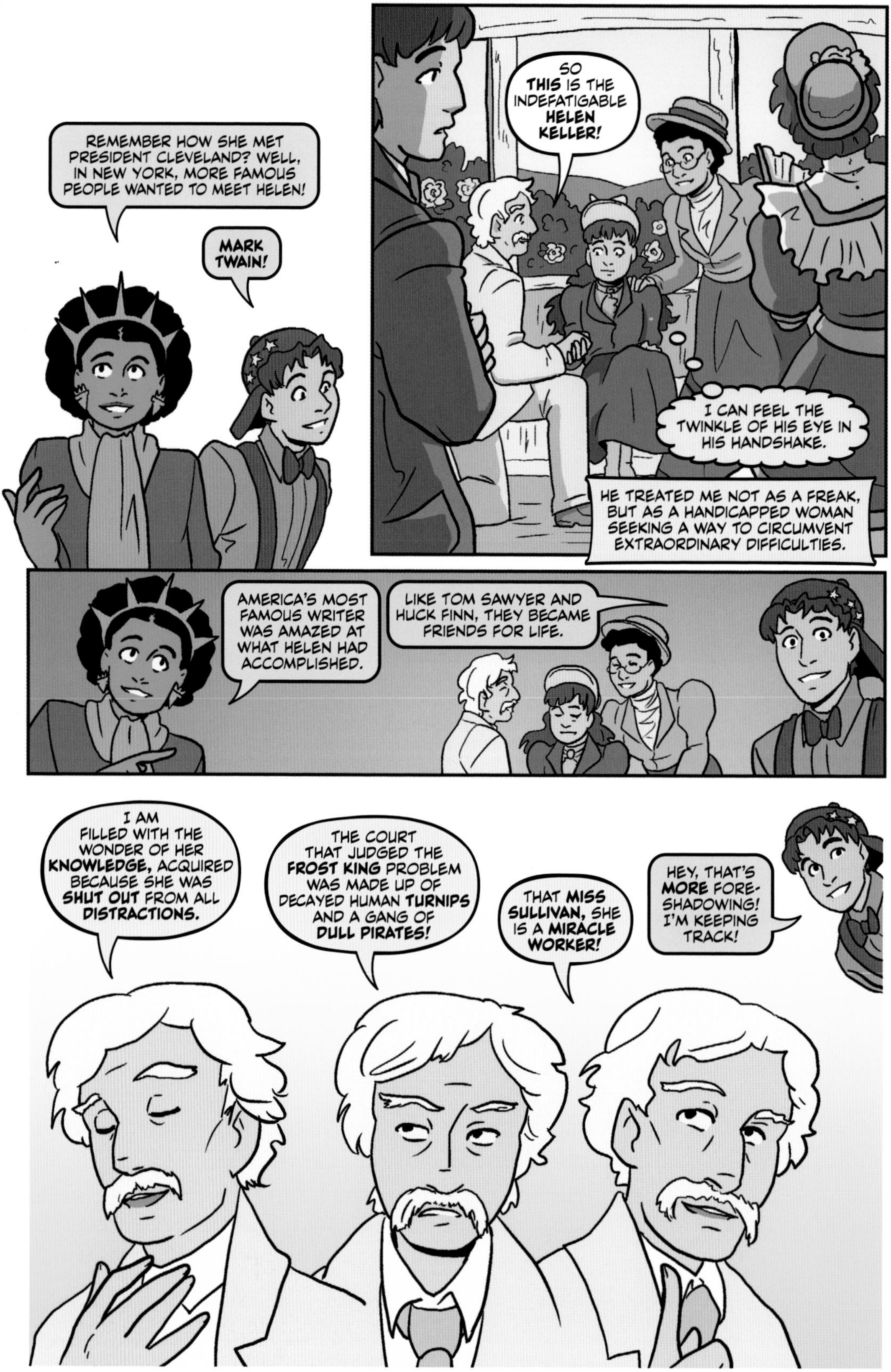
REMEMBER HOW SHE MET PRESIDENT CLEVELAND? WELL, IN NEW YORK, MORE FAMOUS PEOPLE WANTED TO MEET HELEN!
MARK TWAIN!
SO **THIS** IS THE INDEFATIGABLE **HELEN KELLER!**
I CAN FEEL THE TWINKLE OF HIS EYE IN HIS HANDSHAKE.
HE TREATED ME NOT AS A FREAK, BUT AS A HANDICAPPED WOMAN SEEKING A WAY TO CIRCUMVENT EXTRAORDINARY DIFFICULTIES.
AMERICA'S MOST FAMOUS WRITER WAS AMAZED AT WHAT HELEN HAD ACCOMPLISHED.
LIKE TOM SAWYER AND HUCK FINN, THEY BECAME FRIENDS FOR LIFE.
I AM FILLED WITH THE WONDER OF HER **KNOWLEDGE,** ACQUIRED BECAUSE SHE WAS **SHUT OUT** FROM ALL **DISTRACTIONS.**
THE COURT THAT JUDGED THE **FROST KING** PROBLEM WAS MADE UP OF DECAYED HUMAN **TURNIPS** AND A GANG OF **DULL PIRATES!**
THAT **MISS SULLIVAN,** SHE IS A **MIRACLE WORKER!**
HEY, THAT'S **MORE** FORE-SHADOWING! I'M KEEPING TRACK!

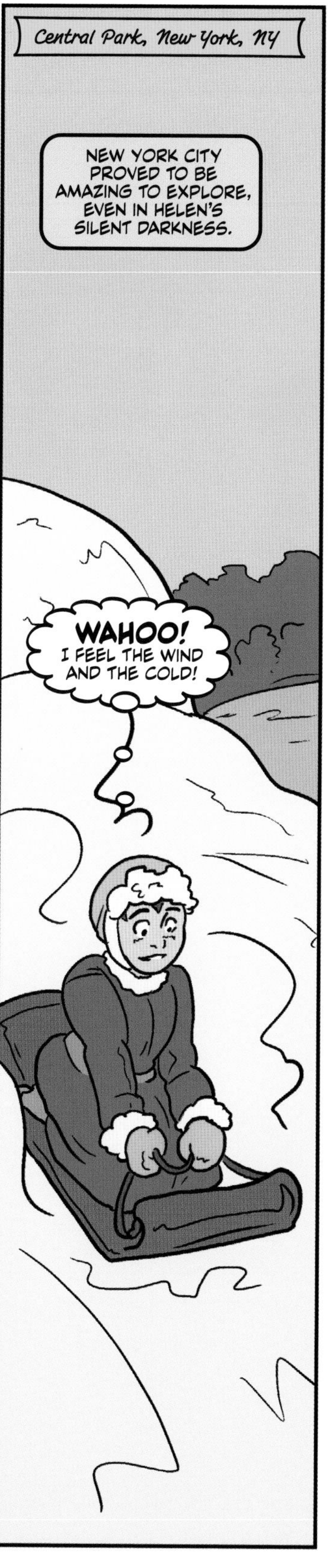
Central Park, New York, NY
NEW YORK CITY PROVED TO BE AMAZING TO EXPLORE, EVEN IN HELEN'S SILENT DARKNESS.
WAHOO! I FEEL THE WIND AND THE COLD!

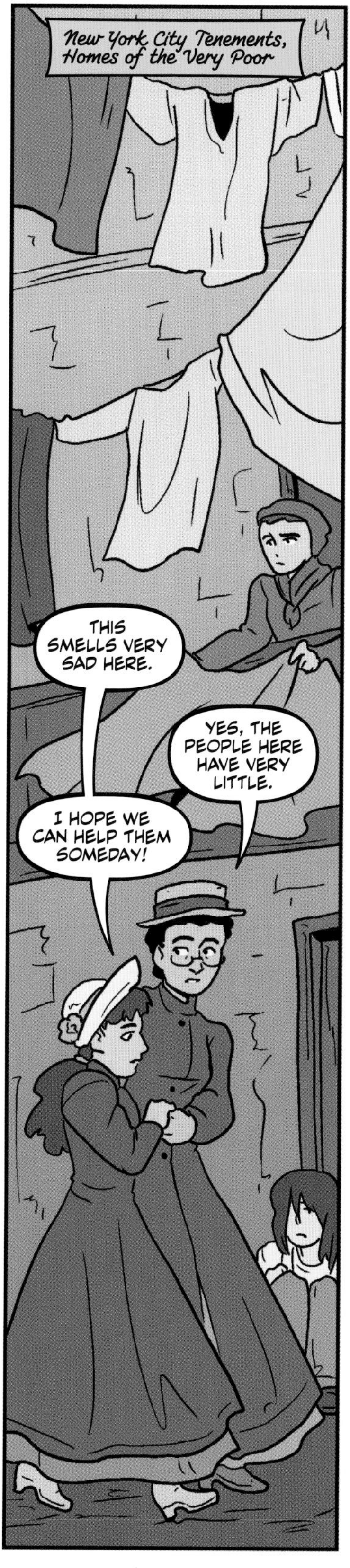
New York City Tenements, Homes of the Very Poor
THIS SMELLS VERY SAD HERE.
YES, THE PEOPLE HERE HAVE VERY LITTLE.
I HOPE WE CAN HELP THEM SOMEDAY!

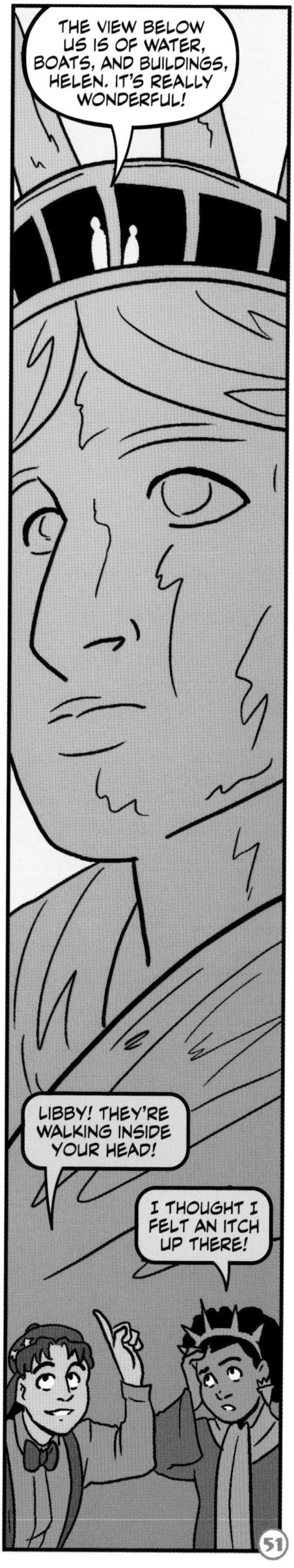
THE VIEW BELOW US IS OF WATER, BOATS, AND BUILDINGS, HELEN. IT'S REALLY WONDERFUL!
LIBBY! THEY'RE WALKING INSIDE YOUR HEAD!
I THOUGHT I FELT AN ITCH UP THERE!

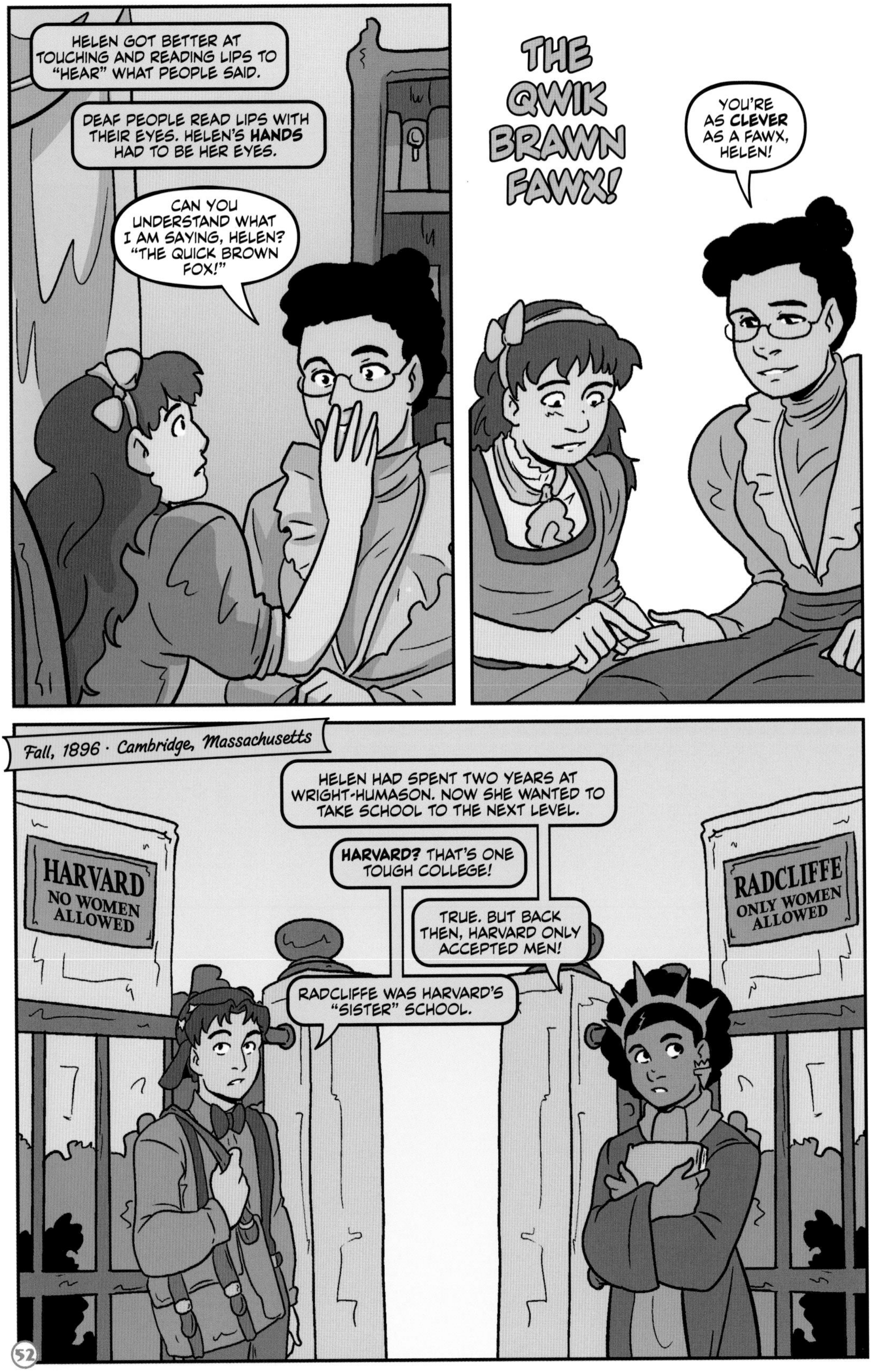
HELEN GOT BETTER AT TOUCHING AND READING LIPS TO "HEAR" WHAT PEOPLE SAID.
DEAF PEOPLE READ LIPS WITH THEIR EYES. HELEN'S **HANDS** HAD TO BE HER EYES.
CAN YOU UNDERSTAND WHAT I AM SAYING, HELEN? "THE QUICK BROWN FOX!"
THE QWIK BRAWN FAWX!
YOU'RE AS **CLEVER** AS A FAWX, HELEN!
Fall, 1896 · Cambridge, Massachusetts
HELEN HAD SPENT TWO YEARS AT WRIGHT-HUMASON. NOW SHE WANTED TO TAKE SCHOOL TO THE NEXT LEVEL.
HARVARD? THAT'S ONE TOUGH COLLEGE!
TRUE. BUT BACK THEN, HARVARD ONLY ACCEPTED MEN!
RADCLIFFE WAS HARVARD'S "SISTER" SCHOOL.
HARVARD NO WOMEN ALLOWED
RADCLIFFE ONLY WOMEN ALLOWED

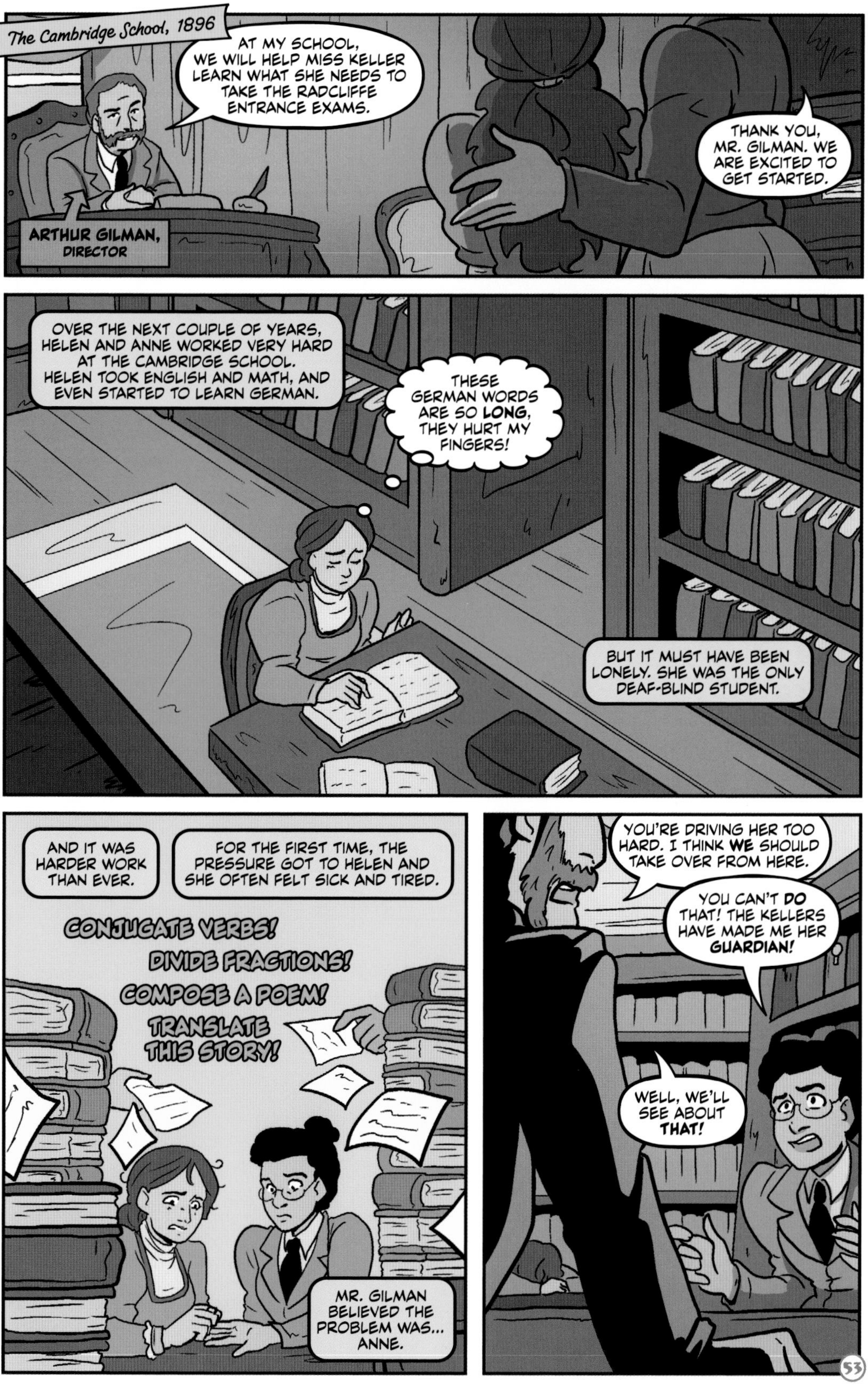
The Cambridge School, 1896
AT MY SCHOOL, WE WILL HELP MISS KELLER LEARN WHAT SHE NEEDS TO TAKE THE RADCLIFFE ENTRANCE EXAMS.
ARTHUR GILMAN, DIRECTOR
THANK YOU, MR. GILMAN. WE ARE EXCITED TO GET STARTED.
OVER THE NEXT COUPLE OF YEARS, HELEN AND ANNE WORKED VERY HARD AT THE CAMBRIDGE SCHOOL. HELEN TOOK ENGLISH AND MATH, AND EVEN STARTED TO LEARN GERMAN.
THESE GERMAN WORDS ARE SO **LONG**, THEY HURT MY FINGERS!
BUT IT MUST HAVE BEEN LONELY. SHE WAS THE ONLY DEAF-BLIND STUDENT.
AND IT WAS HARDER WORK THAN EVER.
FOR THE FIRST TIME, THE PRESSURE GOT TO HELEN AND SHE OFTEN FELT SICK AND TIRED.
CONJUGATE VERBS!
DIVIDE FRACTIONS!
COMPOSE A POEM!
TRANSLATE THIS STORY!
MR. GILMAN BELIEVED THE PROBLEM WAS... ANNE.
YOU'RE DRIVING HER TOO HARD. I THINK **WE** SHOULD TAKE OVER FROM HERE.
YOU CAN'T **DO** THAT! THE KELLERS HAVE MADE ME HER **GUARDIAN!**
WELL, WE'LL SEE ABOUT **THAT!**

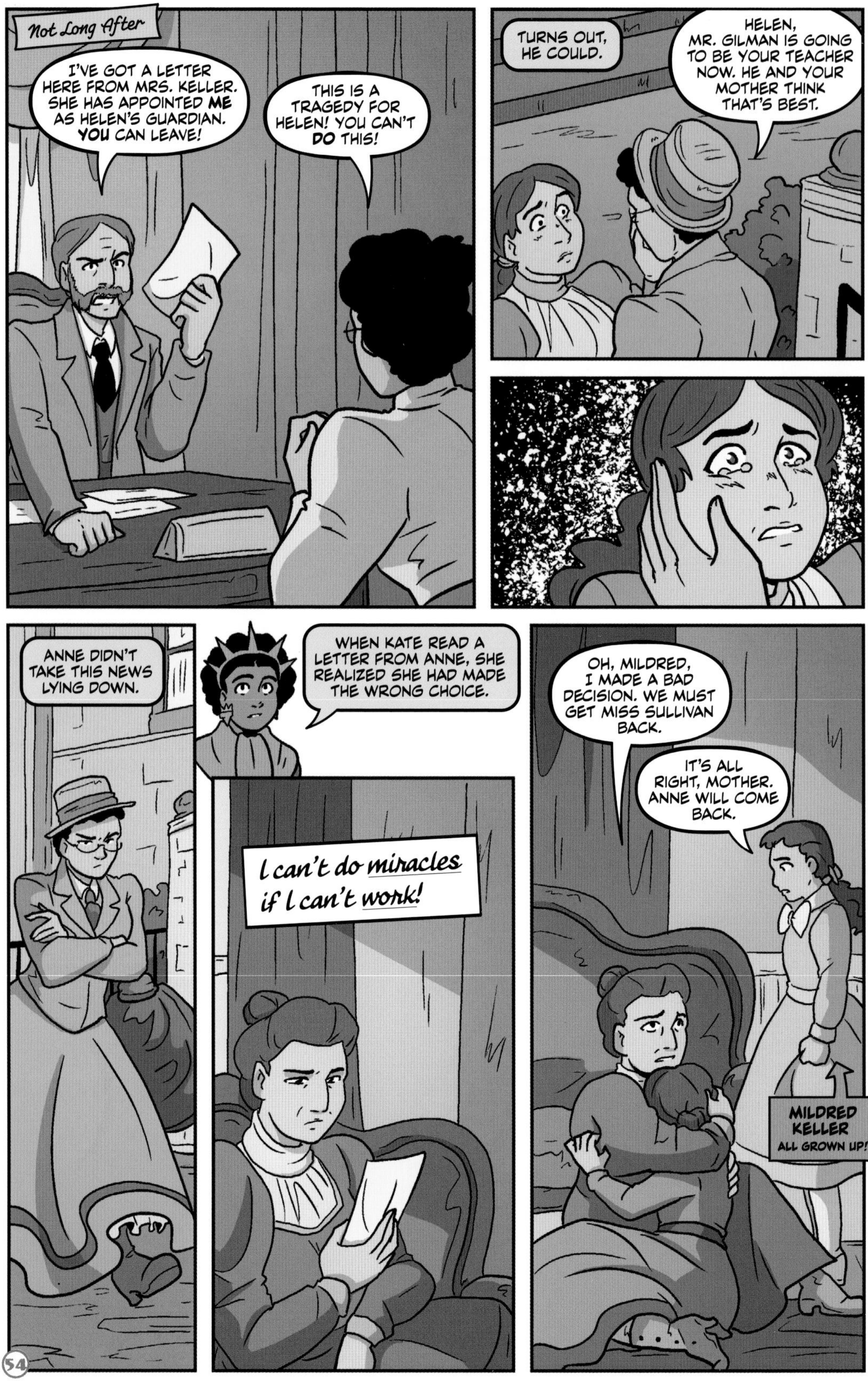
Not Long After
I'VE GOT A LETTER HERE FROM MRS. KELLER. SHE HAS APPOINTED **ME** AS HELEN'S GUARDIAN. **YOU** CAN LEAVE!
THIS IS A TRAGEDY FOR HELEN! YOU CAN'T **DO** THIS!
TURNS OUT, HE COULD.
HELEN, MR. GILMAN IS GOING TO BE YOUR TEACHER NOW. HE AND YOUR MOTHER THINK THAT'S BEST.
ANNE DIDN'T TAKE THIS NEWS LYING DOWN.
WHEN KATE READ A LETTER FROM ANNE, SHE REALIZED SHE HAD MADE THE WRONG CHOICE.
I can't do miracles if I can't work!
OH, MILDRED, I MADE A BAD DECISION. WE MUST GET MISS SULLIVAN BACK.
IT'S ALL RIGHT, MOTHER. ANNE WILL COME BACK.
MILDRED KELLER ALL GROWN UP!

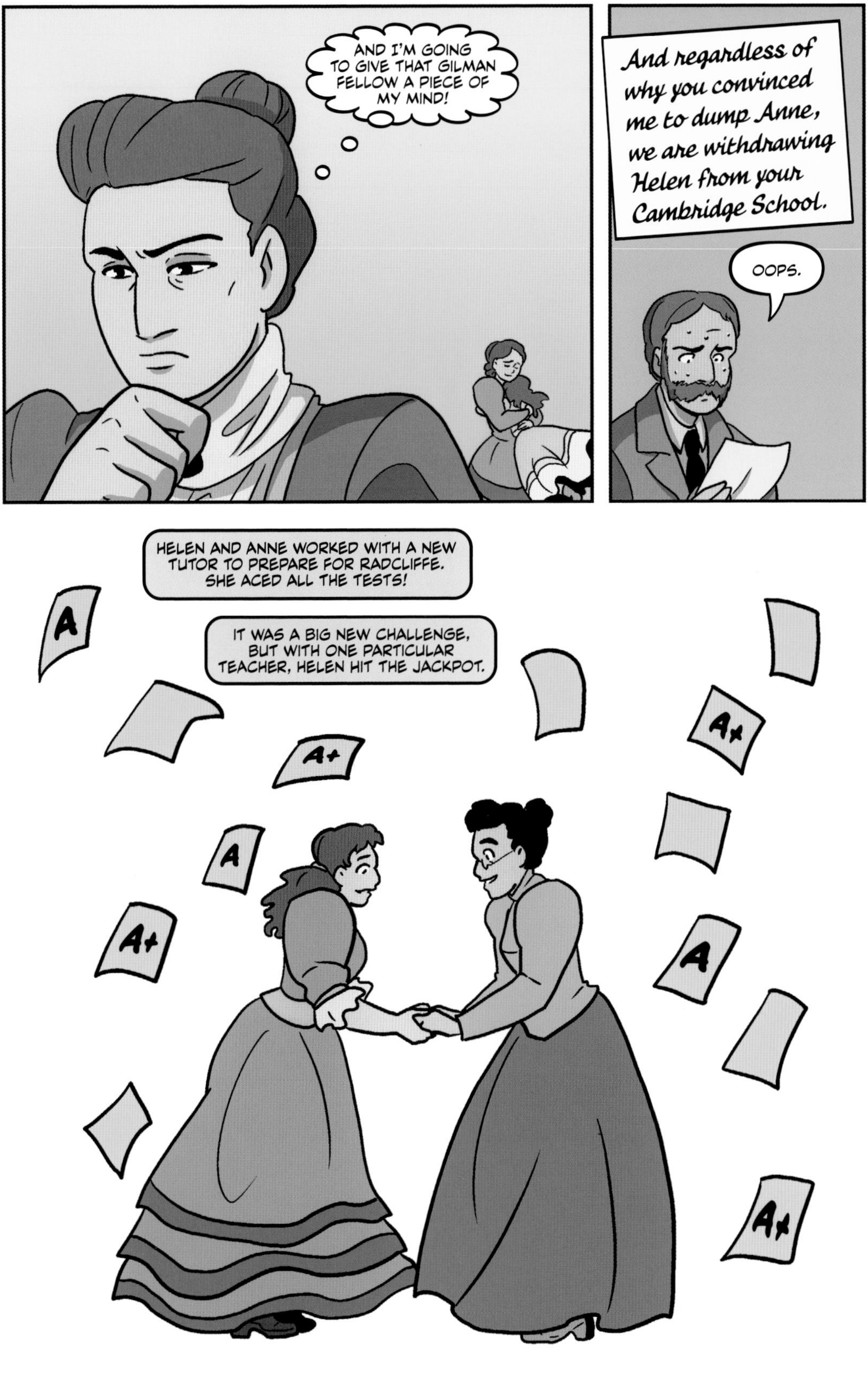
AND I'M GOING TO GIVE THAT GILMAN FELLOW A PIECE OF MY MIND!
And regardless of why you convinced me to dump Anne, we are withdrawing Helen from your Cambridge School.
OOPS.
HELEN AND ANNE WORKED WITH A NEW TUTOR TO PREPARE FOR RADCLIFFE. SHE ACED ALL THE TESTS!
IT WAS A BIG NEW CHALLENGE, BUT WITH ONE PARTICULAR TEACHER, HELEN HIT THE JACKPOT.
A
A+
A
A+
A+
A
A+

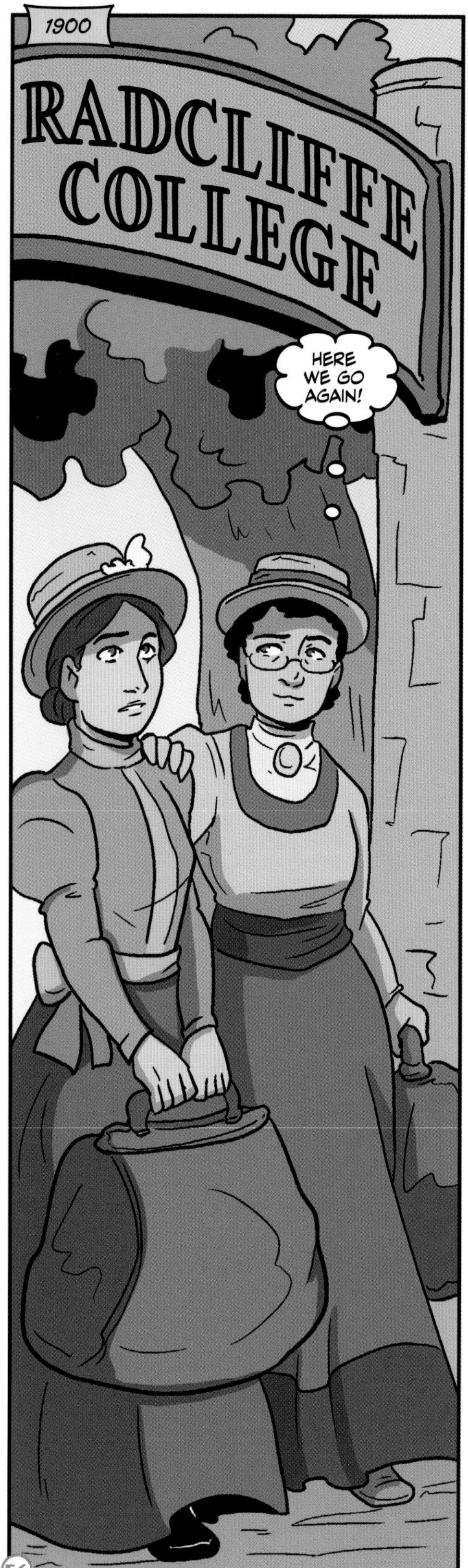
1900
RADCLIFFE COLLEGE
HERE WE GO AGAIN!

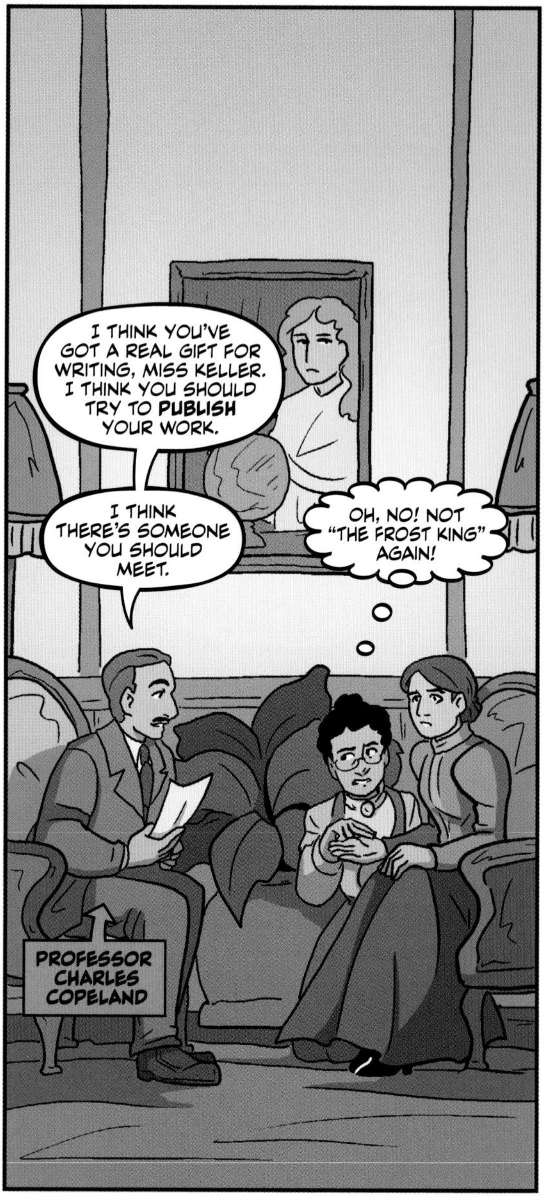
I THINK YOU'VE GOT A REAL GIFT FOR WRITING, MISS KELLER. I THINK YOU SHOULD TRY TO **PUBLISH** YOUR WORK.
I THINK THERE'S SOMEONE YOU SHOULD MEET.
OH, NO! NOT "THE FROST KING" AGAIN!
PROFESSOR CHARLES COPELAND

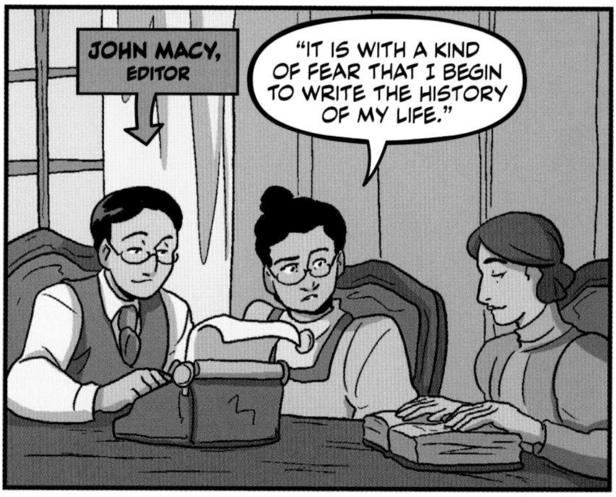
JOHN MACY, EDITOR
"IT IS WITH A KIND OF FEAR THAT I BEGIN TO WRITE THE HISTORY OF MY LIFE."

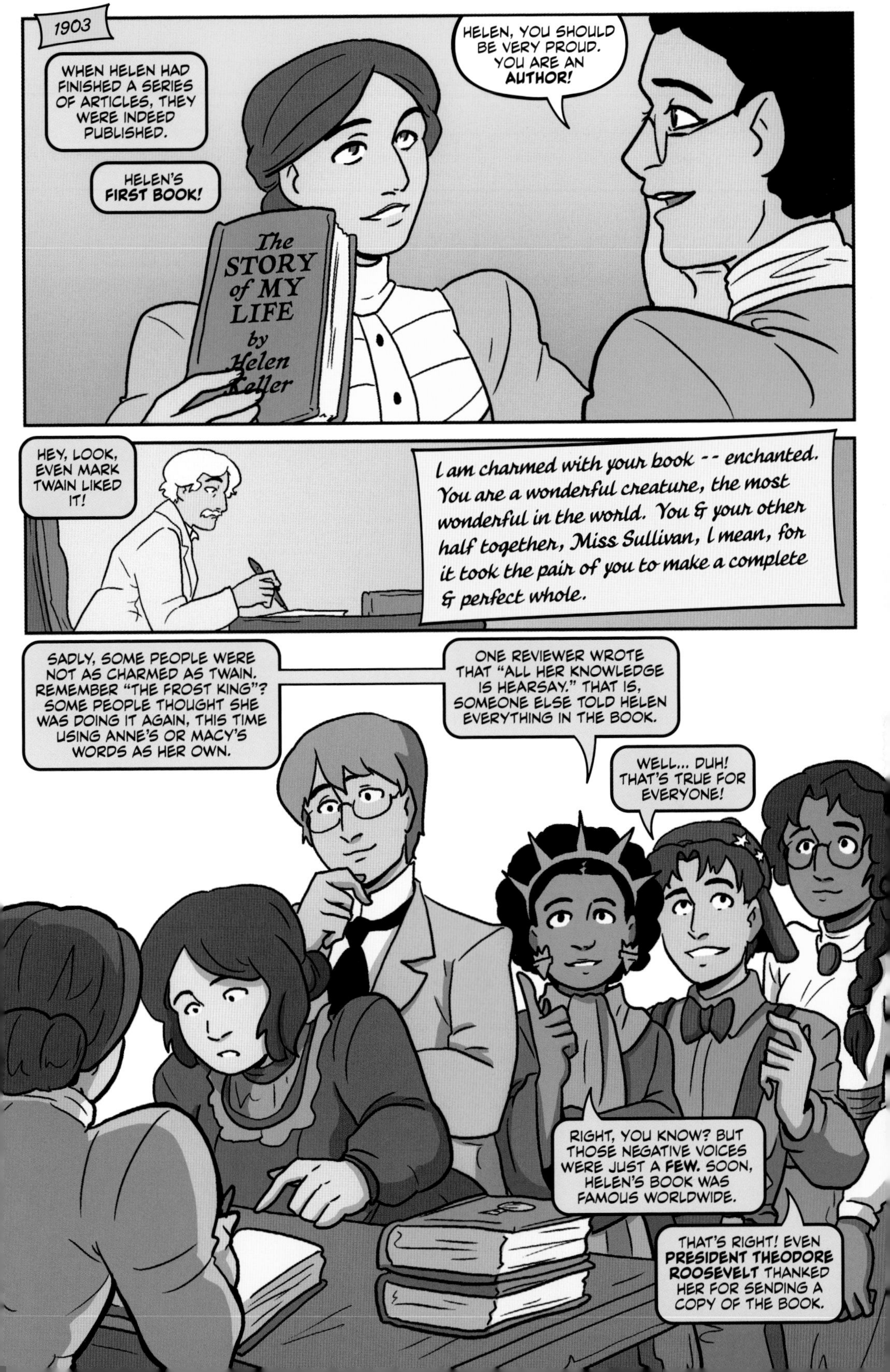

1903
WHEN HELEN HAD FINISHED A SERIES OF ARTICLES, THEY WERE INDEED PUBLISHED.
HELEN'S FIRST BOOK!
HELEN, YOU SHOULD BE VERY PROUD. YOU ARE AN AUTHOR!
The STORY of MY LIFE by Helen Keller
HEY, LOOK, EVEN MARK TWAIN LIKED IT!
I am charmed with your book -- enchanted. You are a wonderful creature, the most wonderful in the world. You & your other half together, Miss Sullivan, I mean, for it took the pair of you to make a complete & perfect whole.
SADLY, SOME PEOPLE WERE NOT AS CHARMED AS TWAIN. REMEMBER "THE FROST KING"? SOME PEOPLE THOUGHT SHE WAS DOING IT AGAIN, THIS TIME USING ANNE'S OR MACY'S WORDS AS HER OWN.
ONE REVIEWER WROTE THAT "ALL HER KNOWLEDGE IS HEARSAY." THAT IS, SOMEONE ELSE TOLD HELEN EVERYTHING IN THE BOOK.
WELL... DUH! THAT'S TRUE FOR EVERYONE!
RIGHT, YOU KNOW? BUT THOSE NEGATIVE VOICES WERE JUST A FEW. SOON, HELEN'S BOOK WAS FAMOUS WORLDWIDE.
THAT'S RIGHT! EVEN PRESIDENT THEODORE ROOSEVELT THANKED HER FOR SENDING A COPY OF THE BOOK.

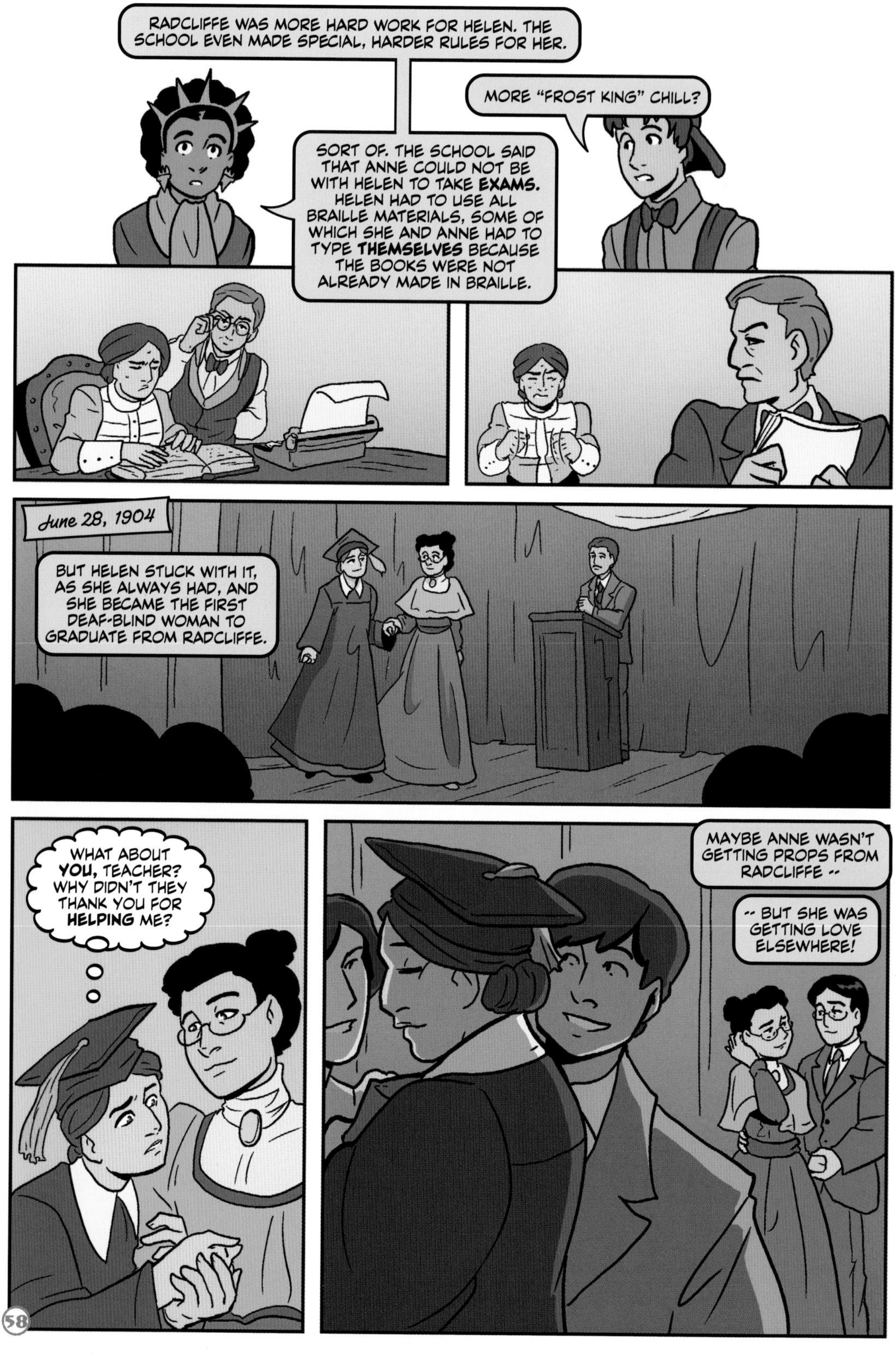

RADCLIFFE WAS MORE HARD WORK FOR HELEN. THE SCHOOL EVEN MADE SPECIAL, HARDER RULES FOR HER.
MORE "FROST KING" CHILL?
SORT OF. THE SCHOOL SAID THAT ANNE COULD NOT BE WITH HELEN TO TAKE EXAMS. HELEN HAD TO USE ALL BRAILLE MATERIALS, SOME OF WHICH SHE AND ANNE HAD TO TYPE THEMSELVES BECAUSE THE BOOKS WERE NOT ALREADY MADE IN BRAILLE.
June 28, 1904
BUT HELEN STUCK WITH IT, AS SHE ALWAYS HAD, AND SHE BECAME THE FIRST DEAF-BLIND WOMAN TO GRADUATE FROM RADCLIFFE.
WHAT ABOUT YOU, TEACHER? WHY DIDN'T THEY THANK YOU FOR HELPING ME?
MAYBE ANNE WASN'T GETTING PROPS FROM RADCLIFFE --
-- BUT SHE WAS GETTING LOVE ELSEWHERE!

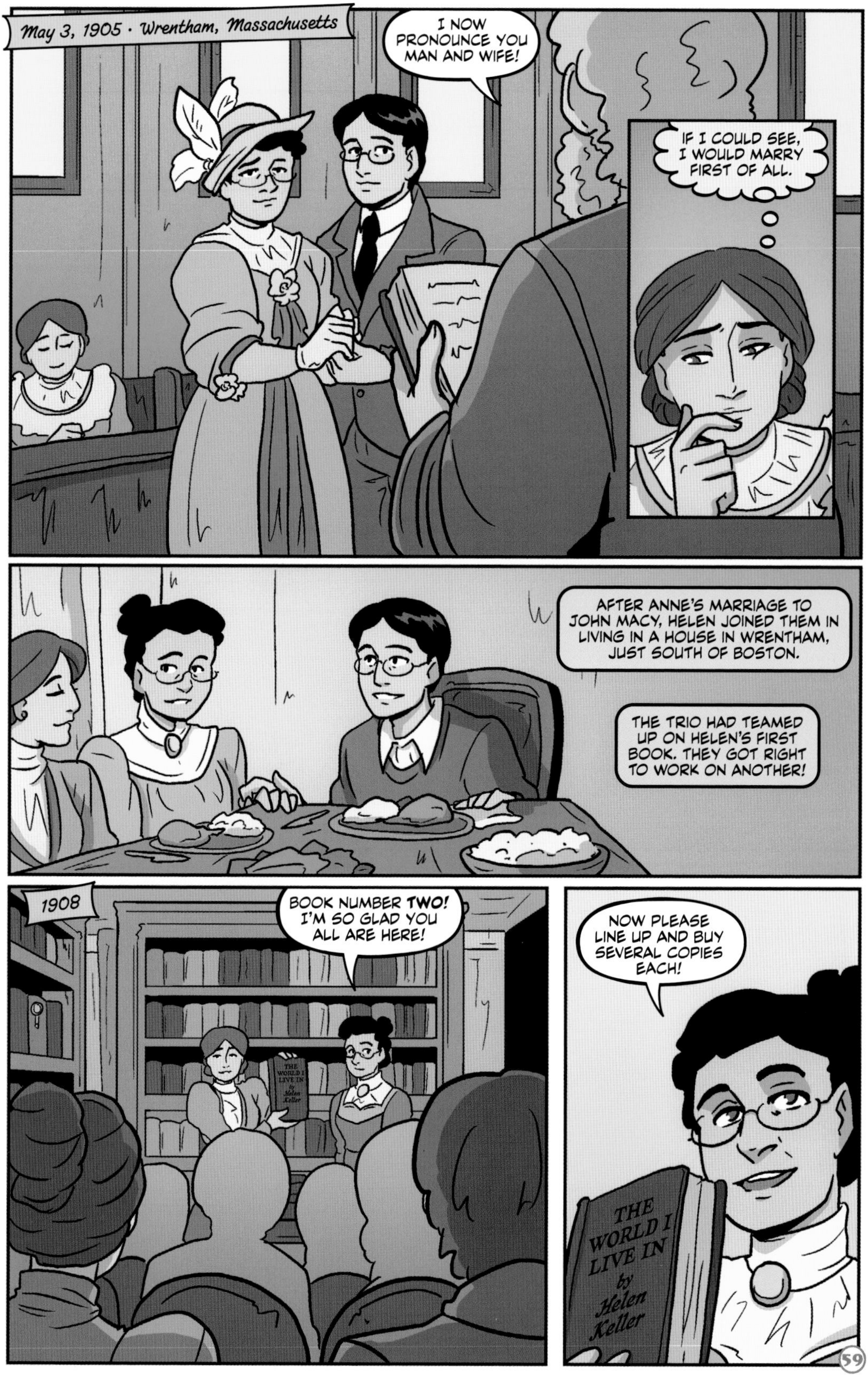
May 3, 1905 · Wrentham, Massachusetts
I NOW PRONOUNCE YOU MAN AND WIFE!
IF I COULD SEE, I WOULD MARRY FIRST OF ALL.
AFTER ANNE'S MARRIAGE TO JOHN MACY, HELEN JOINED THEM IN LIVING IN A HOUSE IN WRENTHAM, JUST SOUTH OF BOSTON.
THE TRIO HAD TEAMED UP ON HELEN'S FIRST BOOK. THEY GOT RIGHT TO WORK ON ANOTHER!
1908
BOOK NUMBER **TWO!** I'M SO GLAD YOU ALL ARE HERE!
THE WORLD I LIVE IN by Helen Keller
NOW PLEASE LINE UP AND BUY SEVERAL COPIES EACH!
THE WORLD I LIVE IN by Helen Keller

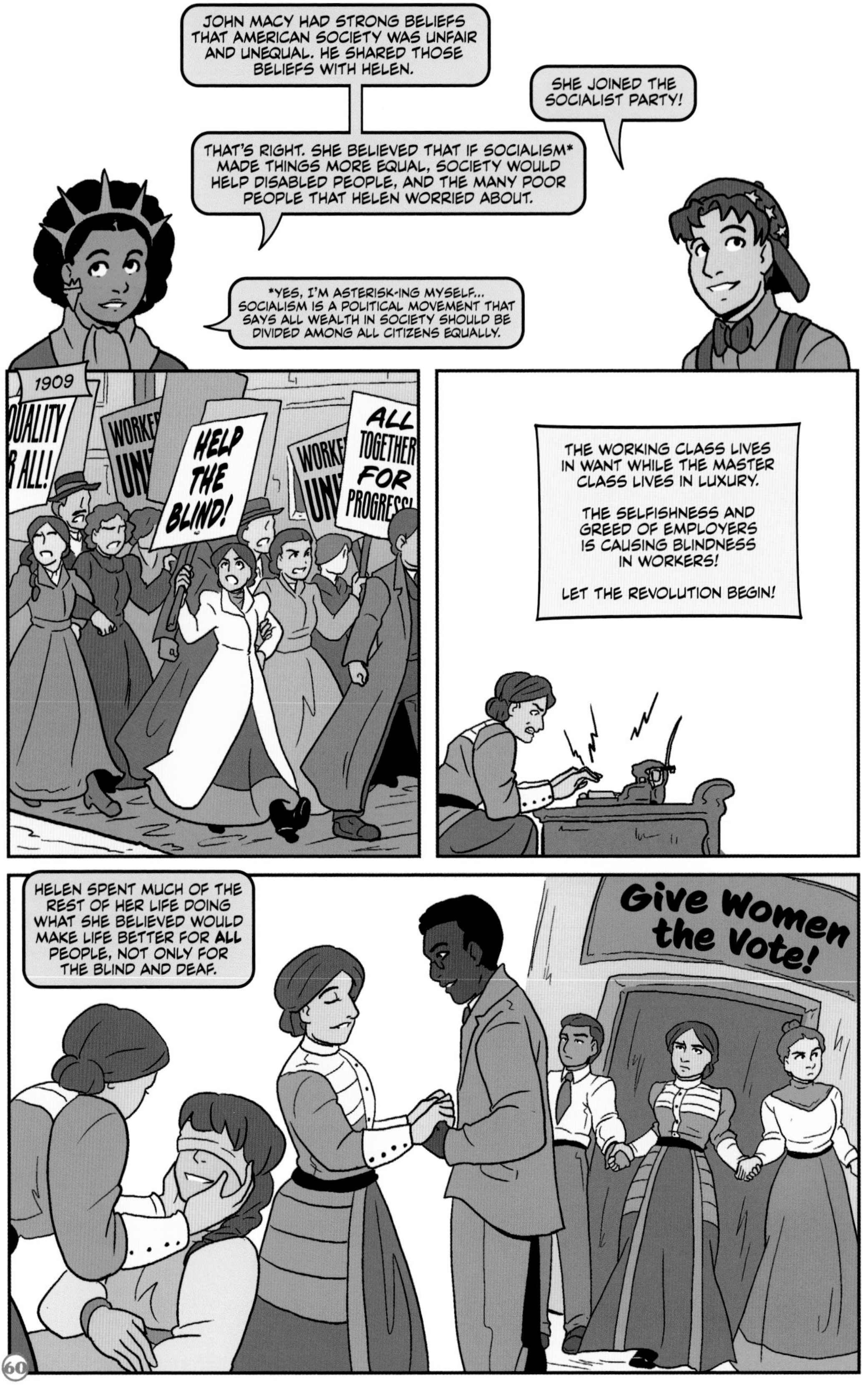
JOHN MACY HAD STRONG BELIEFS THAT AMERICAN SOCIETY WAS UNFAIR AND UNEQUAL. HE SHARED THOSE BELIEFS WITH HELEN.
SHE JOINED THE SOCIALIST PARTY!
THAT'S RIGHT. SHE BELIEVED THAT IF SOCIALISM* MADE THINGS MORE EQUAL, SOCIETY WOULD HELP DISABLED PEOPLE, AND THE MANY POOR PEOPLE THAT HELEN WORRIED ABOUT.
*YES, I'M ASTERISK-ING MYSELF... SOCIALISM IS A POLITICAL MOVEMENT THAT SAYS ALL WEALTH IN SOCIETY SHOULD BE DIVIDED AMONG ALL CITIZENS EQUALLY.
1909
HELP THE BLIND!
ALL TOGETHER FOR PROGRESS!
THE WORKING CLASS LIVES IN WANT WHILE THE MASTER CLASS LIVES IN LUXURY.
THE SELFISHNESS AND GREED OF EMPLOYERS IS CAUSING BLINDNESS IN WORKERS!
LET THE REVOLUTION BEGIN!
HELEN SPENT MUCH OF THE REST OF HER LIFE DOING WHAT SHE BELIEVED WOULD MAKE LIFE BETTER FOR ALL PEOPLE, NOT ONLY FOR THE BLIND AND DEAF.
Give Women the Vote!

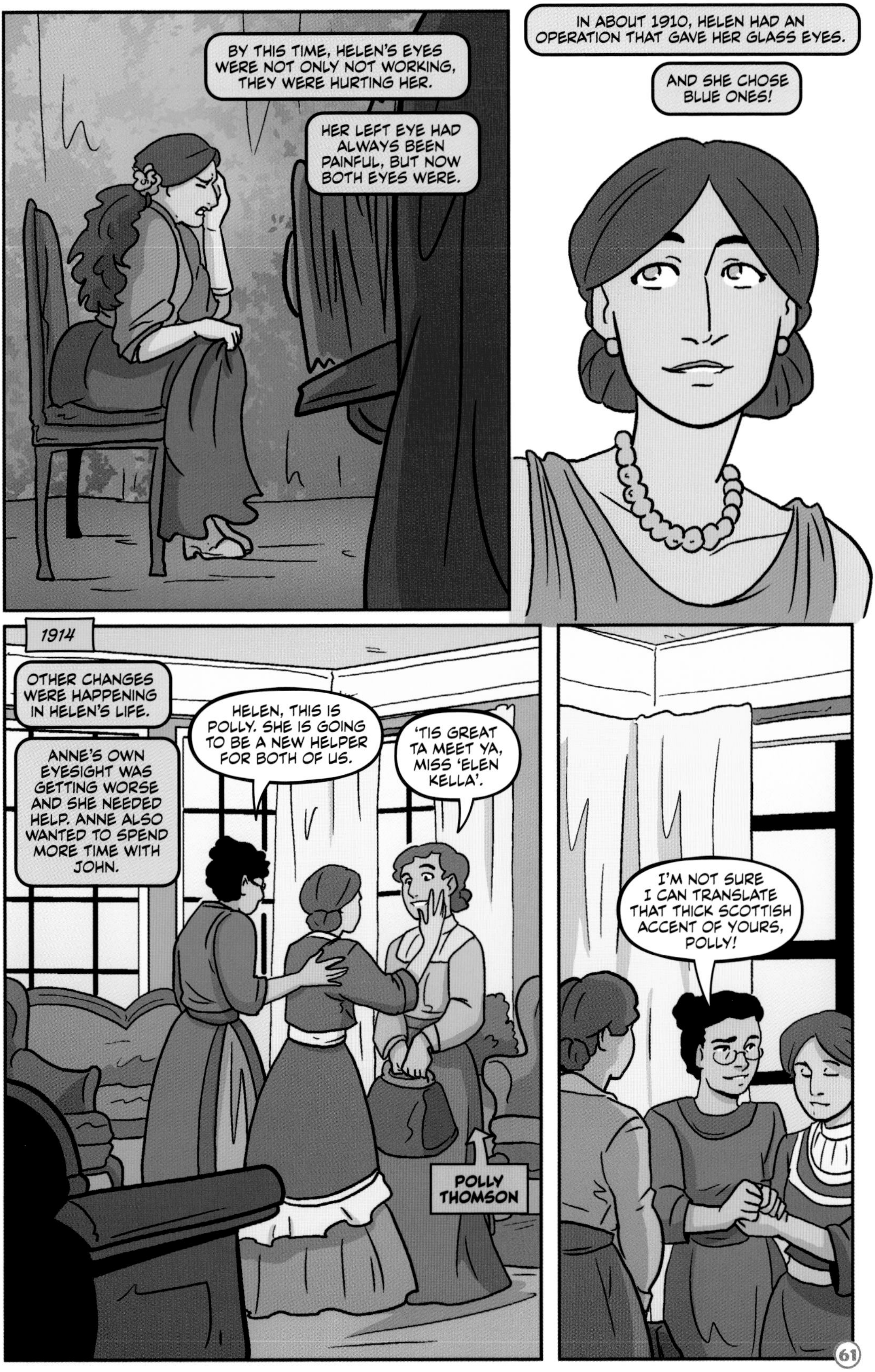

BY THIS TIME, HELEN'S EYES WERE NOT ONLY NOT WORKING, THEY WERE HURTING HER.
HER LEFT EYE HAD ALWAYS BEEN PAINFUL, BUT NOW BOTH EYES WERE.
IN ABOUT 1910, HELEN HAD AN OPERATION THAT GAVE HER GLASS EYES.
AND SHE CHOSE BLUE ONES!
1914
OTHER CHANGES WERE HAPPENING IN HELEN'S LIFE.
ANNE'S OWN EYESIGHT WAS GETTING WORSE AND SHE NEEDED HELP. ANNE ALSO WANTED TO SPEND MORE TIME WITH JOHN.
HELEN, THIS IS POLLY. SHE IS GOING TO BE A NEW HELPER FOR BOTH OF US.
'TIS GREAT TA MEET YA, MISS 'ELEN KELLA'.
POLLY THOMSON
I'M NOT SURE I CAN TRANSLATE THAT THICK SCOTTISH ACCENT OF YOURS, POLLY!

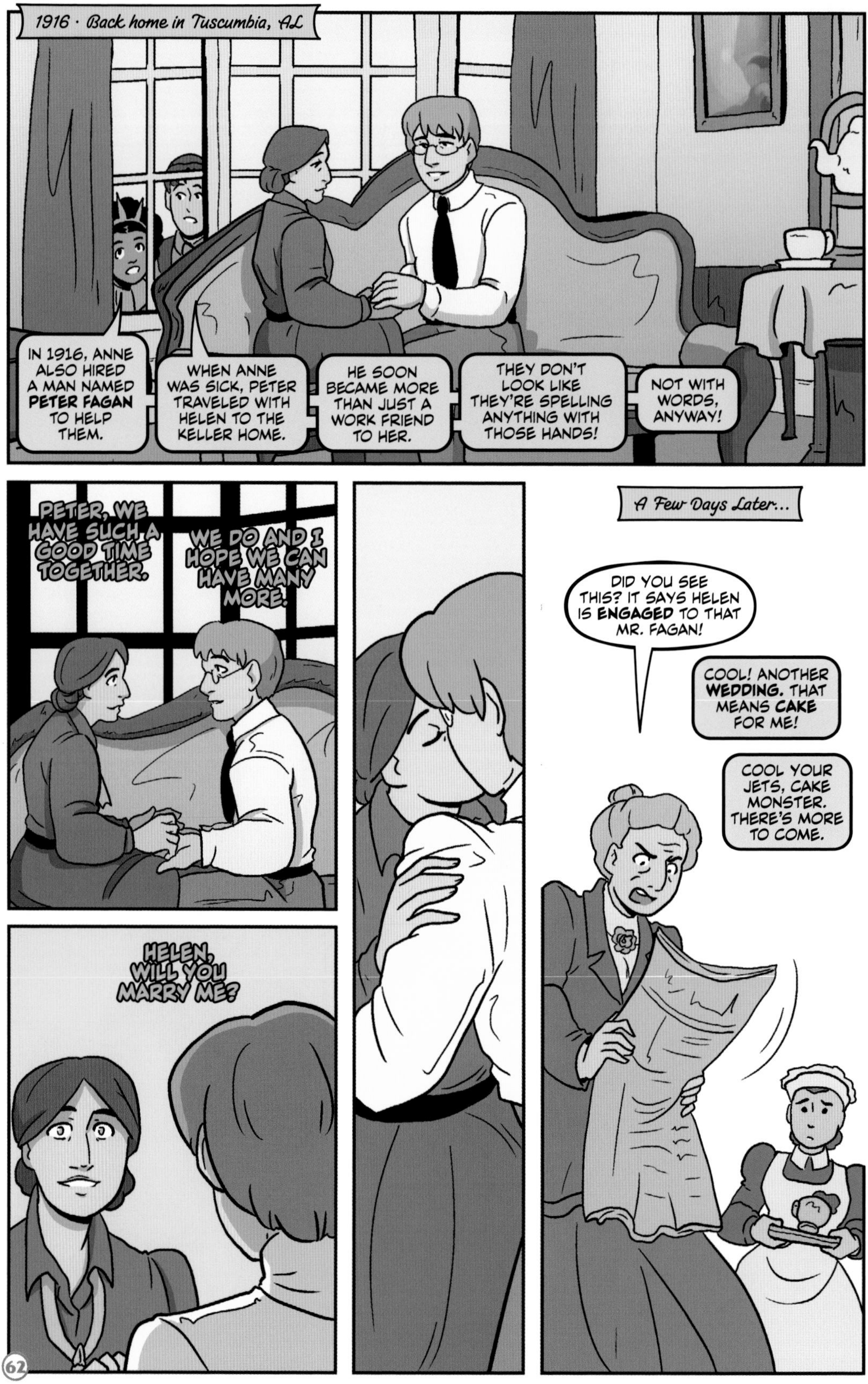
1916 · Back home in Tuscumbia, AL
IN 1916, ANNE ALSO HIRED A MAN NAMED PETER FAGAN TO HELP THEM.
WHEN ANNE WAS SICK, PETER TRAVELED WITH HELEN TO THE KELLER HOME.
HE SOON BECAME MORE THAN JUST A WORK FRIEND TO HER.
THEY DON'T LOOK LIKE THEY'RE SPELLING ANYTHING WITH THOSE HANDS!
NOT WITH WORDS, ANYWAY!
PETER, WE HAVE SUCH A GOOD TIME TOGETHER.
WE DO AND I HOPE WE CAN HAVE MANY MORE.
HELEN, WILL YOU MARRY ME?
A Few Days Later...
DID YOU SEE THIS? IT SAYS HELEN IS ENGAGED TO THAT MR. FAGAN!
COOL! ANOTHER WEDDING. THAT MEANS CAKE FOR ME!
COOL YOUR JETS, CAKE MONSTER. THERE'S MORE TO COME.

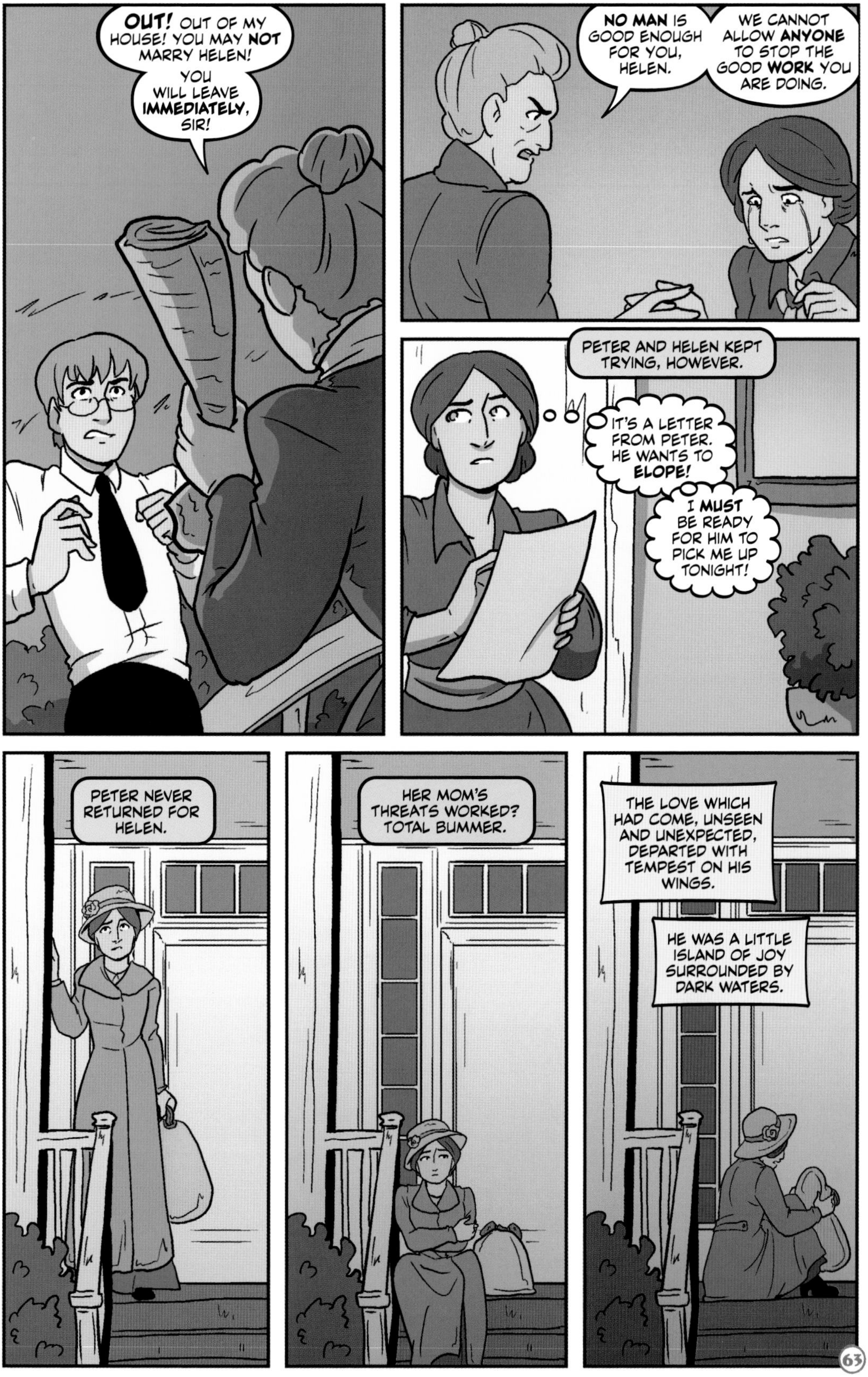
OUT! OUT OF MY HOUSE! YOU MAY NOT MARRY HELEN!
YOU WILL LEAVE IMMEDIATELY, SIR!
NO MAN IS GOOD ENOUGH FOR YOU, HELEN.
WE CANNOT ALLOW ANYONE TO STOP THE GOOD WORK YOU ARE DOING.
PETER AND HELEN KEPT TRYING, HOWEVER.
IT'S A LETTER FROM PETER. HE WANTS TO ELOPE!
I MUST BE READY FOR HIM TO PICK ME UP TONIGHT!
PETER NEVER RETURNED FOR HELEN.
HER MOM'S THREATS WORKED? TOTAL BUMMER.
THE LOVE WHICH HAD COME, UNSEEN AND UNEXPECTED, DEPARTED WITH TEMPEST ON HIS WINGS.
HE WAS A LITTLE ISLAND OF JOY SURROUNDED BY DARK WATERS.

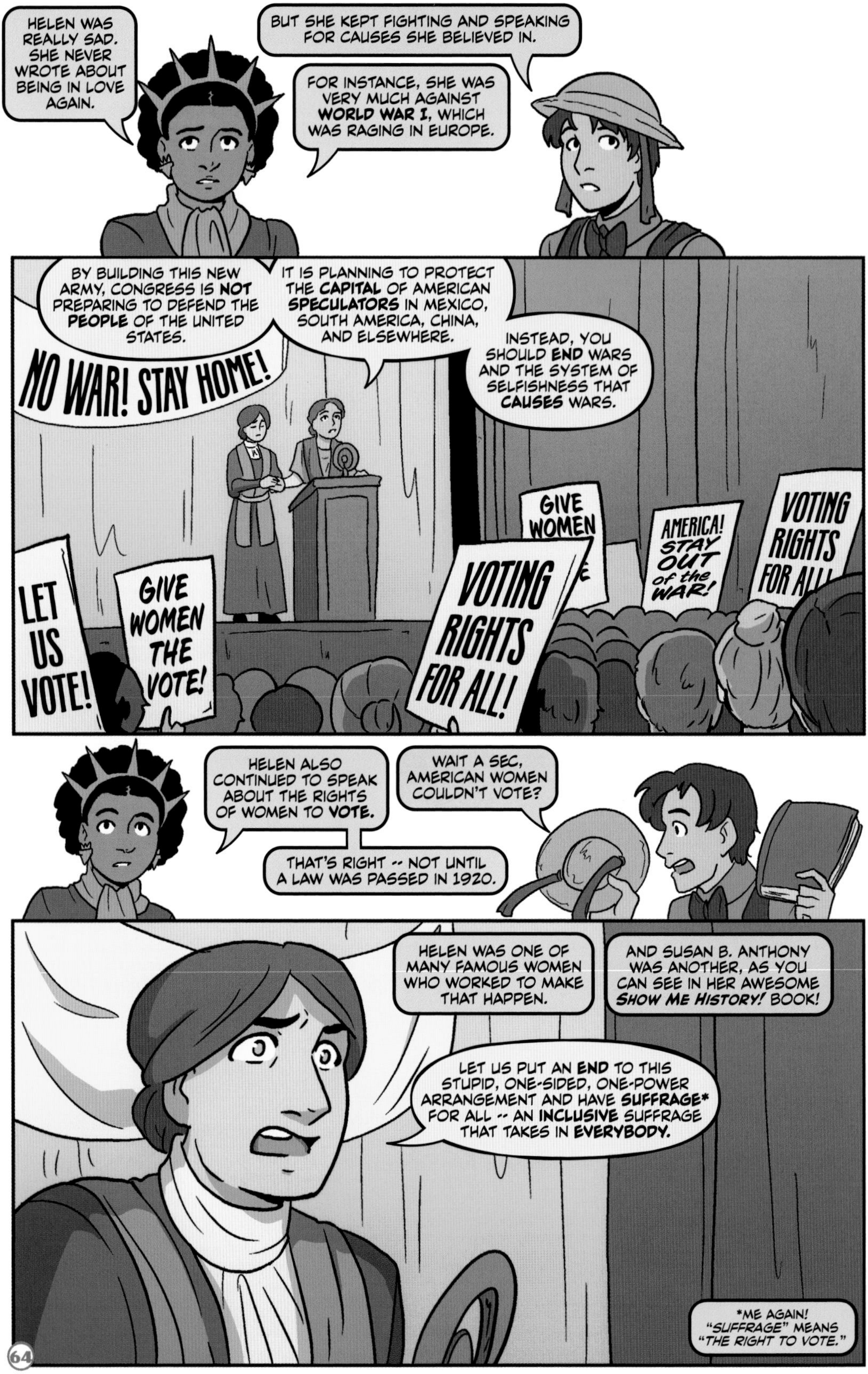
HELEN WAS REALLY SAD. SHE NEVER WROTE ABOUT BEING IN LOVE AGAIN.
BUT SHE KEPT FIGHTING AND SPEAKING FOR CAUSES SHE BELIEVED IN.
FOR INSTANCE, SHE WAS VERY MUCH AGAINST **WORLD WAR I**, WHICH WAS RAGING IN EUROPE.
BY BUILDING THIS NEW ARMY, CONGRESS IS **NOT** PREPARING TO DEFEND THE **PEOPLE** OF THE UNITED STATES.
IT IS PLANNING TO PROTECT THE **CAPITAL** OF AMERICAN **SPECULATORS** IN MEXICO, SOUTH AMERICA, CHINA, AND ELSEWHERE.
INSTEAD, YOU SHOULD **END** WARS AND THE SYSTEM OF SELFISHNESS THAT **CAUSES** WARS.
NO WAR! STAY HOME!
LET US VOTE!
GIVE WOMEN THE VOTE!
VOTING RIGHTS FOR ALL!
GIVE WOMEN
AMERICA! STAY OUT of the WAR!
VOTING RIGHTS FOR ALL
HELEN ALSO CONTINUED TO SPEAK ABOUT THE RIGHTS OF WOMEN TO **VOTE.**
THAT'S RIGHT -- NOT UNTIL A LAW WAS PASSED IN 1920.
WAIT A SEC, AMERICAN WOMEN COULDN'T VOTE?
HELEN WAS ONE OF MANY FAMOUS WOMEN WHO WORKED TO MAKE THAT HAPPEN.
AND SUSAN B. ANTHONY WAS ANOTHER, AS YOU CAN SEE IN HER AWESOME ***SHOW ME HISTORY!*** BOOK!
LET US PUT AN **END** TO THIS STUPID, ONE-SIDED, ONE-POWER ARRANGEMENT AND HAVE **SUFFRAGE*** FOR ALL -- AN **INCLUSIVE** SUFFRAGE THAT TAKES IN **EVERYBODY.**
*ME AGAIN! *"SUFFRAGE"* MEANS *"THE RIGHT TO VOTE."*

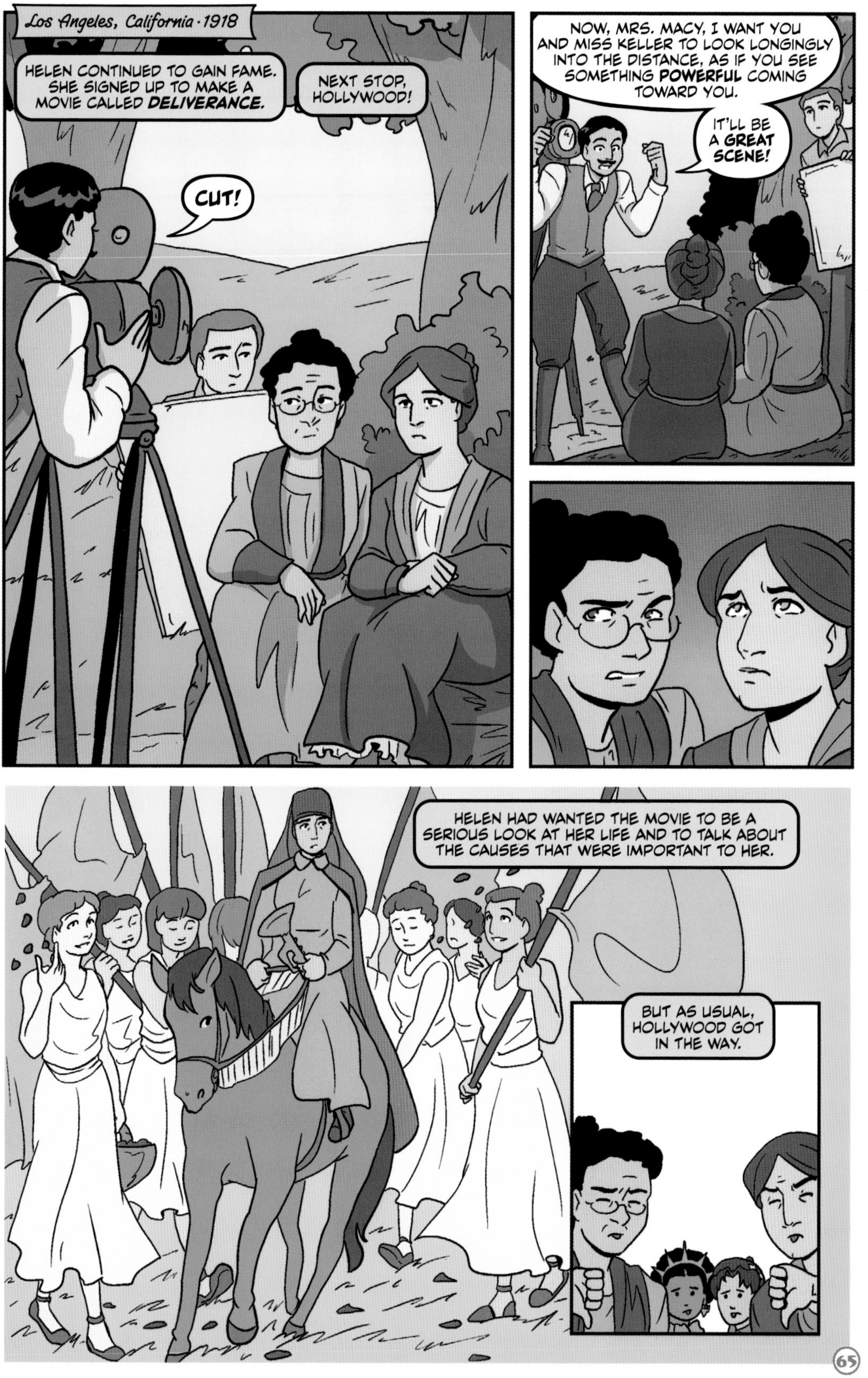
Los Angeles, California · 1918
HELEN CONTINUED TO GAIN FAME. SHE SIGNED UP TO MAKE A MOVIE CALLED DELIVERANCE.
NEXT STOP, HOLLYWOOD!
CUT!
NOW, MRS. MACY, I WANT YOU AND MISS KELLER TO LOOK LONGINGLY INTO THE DISTANCE, AS IF YOU SEE SOMETHING POWERFUL COMING TOWARD YOU.
IT'LL BE A GREAT SCENE!
HELEN HAD WANTED THE MOVIE TO BE A SERIOUS LOOK AT HER LIFE AND TO TALK ABOUT THE CAUSES THAT WERE IMPORTANT TO HER.
BUT AS USUAL, HOLLYWOOD GOT IN THE WAY.

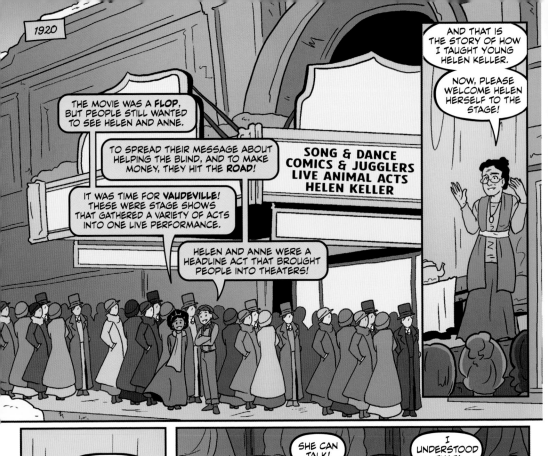

1920

AND THAT IS THE STORY OF HOW I TAUGHT YOUNG HELEN KELLER.

NOW, PLEASE WELCOME HELEN HERSELF TO THE STAGE!

THE MOVIE WAS A **FLOP**, BUT PEOPLE STILL WANTED TO SEE HELEN AND ANNE.

TO SPREAD THEIR MESSAGE ABOUT HELPING THE BLIND, AND TO MAKE MONEY, THEY HIT THE **ROAD**!

IT WAS TIME FOR **VAUDEVILLE**! THESE WERE STAGE SHOWS THAT GATHERED A VARIETY OF ACTS INTO ONE LIVE PERFORMANCE.

HELEN AND ANNE WERE A HEADLINE ACT THAT BROUGHT PEOPLE INTO THEATERS!

SONG & DANCE
COMICS & JUGGLERS
LIVE ANIMAL ACTS
HELEN KELLER

ISN'T THIS B-B-BEAUTIFUL!

SHE CAN TALK!

I UNDERSTOOD THAT!

IS SHE FOR REAL?

WHAT AN ACT!

ANNE AND HELEN TALKED TO EACH AUDIENCE, TELLING THEIR STORY DOZENS OF TIMES IN MANY CITIES.

AND THEY TOOK HOME BIG MONEY -- $2,000 A WEEK! THAT WOULD BE MORE THAN $28,000 TODAY!

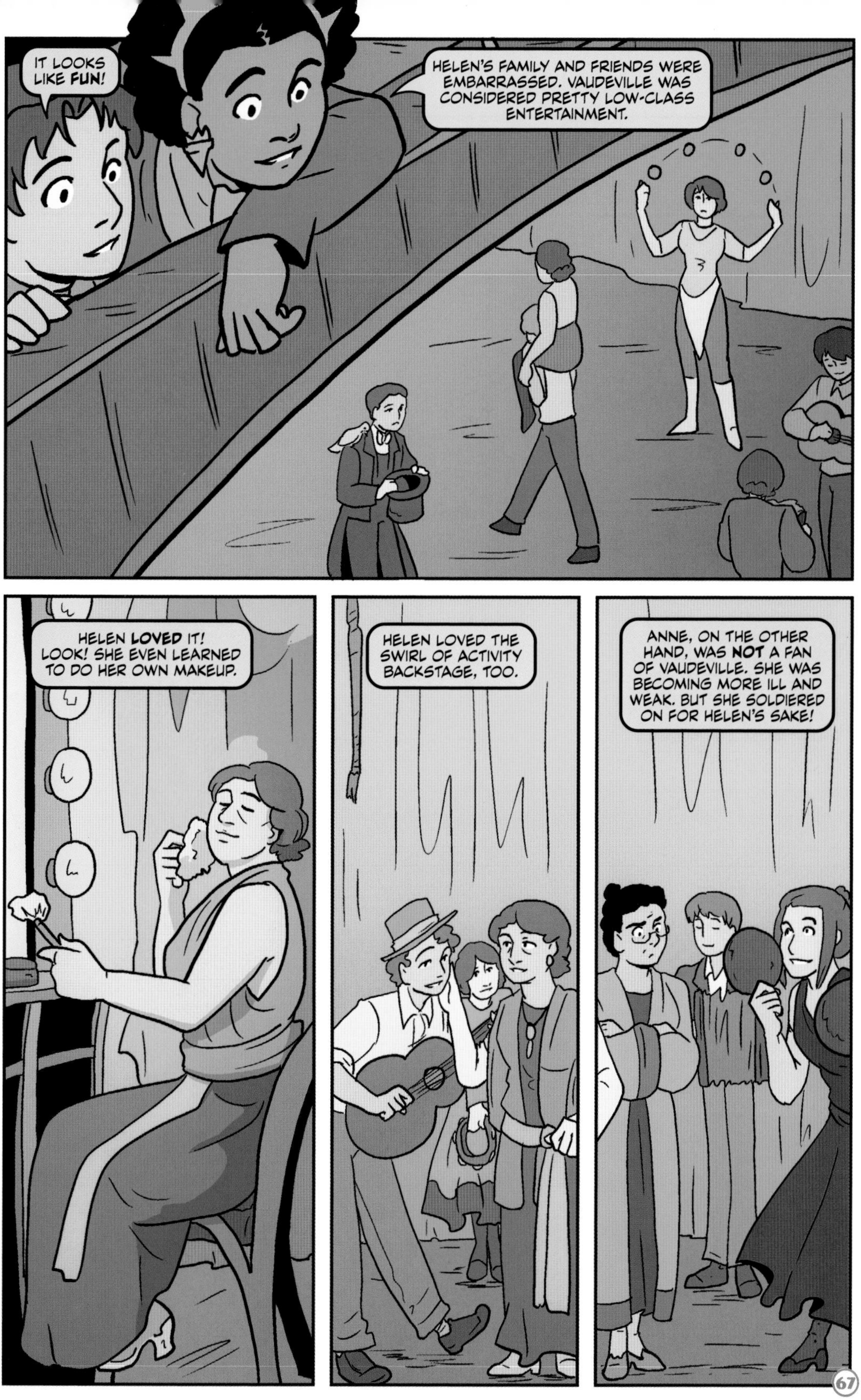

IT LOOKS LIKE **FUN**!
HELEN'S FAMILY AND FRIENDS WERE EMBARRASSED. VAUDEVILLE WAS CONSIDERED PRETTY LOW-CLASS ENTERTAINMENT.
HELEN **LOVED** IT! LOOK! SHE EVEN LEARNED TO DO HER OWN MAKEUP.
HELEN LOVED THE SWIRL OF ACTIVITY BACKSTAGE, TOO.
ANNE, ON THE OTHER HAND, WAS **NOT** A FAN OF VAUDEVILLE. SHE WAS BECOMING MORE ILL AND WEAK. BUT SHE SOLDIERED ON FOR HELEN'S SAKE!

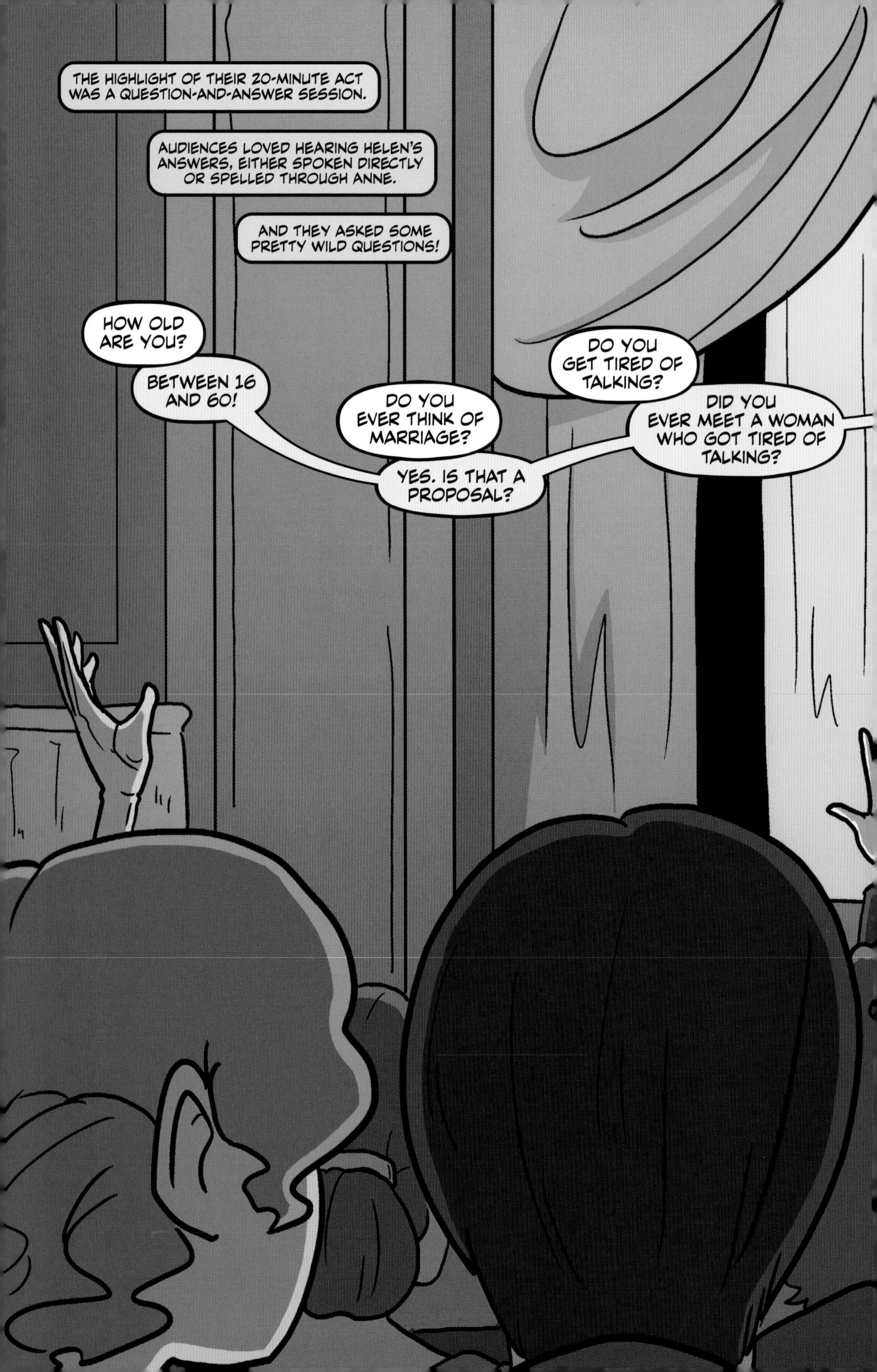
THE HIGHLIGHT OF THEIR 20-MINUTE ACT WAS A QUESTION-AND-ANSWER SESSION.
AUDIENCES LOVED HEARING HELEN'S ANSWERS, EITHER SPOKEN DIRECTLY OR SPELLED THROUGH ANNE.
AND THEY ASKED SOME PRETTY WILD QUESTIONS!
HOW OLD ARE YOU?
BETWEEN 16 AND 60!
DO YOU EVER THINK OF MARRIAGE?
YES. IS THAT A PROPOSAL?
DO YOU GET TIRED OF TALKING?
DID YOU EVER MEET A WOMAN WHO GOT TIRED OF TALKING?

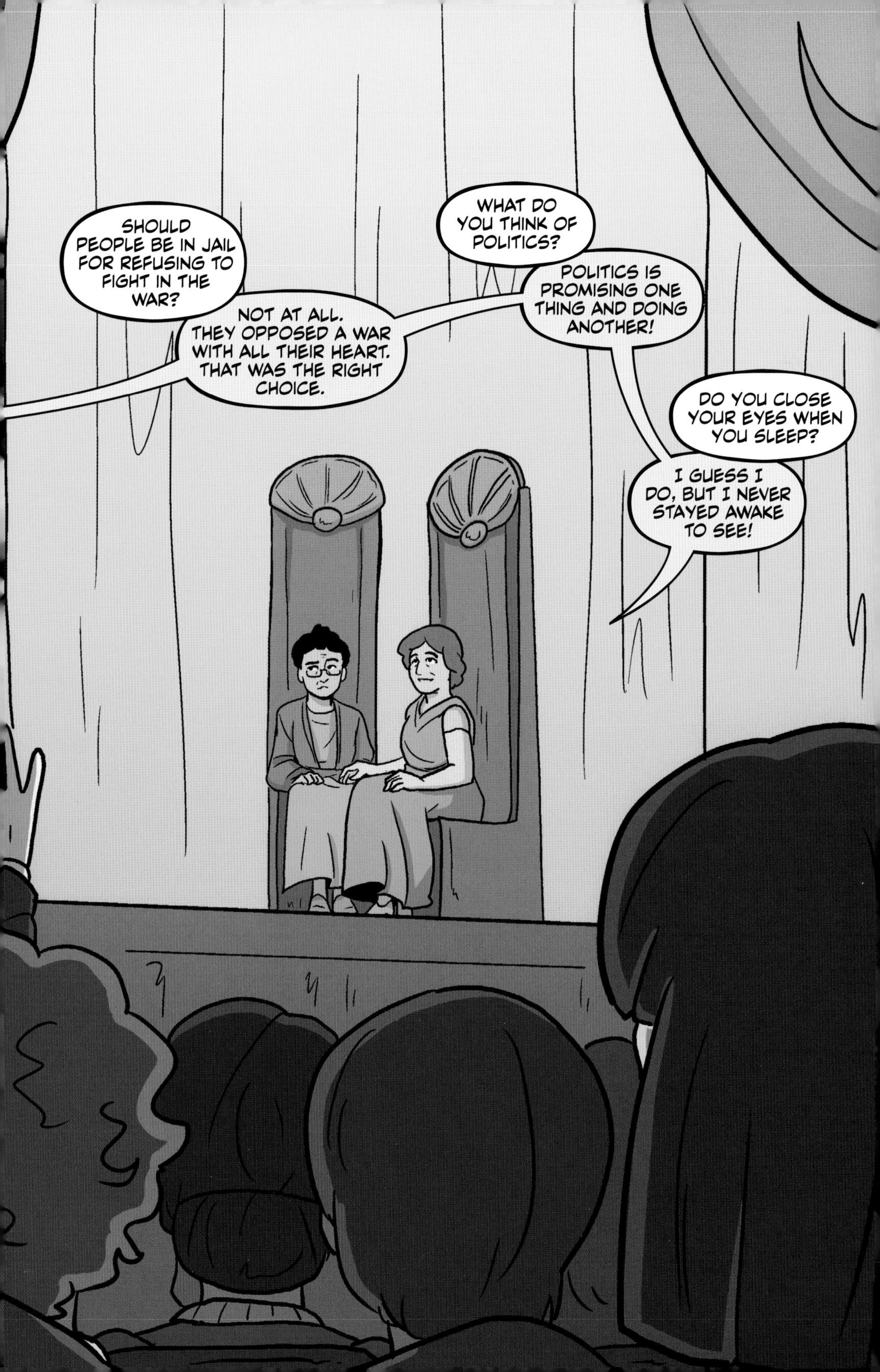
SHOULD PEOPLE BE IN JAIL FOR REFUSING TO FIGHT IN THE WAR?
NOT AT ALL. THEY OPPOSED A WAR WITH ALL THEIR HEART. THAT WAS THE RIGHT CHOICE.
WHAT DO YOU THINK OF POLITICS?
POLITICS IS PROMISING ONE THING AND DOING ANOTHER!
DO YOU CLOSE YOUR EYES WHEN YOU SLEEP?
I GUESS I DO, BUT I NEVER STAYED AWAKE TO SEE!

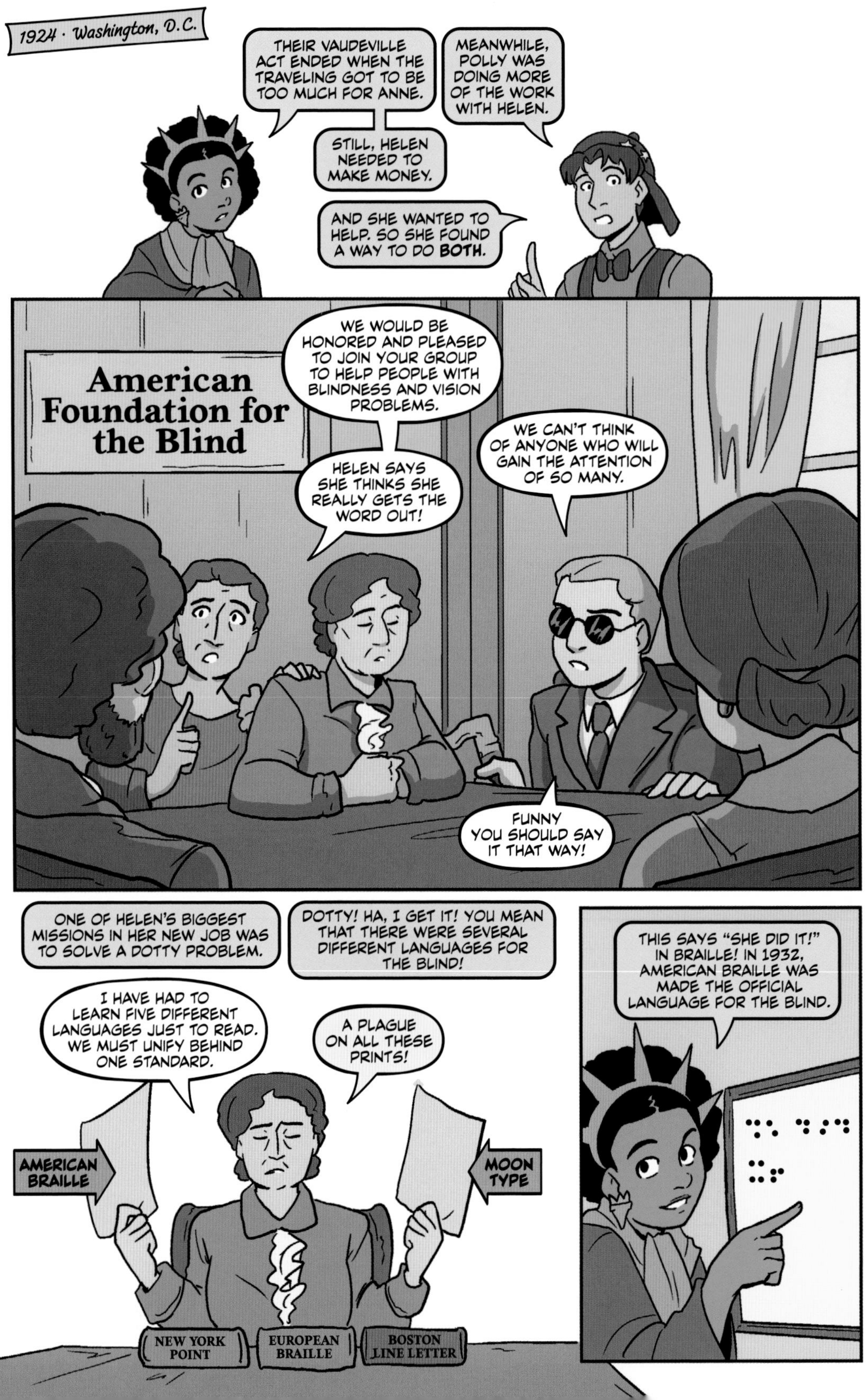
1924 · Washington, D.C.
THEIR VAUDEVILLE ACT ENDED WHEN THE TRAVELING GOT TO BE TOO MUCH FOR ANNE.
STILL, HELEN NEEDED TO MAKE MONEY.
MEANWHILE, POLLY WAS DOING MORE OF THE WORK WITH HELEN.
AND SHE WANTED TO HELP. SO SHE FOUND A WAY TO DO BOTH.
American Foundation for the Blind
WE WOULD BE HONORED AND PLEASED TO JOIN YOUR GROUP TO HELP PEOPLE WITH BLINDNESS AND VISION PROBLEMS.
HELEN SAYS SHE THINKS SHE REALLY GETS THE WORD OUT!
WE CAN'T THINK OF ANYONE WHO WILL GAIN THE ATTENTION OF SO MANY.
FUNNY YOU SHOULD SAY IT THAT WAY!
ONE OF HELEN'S BIGGEST MISSIONS IN HER NEW JOB WAS TO SOLVE A DOTTY PROBLEM.
DOTTY! HA, I GET IT! YOU MEAN THAT THERE WERE SEVERAL DIFFERENT LANGUAGES FOR THE BLIND!
I HAVE HAD TO LEARN FIVE DIFFERENT LANGUAGES JUST TO READ. WE MUST UNIFY BEHIND ONE STANDARD.
A PLAGUE ON ALL THESE PRINTS!
AMERICAN BRAILLE
MOON TYPE
NEW YORK POINT
EUROPEAN BRAILLE
BOSTON LINE LETTER
THIS SAYS "SHE DID IT!" IN BRAILLE! IN 1932, AMERICAN BRAILLE WAS MADE THE OFFICIAL LANGUAGE FOR THE BLIND.

1931

HELEN'S WORK ALWAYS TOOK HER BACK TO A FAMILIAR PLACE -- THE WHITE HOUSE!

PRESIDENT HERBERT HOOVER

MISS KELLER, AT THIS MEETING TO START A NEW ORGANIZATION THAT HELPS THE BLIND, I KNOW THAT YOUR LEADERSHIP WILL MAKE A HUGE DIFFERENCE.

I HOPE SO. AND BY THE WAY, YOU'RE THE 8TH PRESIDENT I'VE MET -- SO FAR!

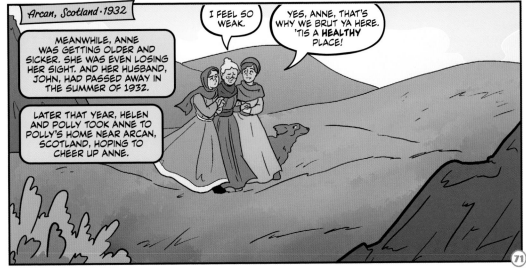

Arcan, Scotland · 1932

MEANWHILE, ANNE WAS GETTING OLDER AND SICKER. SHE WAS EVEN LOSING HER SIGHT. AND HER HUSBAND, JOHN, HAD PASSED AWAY IN THE SUMMER OF 1932.

LATER THAT YEAR, HELEN AND POLLY TOOK ANNE TO POLLY'S HOME NEAR ARCAN, SCOTLAND, HOPING TO CHEER UP ANNE.

I FEEL SO WEAK.

YES, ANNE, THAT'S WHY WE BRUT YA HERE. 'TIS A HEALTHY PLACE!

71

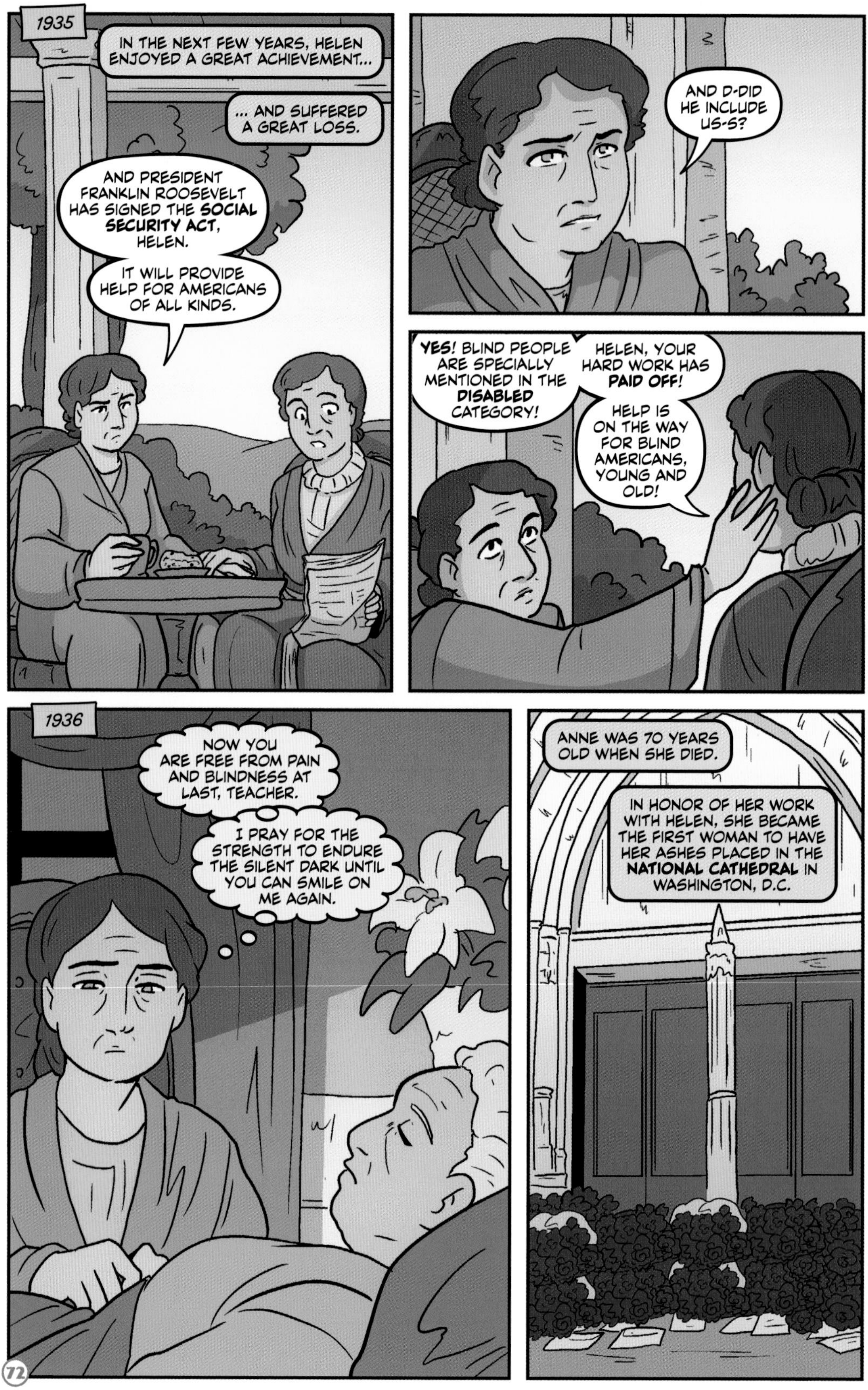
1935
IN THE NEXT FEW YEARS, HELEN ENJOYED A GREAT ACHIEVEMENT...
... AND SUFFERED A GREAT LOSS.
AND PRESIDENT FRANKLIN ROOSEVELT HAS SIGNED THE **SOCIAL SECURITY ACT**, HELEN.
IT WILL PROVIDE HELP FOR AMERICANS OF ALL KINDS.
AND D-DID HE INCLUDE US-S?
YES! BLIND PEOPLE ARE SPECIALLY MENTIONED IN THE **DISABLED** CATEGORY!
HELEN, YOUR HARD WORK HAS **PAID OFF!**
HELP IS ON THE WAY FOR BLIND AMERICANS, YOUNG AND OLD!
1936
NOW YOU ARE FREE FROM PAIN AND BLINDNESS AT LAST, TEACHER.
I PRAY FOR THE STRENGTH TO ENDURE THE SILENT DARK UNTIL YOU CAN SMILE ON ME AGAIN.
ANNE WAS 70 YEARS OLD WHEN SHE DIED.
IN HONOR OF HER WORK WITH HELEN, SHE BECAME THE FIRST WOMAN TO HAVE HER ASHES PLACED IN THE **NATIONAL CATHEDRAL** IN WASHINGTON, D.C.

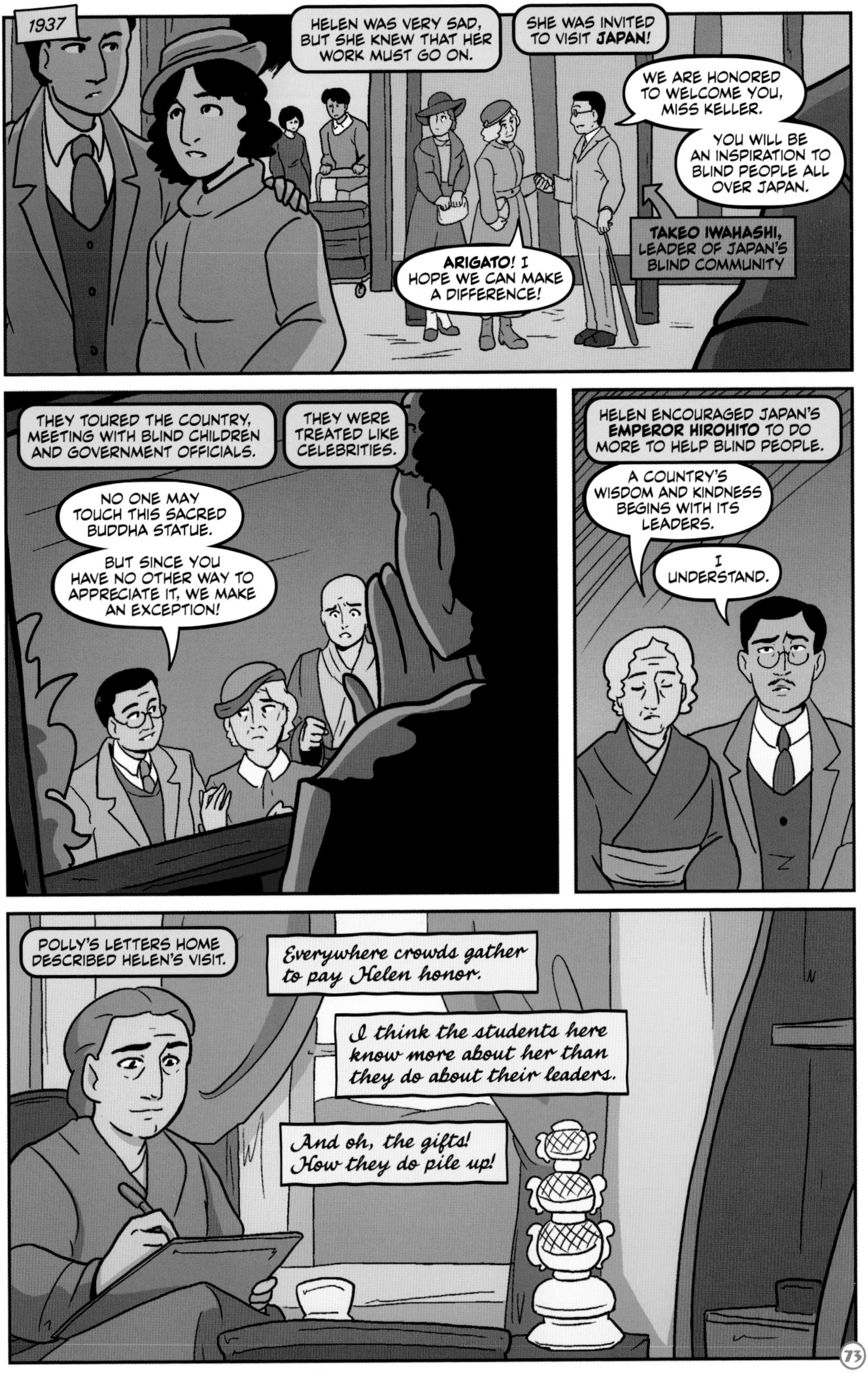
1937
HELEN WAS VERY SAD, BUT SHE KNEW THAT HER WORK MUST GO ON.
SHE WAS INVITED TO VISIT **JAPAN**!
WE ARE HONORED TO WELCOME YOU, MISS KELLER.
YOU WILL BE AN INSPIRATION TO BLIND PEOPLE ALL OVER JAPAN.
TAKEO IWAHASHI, LEADER OF JAPAN'S BLIND COMMUNITY
ARIGATO! I HOPE WE CAN MAKE A DIFFERENCE!
THEY TOURED THE COUNTRY, MEETING WITH BLIND CHILDREN AND GOVERNMENT OFFICIALS.
THEY WERE TREATED LIKE CELEBRITIES.
NO ONE MAY TOUCH THIS SACRED BUDDHA STATUE.
BUT SINCE YOU HAVE NO OTHER WAY TO APPRECIATE IT, WE MAKE AN EXCEPTION!
HELEN ENCOURAGED JAPAN'S **EMPEROR HIROHITO** TO DO MORE TO HELP BLIND PEOPLE.
A COUNTRY'S WISDOM AND KINDNESS BEGINS WITH ITS LEADERS.
I UNDERSTAND.
POLLY'S LETTERS HOME DESCRIBED HELEN'S VISIT.
Everywhere crowds gather to pay Helen honor.
I think the students here know more about her than they do about their leaders.
And oh, the gifts! How they do pile up!

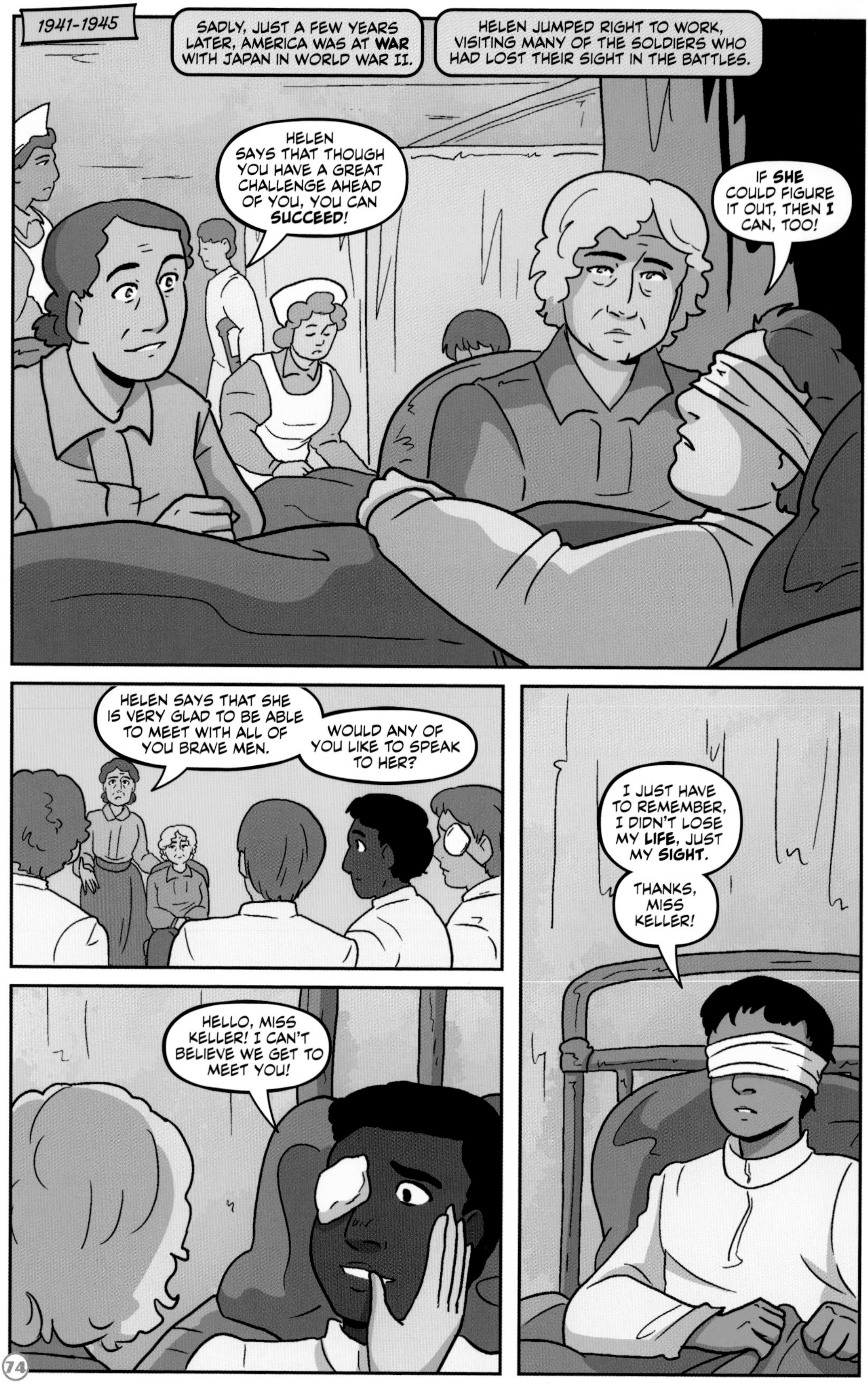
1941-1945
SADLY, JUST A FEW YEARS LATER, AMERICA WAS AT **WAR** WITH JAPAN IN WORLD WAR II.
HELEN JUMPED RIGHT TO WORK, VISITING MANY OF THE SOLDIERS WHO HAD LOST THEIR SIGHT IN THE BATTLES.
HELEN SAYS THAT THOUGH YOU HAVE A GREAT CHALLENGE AHEAD OF YOU, YOU CAN **SUCCEED**!
IF **SHE** COULD FIGURE IT OUT, THEN **I** CAN, TOO!
HELEN SAYS THAT SHE IS VERY GLAD TO BE ABLE TO MEET WITH ALL OF YOU BRAVE MEN.
WOULD ANY OF YOU LIKE TO SPEAK TO HER?
HELLO, MISS KELLER! I CAN'T BELIEVE WE GET TO MEET YOU!
I JUST HAVE TO REMEMBER, I DIDN'T LOSE MY **LIFE**, JUST MY **SIGHT**.
THANKS, MISS KELLER!

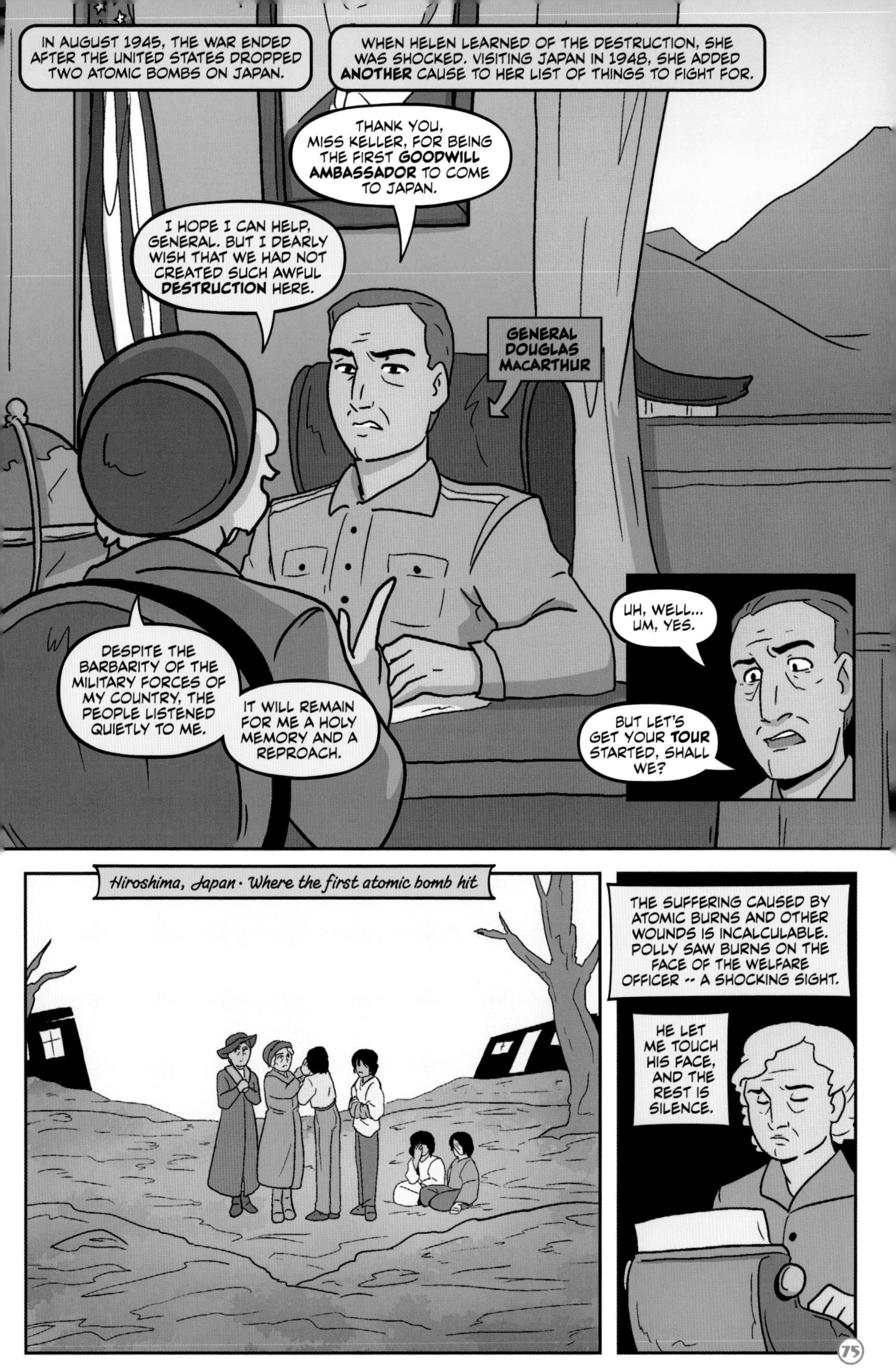

IN AUGUST 1945, THE WAR ENDED AFTER THE UNITED STATES DROPPED TWO ATOMIC BOMBS ON JAPAN.
WHEN HELEN LEARNED OF THE DESTRUCTION, SHE WAS SHOCKED. VISITING JAPAN IN 1948, SHE ADDED **ANOTHER** CAUSE TO HER LIST OF THINGS TO FIGHT FOR.
THANK YOU, MISS KELLER, FOR BEING THE FIRST **GOODWILL AMBASSADOR** TO COME TO JAPAN.
I HOPE I CAN HELP, GENERAL. BUT I DEARLY WISH THAT WE HAD NOT CREATED SUCH AWFUL **DESTRUCTION** HERE.
GENERAL DOUGLAS MacARTHUR
DESPITE THE BARBARITY OF THE MILITARY FORCES OF MY COUNTRY, THE PEOPLE LISTENED QUIETLY TO ME.
IT WILL REMAIN FOR ME A HOLY MEMORY AND A REPROACH.
UH, WELL... UM, YES.
BUT LET'S GET YOUR **TOUR** STARTED, SHALL WE?
Hiroshima, Japan · Where the first atomic bomb hit
THE SUFFERING CAUSED BY ATOMIC BURNS AND OTHER WOUNDS IS INCALCULABLE. POLLY SAW BURNS ON THE FACE OF THE WELFARE OFFICER -- A SHOCKING SIGHT.
HE LET ME TOUCH HIS FACE, AND THE REST IS SILENCE.

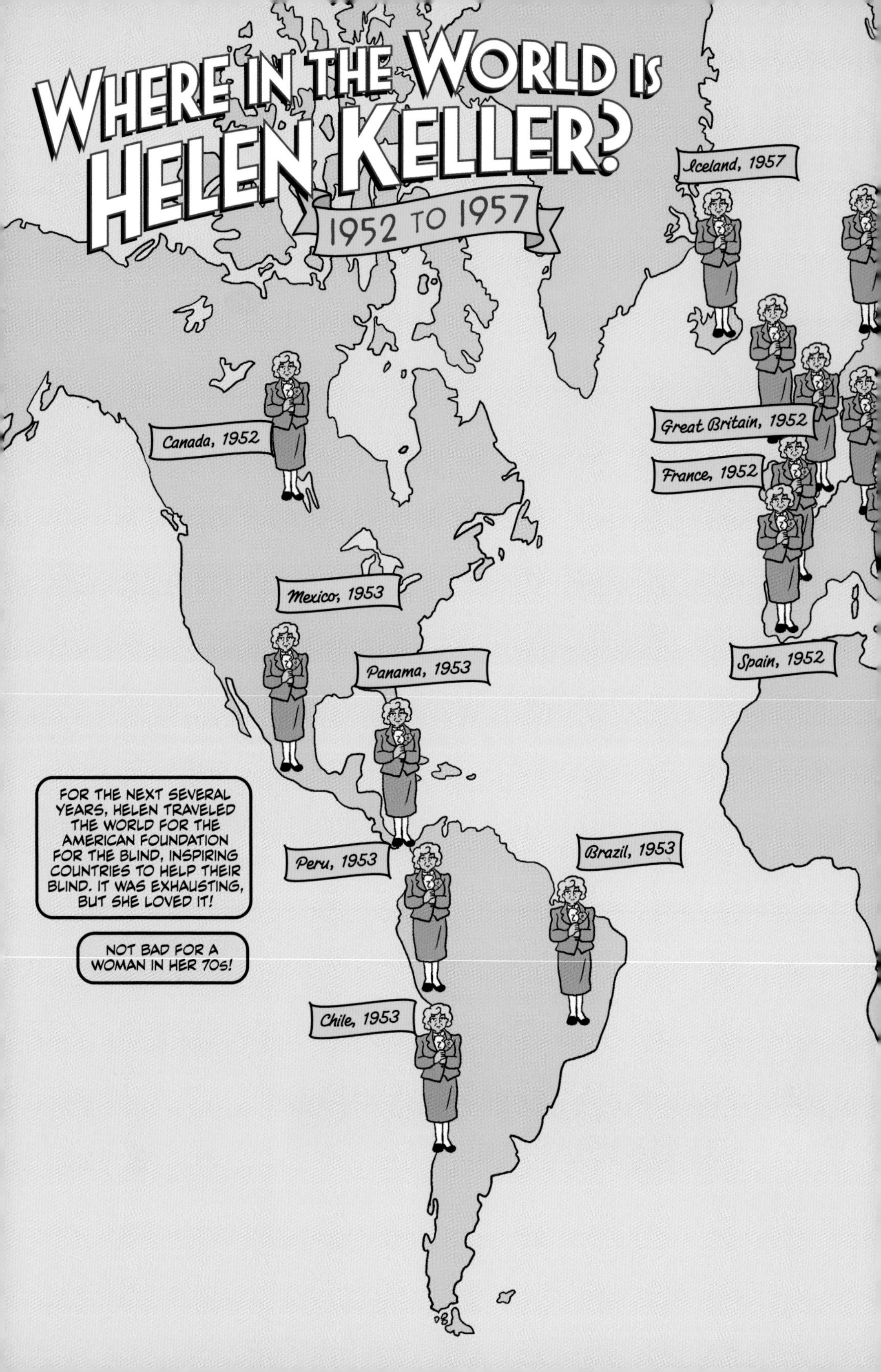

WHERE IN THE WORLD IS HELEN KELLER?
1952 TO 1957
Iceland, 1957
Canada, 1952
Great Britain, 1952
France, 1952
Mexico, 1953
Panama, 1953
Spain, 1952
FOR THE NEXT SEVERAL YEARS, HELEN TRAVELED THE WORLD FOR THE AMERICAN FOUNDATION FOR THE BLIND, INSPIRING COUNTRIES TO HELP THEIR BLIND. IT WAS EXHAUSTING, BUT SHE LOVED IT!
Peru, 1953
Brazil, 1953
NOT BAD FOR A WOMAN IN HER 70S!
Chile, 1953

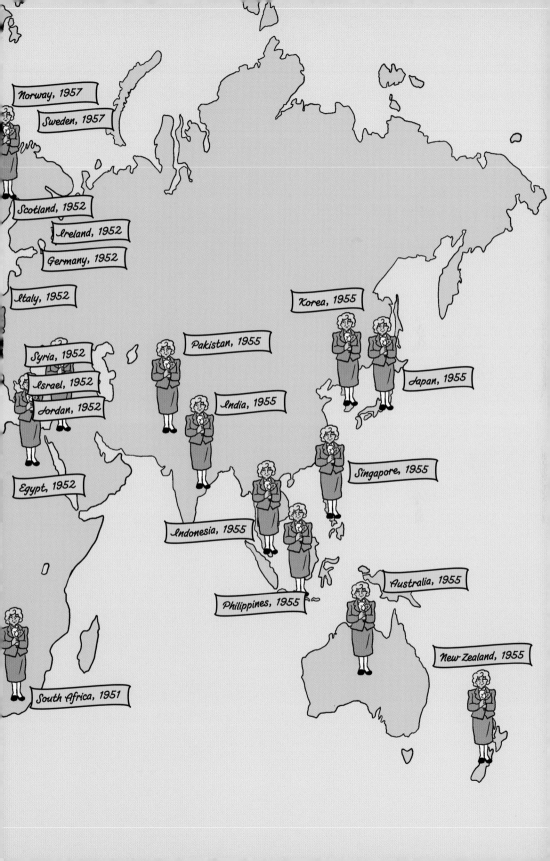

Norway, 1957

Sweden, 1957

Scotland, 1952

Ireland, 1952

Germany, 1952

Italy, 1952

Korea, 1955

Syria, 1952

Pakistan, 1955

Israel, 1952

Japan, 1955

Jordan, 1952

India, 1955

Egypt, 1952

Singapore, 1955

Indonesia, 1955

Philippines, 1955

Australia, 1955

New Zealand, 1955

South Africa, 1951

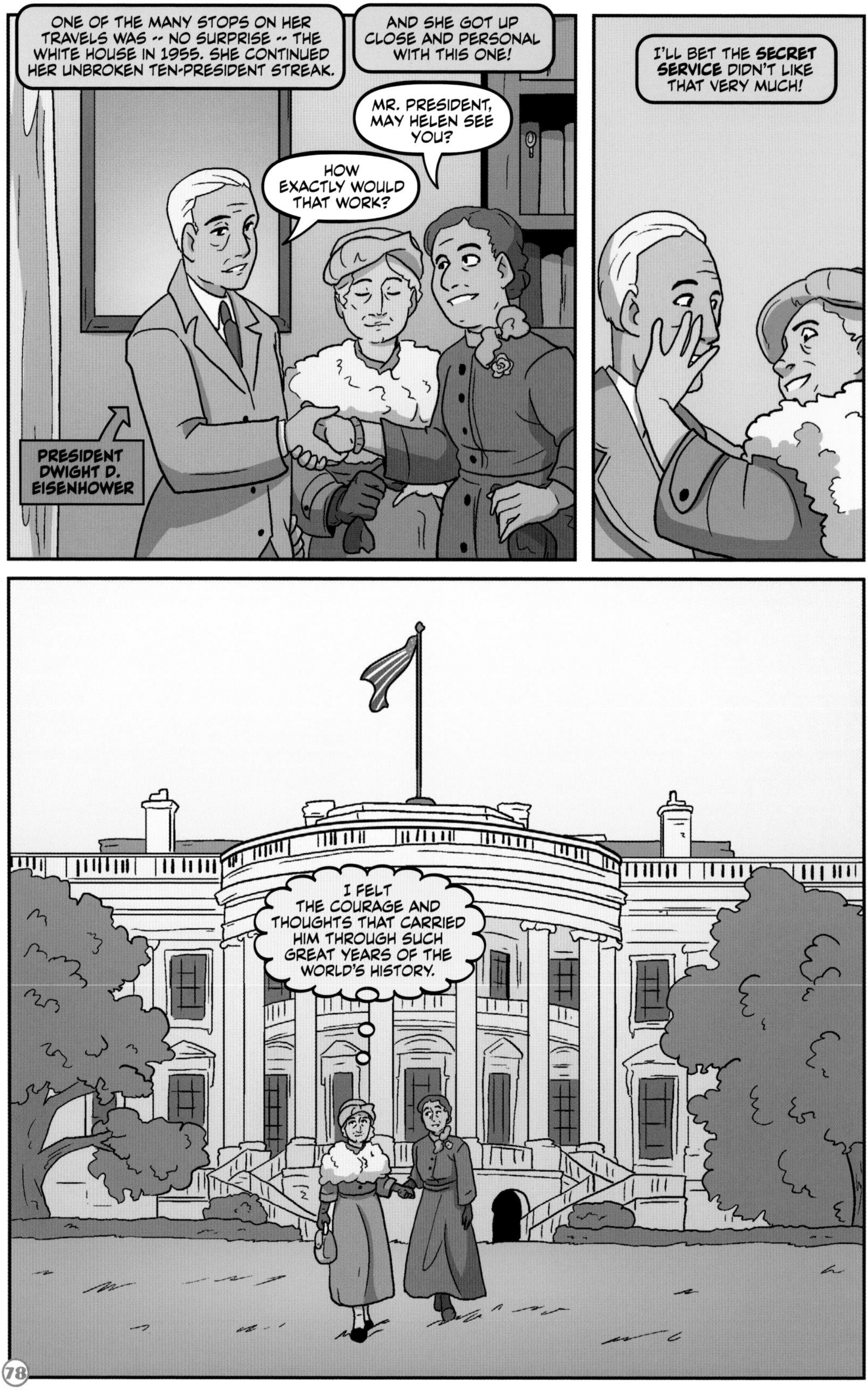

ONE OF THE MANY STOPS ON HER TRAVELS WAS -- NO SURPRISE -- THE WHITE HOUSE IN 1955. SHE CONTINUED HER UNBROKEN TEN-PRESIDENT STREAK.
AND SHE GOT UP CLOSE AND PERSONAL WITH THIS ONE!
MR. PRESIDENT, MAY HELEN SEE YOU?
HOW EXACTLY WOULD THAT WORK?
PRESIDENT DWIGHT D. EISENHOWER
I'LL BET THE **SECRET SERVICE** DIDN'T LIKE THAT VERY MUCH!
I FELT THE COURAGE AND THOUGHTS THAT CARRIED HIM THROUGH SUCH GREAT YEARS OF THE WORLD'S HISTORY.

Helen Becomes A MOVIE STAR!

AGAIN!

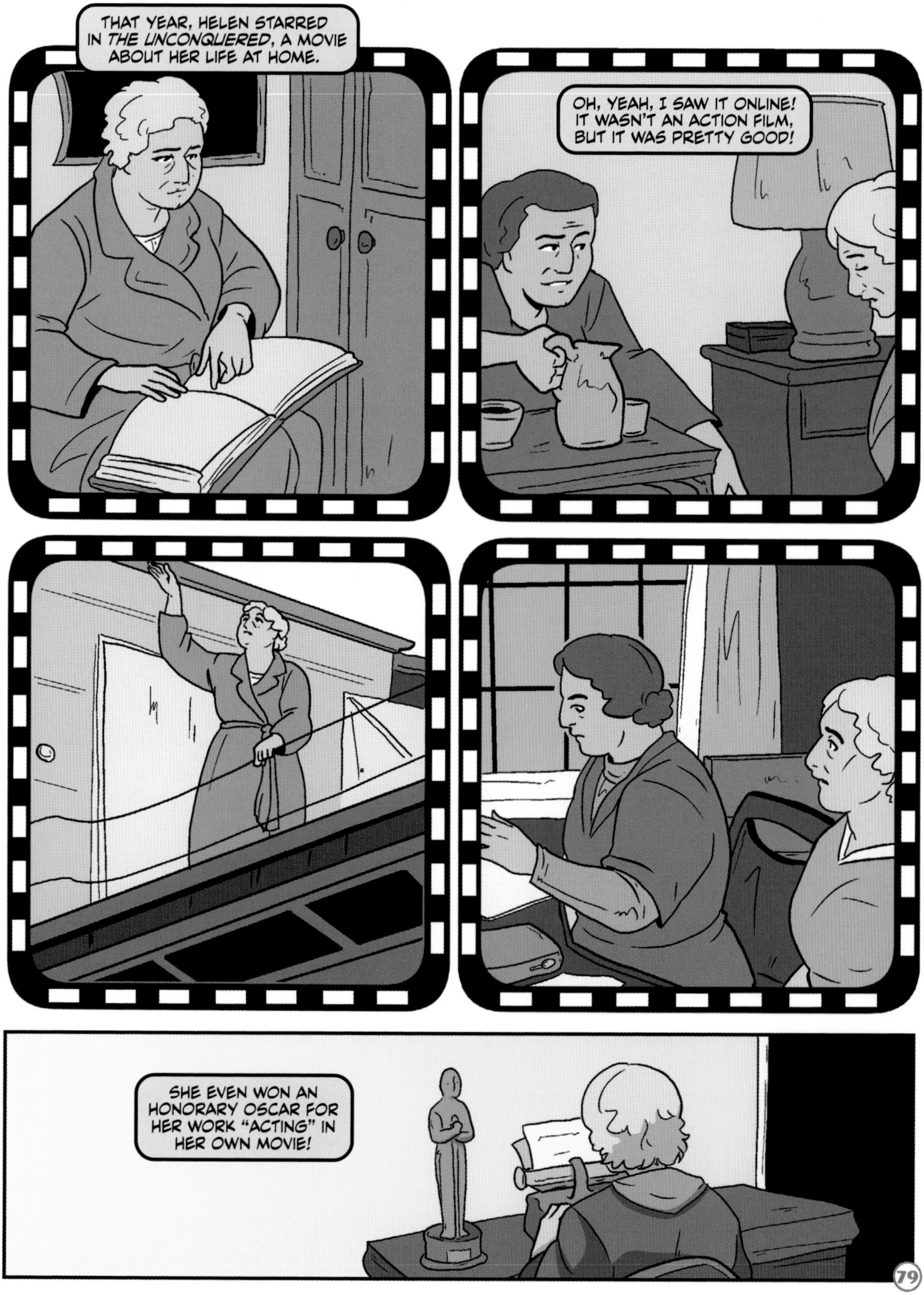

THAT YEAR, HELEN STARRED IN *THE UNCONQUERED*, A MOVIE ABOUT HER LIFE AT HOME.
OH, YEAH, I SAW IT ONLINE! IT WASN'T AN ACTION FILM, BUT IT WAS PRETTY GOOD!
SHE EVEN WON AN HONORARY OSCAR FOR HER WORK "ACTING" IN HER OWN MOVIE!

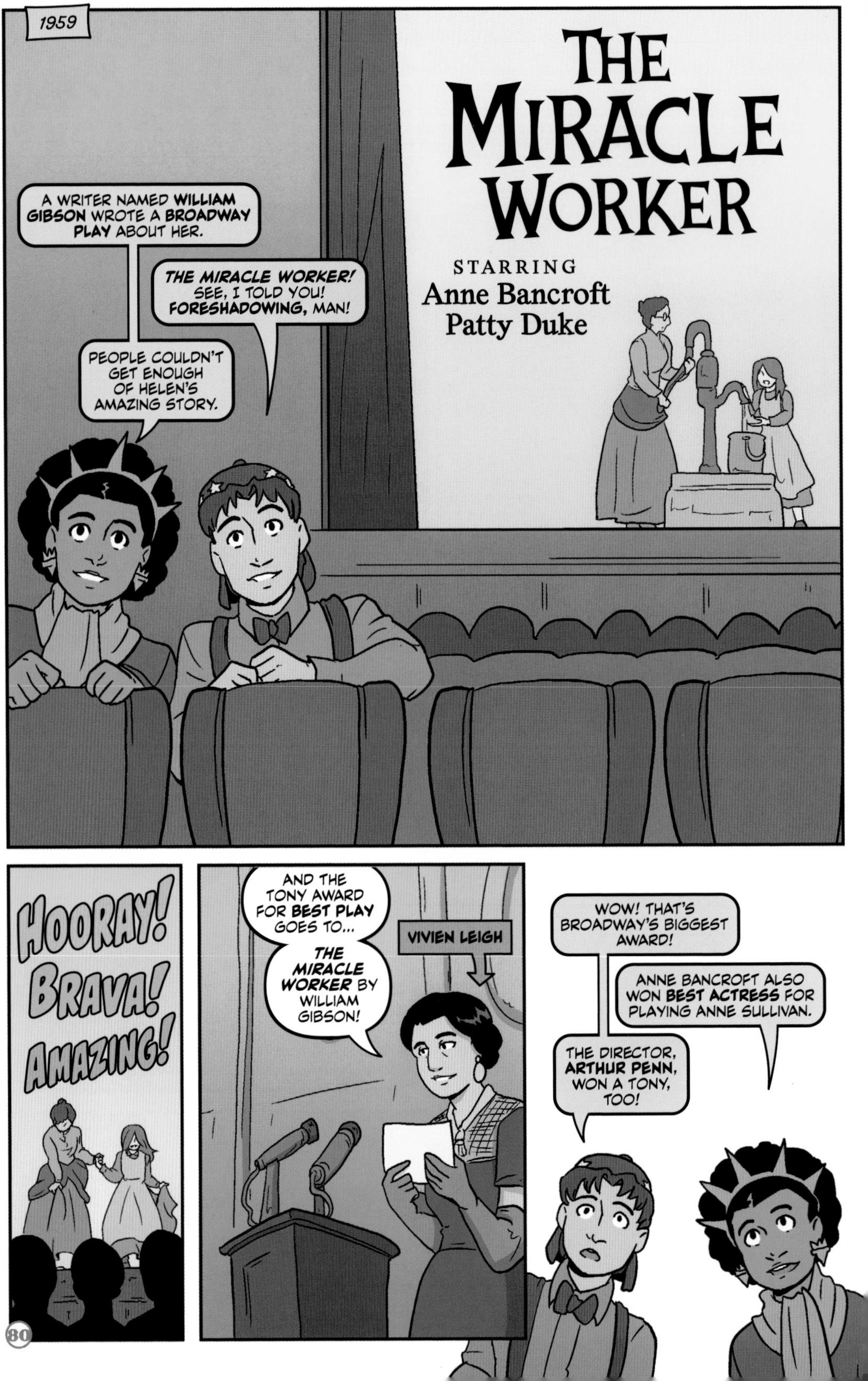
1959
THE MIRACLE WORKER
STARRING
Anne Bancroft
Patty Duke
A WRITER NAMED WILLIAM GIBSON WROTE A BROADWAY PLAY ABOUT HER.
THE MIRACLE WORKER! SEE, I TOLD YOU! FORESHADOWING, MAN!
PEOPLE COULDN'T GET ENOUGH OF HELEN'S AMAZING STORY.
HOORAY! BRAVA! AMAZING!
AND THE TONY AWARD FOR BEST PLAY GOES TO...
THE MIRACLE WORKER BY WILLIAM GIBSON!
VIVIEN LEIGH
WOW! THAT'S BROADWAY'S BIGGEST AWARD!
ANNE BANCROFT ALSO WON BEST ACTRESS FOR PLAYING ANNE SULLIVAN.
THE DIRECTOR, ARTHUR PENN, WON A TONY, TOO!

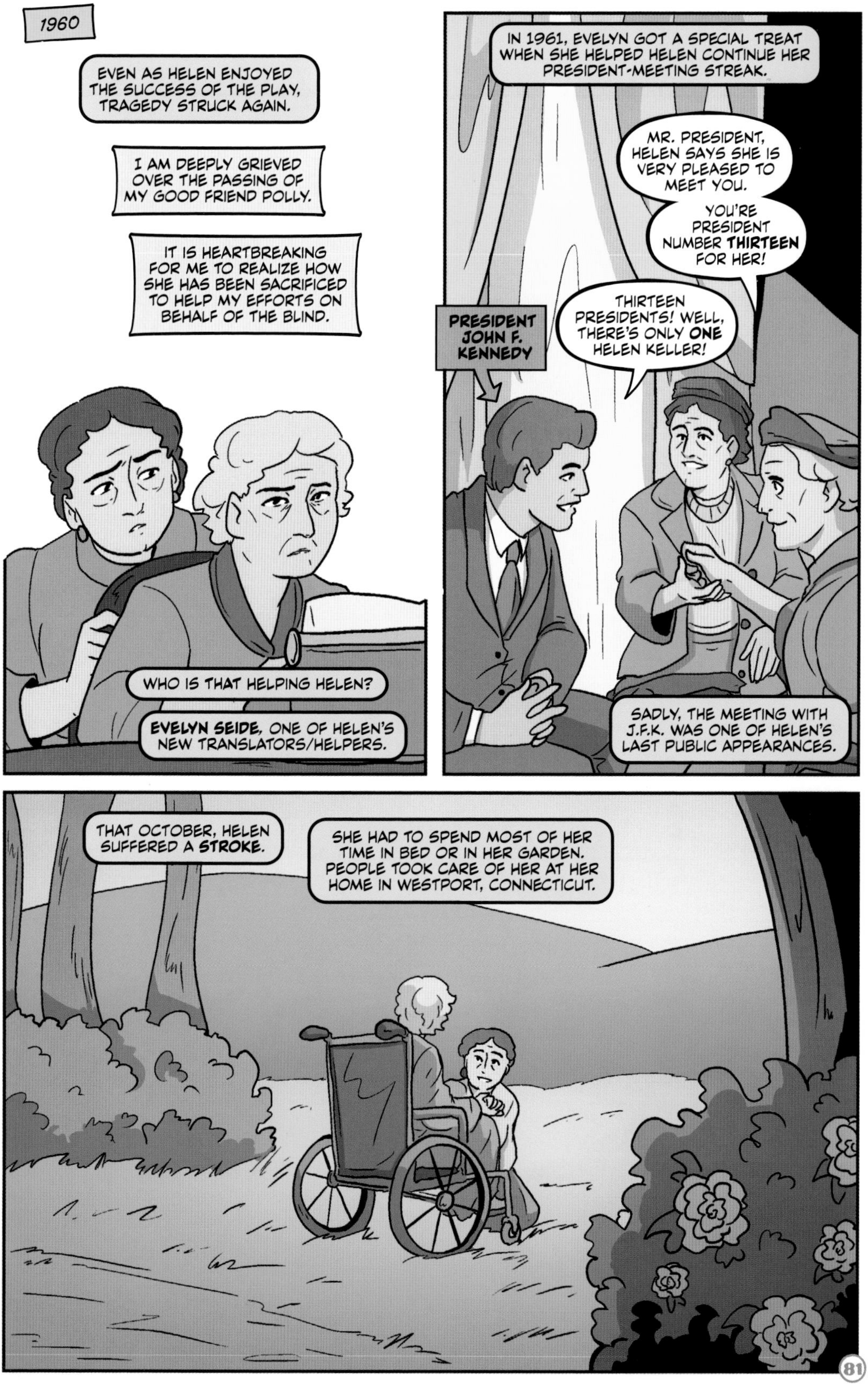
1960
EVEN AS HELEN ENJOYED THE SUCCESS OF THE PLAY, TRAGEDY STRUCK AGAIN.
I AM DEEPLY GRIEVED OVER THE PASSING OF MY GOOD FRIEND POLLY.
IT IS HEARTBREAKING FOR ME TO REALIZE HOW SHE HAS BEEN SACRIFICED TO HELP MY EFFORTS ON BEHALF OF THE BLIND.
WHO IS THAT HELPING HELEN?
EVELYN SEIDE, ONE OF HELEN'S NEW TRANSLATORS/HELPERS.
IN 1961, EVELYN GOT A SPECIAL TREAT WHEN SHE HELPED HELEN CONTINUE HER PRESIDENT-MEETING STREAK.
MR. PRESIDENT, HELEN SAYS SHE IS VERY PLEASED TO MEET YOU.
YOU'RE PRESIDENT NUMBER **THIRTEEN** FOR HER!
PRESIDENT JOHN F. KENNEDY
THIRTEEN PRESIDENTS! WELL, THERE'S ONLY **ONE** HELEN KELLER!
SADLY, THE MEETING WITH J.F.K. WAS ONE OF HELEN'S LAST PUBLIC APPEARANCES.
THAT OCTOBER, HELEN SUFFERED A **STROKE**.
SHE HAD TO SPEND MOST OF HER TIME IN BED OR IN HER GARDEN. PEOPLE TOOK CARE OF HER AT HER HOME IN WESTPORT, CONNECTICUT.

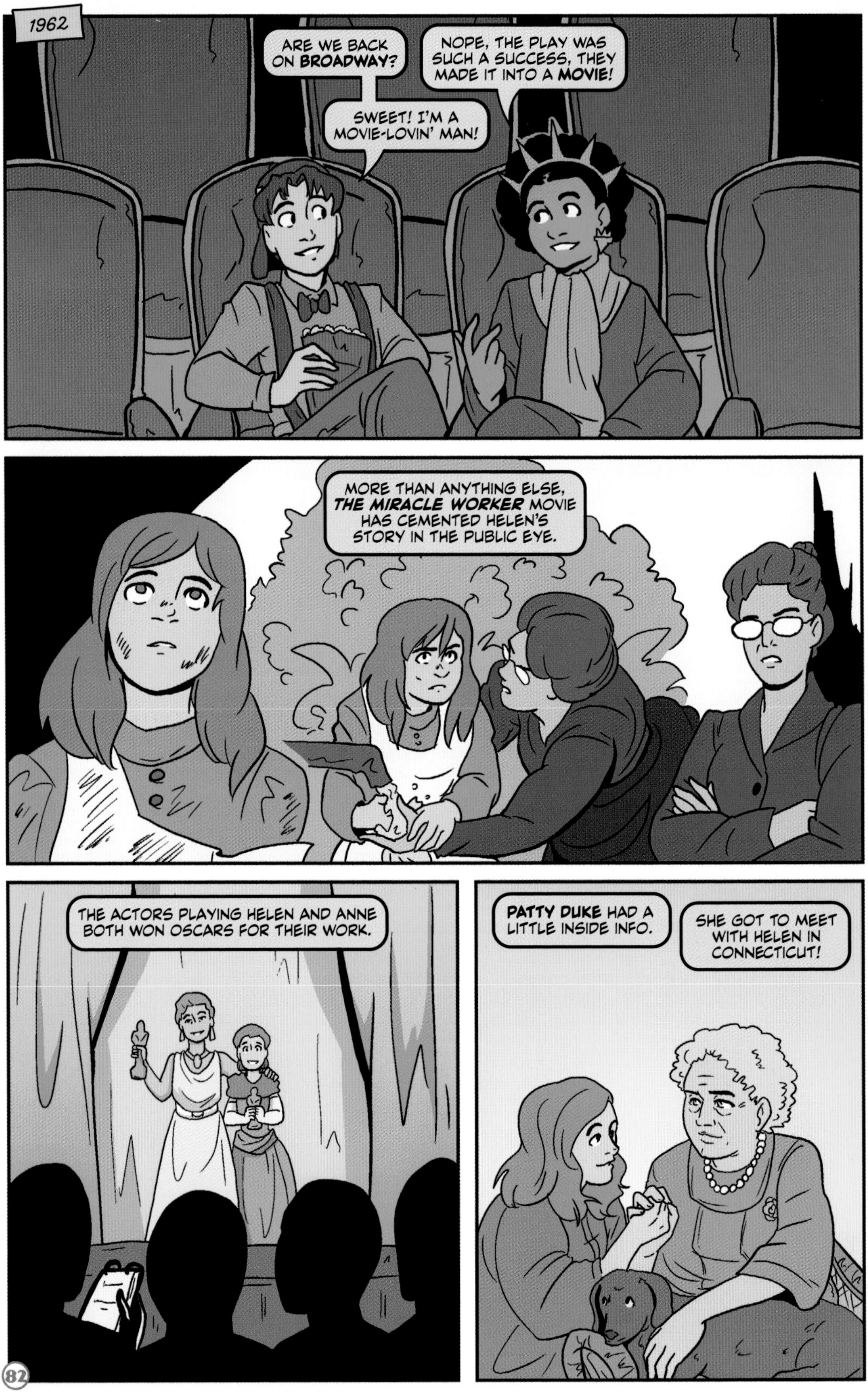
1962
ARE WE BACK ON BROADWAY?
SWEET! I'M A MOVIE-LOVIN' MAN!
NOPE, THE PLAY WAS SUCH A SUCCESS, THEY MADE IT INTO A MOVIE!
MORE THAN ANYTHING ELSE, THE MIRACLE WORKER MOVIE HAS CEMENTED HELEN'S STORY IN THE PUBLIC EYE.
THE ACTORS PLAYING HELEN AND ANNE BOTH WON OSCARS FOR THEIR WORK.
PATTY DUKE HAD A LITTLE INSIDE INFO.
SHE GOT TO MEET WITH HELEN IN CONNECTICUT!

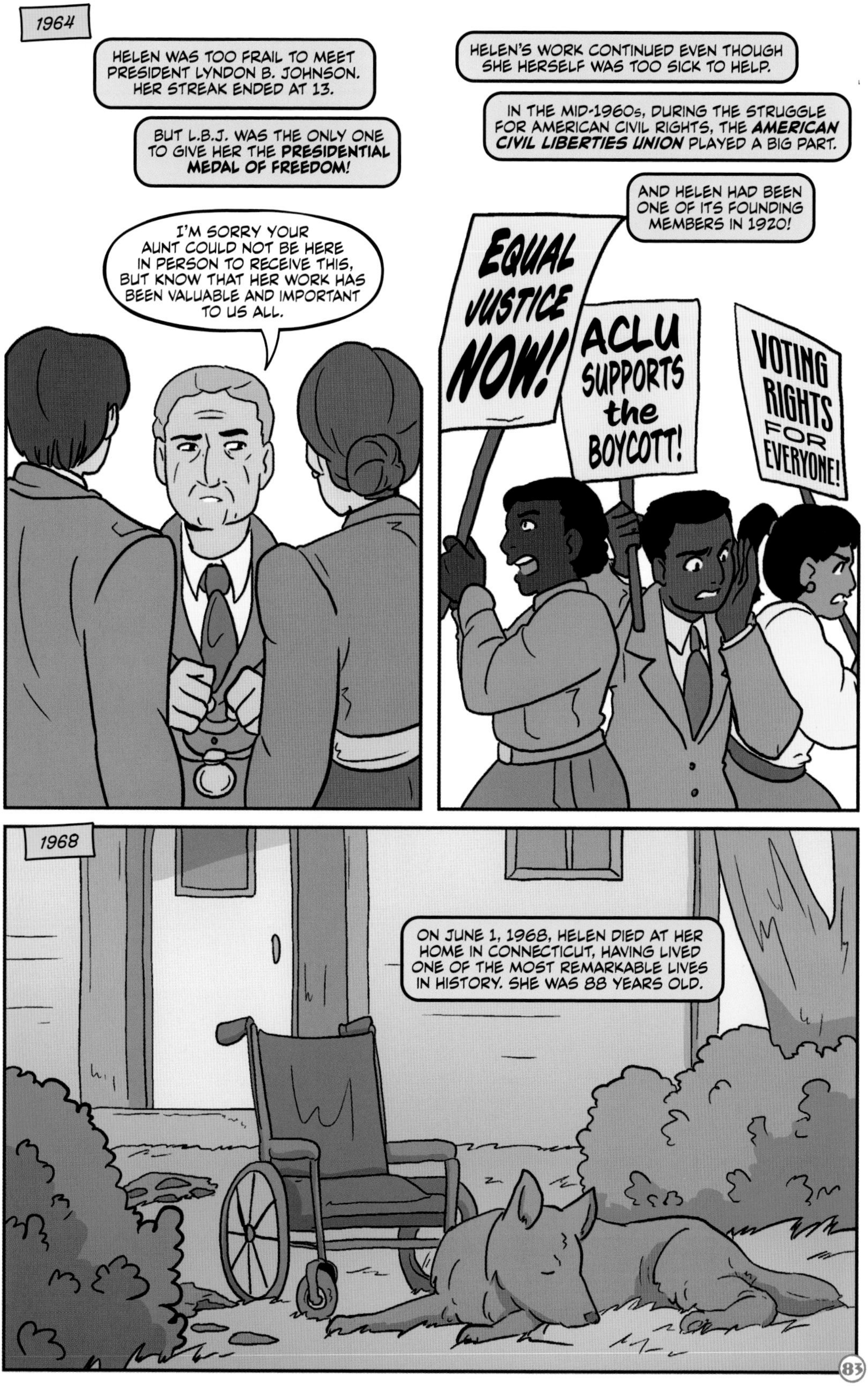
1964
HELEN WAS TOO FRAIL TO MEET PRESIDENT LYNDON B. JOHNSON. HER STREAK ENDED AT 13.
BUT L.B.J. WAS THE ONLY ONE TO GIVE HER THE **PRESIDENTIAL MEDAL OF FREEDOM!**
I'M SORRY YOUR AUNT COULD NOT BE HERE IN PERSON TO RECEIVE THIS, BUT KNOW THAT HER WORK HAS BEEN VALUABLE AND IMPORTANT TO US ALL.
HELEN'S WORK CONTINUED EVEN THOUGH SHE HERSELF WAS TOO SICK TO HELP.
IN THE MID-1960s, DURING THE STRUGGLE FOR AMERICAN CIVIL RIGHTS, THE ***AMERICAN CIVIL LIBERTIES UNION*** PLAYED A BIG PART.
AND HELEN HAD BEEN ONE OF ITS FOUNDING MEMBERS IN 1920!
EQUAL JUSTICE NOW!
ACLU SUPPORTS the BOYCOTT!
VOTING RIGHTS FOR EVERYONE!
1968
ON JUNE 1, 1968, HELEN DIED AT HER HOME IN CONNECTICUT, HAVING LIVED ONE OF THE MOST REMARKABLE LIVES IN HISTORY. SHE WAS 88 YEARS OLD.

National Cathedral, Washington, D.C.

SHE WILL **LIVE ON,** ONE OF THE FEW, THE IMMORTAL NAMES NOT BORN TO DIE.

HER SPIRIT WILL ENDURE AS LONG AS MAN CAN **READ** AND STORIES CAN BE TOLD OF THE WOMAN WHO SHOWED THE WORLD THERE ARE NO BOUNDARIES TO **COURAGE** AND **FAITH.**

ALABAMA SENATOR LISTER HILL

THE CHOIR FROM THE **PERKINS SCHOOL FOR THE BLIND** PERFORMED AT HELEN'S FUNERAL SERVICE.

HELEN'S ASHES WERE PLACED ALONGSIDE ANNE'S IN THE CATHEDRAL.

HELEN KELLER AND HER LIFELONG COMPANION ANNE SULLIVAN

ID HER LIFELON COMPANION ANNE SULLIVAN

TODAY, YOU CAN STILL FIND A PLAQUE WITH HER NAME IN BRAILLE, WORN DOWN FROM THOUSANDS OF HANDS READING IT OVER THE YEARS.

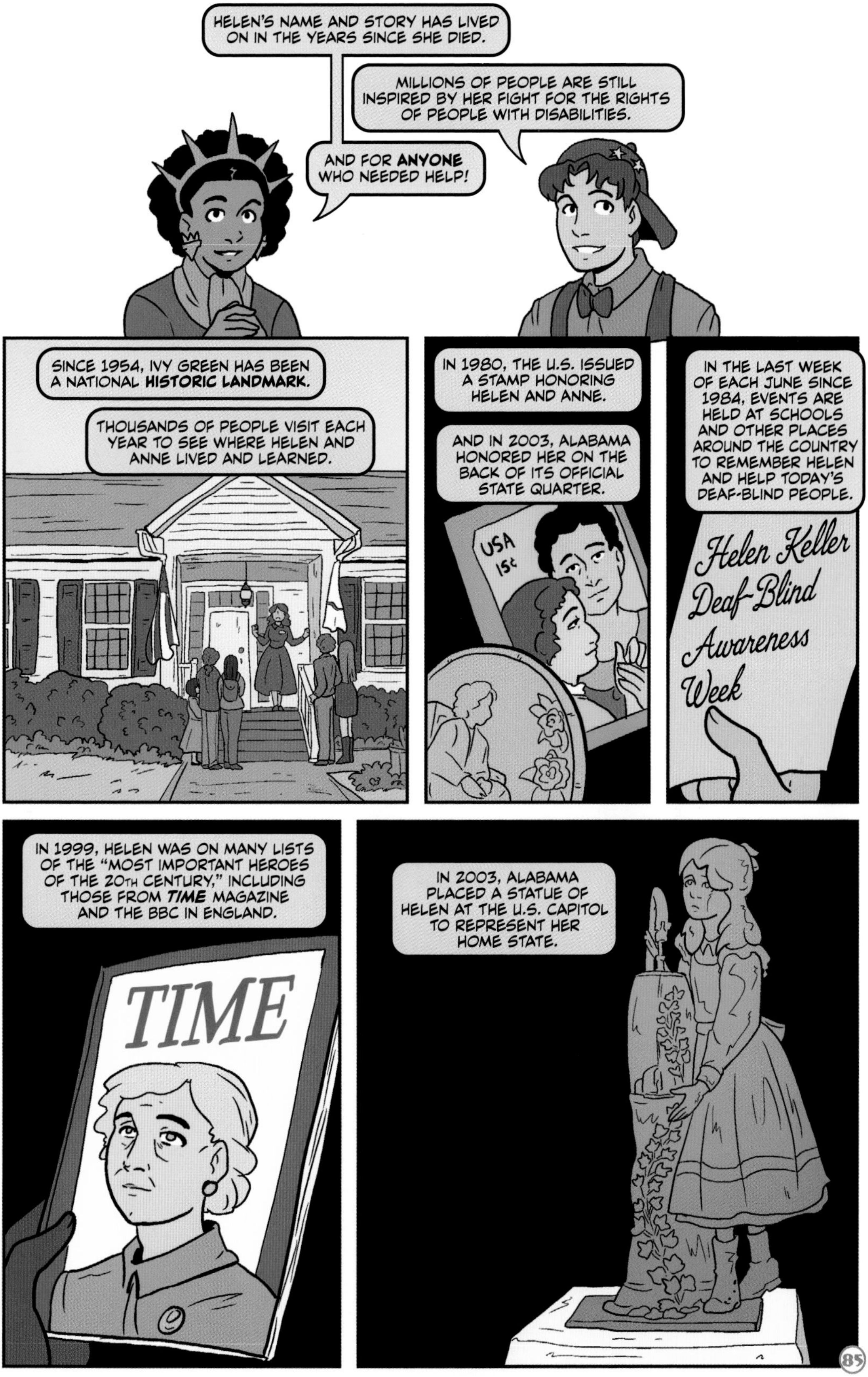
HELEN'S NAME AND STORY HAS LIVED ON IN THE YEARS SINCE SHE DIED.
MILLIONS OF PEOPLE ARE STILL INSPIRED BY HER FIGHT FOR THE RIGHTS OF PEOPLE WITH DISABILITIES.
AND FOR ANYONE WHO NEEDED HELP!
SINCE 1954, IVY GREEN HAS BEEN A NATIONAL HISTORIC LANDMARK.
THOUSANDS OF PEOPLE VISIT EACH YEAR TO SEE WHERE HELEN AND ANNE LIVED AND LEARNED.
IN 1980, THE U.S. ISSUED A STAMP HONORING HELEN AND ANNE.
AND IN 2003, ALABAMA HONORED HER ON THE BACK OF ITS OFFICIAL STATE QUARTER.
USA 15¢
IN THE LAST WEEK OF EACH JUNE SINCE 1984, EVENTS ARE HELD AT SCHOOLS AND OTHER PLACES AROUND THE COUNTRY TO REMEMBER HELEN AND HELP TODAY'S DEAF-BLIND PEOPLE.
Helen Keller Deaf-Blind Awareness Week
IN 1999, HELEN WAS ON MANY LISTS OF THE "MOST IMPORTANT HEROES OF THE 20TH CENTURY," INCLUDING THOSE FROM TIME MAGAZINE AND THE BBC IN ENGLAND.
TIME
IN 2003, ALABAMA PLACED A STATUE OF HELEN AT THE U.S. CAPITOL TO REPRESENT HER HOME STATE.

IT TOOK A LONG TIME, BUT IN 1990, AMERICA FINALLY PASSED A LAW THAT HAS IMPROVED THE LIVES OF MILLIONS OF PEOPLE WITH DISABILITIES OF ALL KINDS.
WITH TODAY'S SIGNING OF THE LANDMARK **AMERICANS WITH DISABILITIES ACT**, EVERY MAN, WOMAN, AND CHILD WITH A DISABILITY CAN NOW PASS THROUGH ONCE-CLOSED DOORS INTO A BRIGHT NEW ERA OF EQUALITY, INDEPENDENCE, AND FREEDOM.
POST OFFICE
PRESIDENT GEORGE H.W. BUSH
AMERICA IS HOME TO MORE THAN 35,000 PEOPLE WHO ARE DEAF-BLIND. ALONG WITH LAWS LIKE THE **ADA**, THEY HAVE BEEN HELPED BY TECHNOLOGY.
IMAGINE WHAT HELEN COULD HAVE DONE WITH SOME OF THESE TOOLS!
TTY DEVICES *CAN BE USED TO MAKE PHONE CALLS.*
AN OPERATOR HEARS THE SPOKEN WORDS AND SENDS THEM IN BRAILLE TO THE DEAF-BLIND PERSON.
THAT PERSON TYPES ANSWERS IN BRAILLE THAT ARE THEN READ OUT LOUD TO THE OTHER CALLER.
SMARTPHONES ARE TRICKY, SINCE YOU NEED TO SEE THE SCREEN. BUT A MIX OF APPS AND TECH HELP DEAF-BLIND PEOPLE USE SOME SMARTPHONES.
OMG! DID YOU SEE WHAT JENN WROTE?
YES! SHE IS SO FUNNY!
YEAH, I AM TOTALLY ROFL.
YEAH, I AM TOTALLY ROFL.

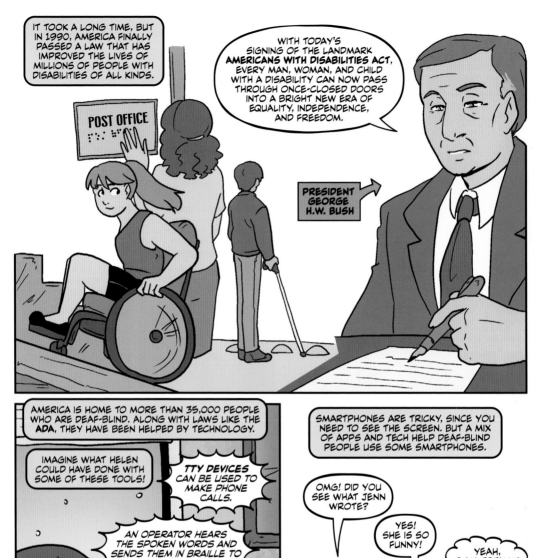

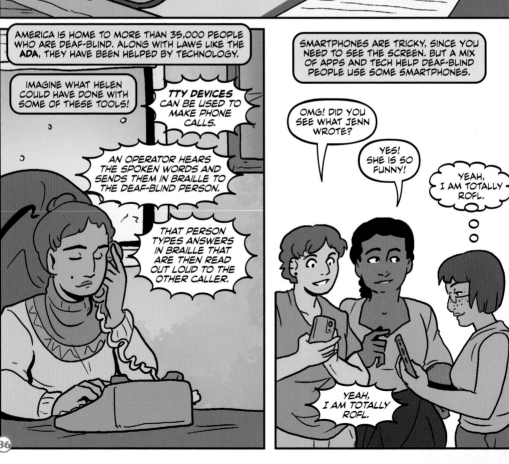

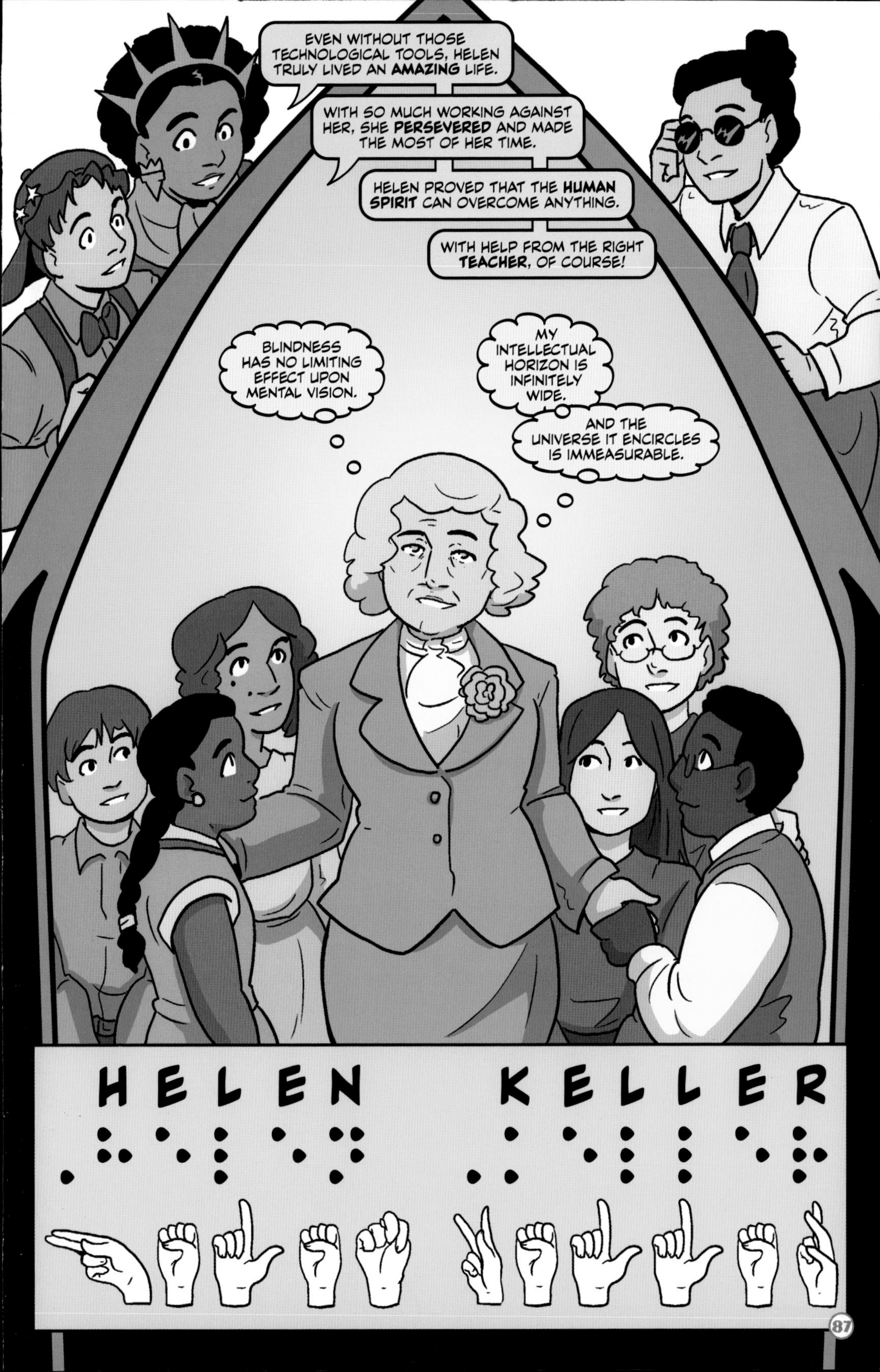

EVEN WITHOUT THOSE TECHNOLOGICAL TOOLS, HELEN TRULY LIVED AN AMAZING LIFE.
WITH SO MUCH WORKING AGAINST HER, SHE PERSEVERED AND MADE THE MOST OF HER TIME.
HELEN PROVED THAT THE HUMAN SPIRIT CAN OVERCOME ANYTHING.
WITH HELP FROM THE RIGHT TEACHER, OF COURSE!
BLINDNESS HAS NO LIMITING EFFECT UPON MENTAL VISION.
MY INTELLECTUAL HORIZON IS INFINITELY WIDE.
AND THE UNIVERSE IT ENCIRCLES IS IMMEASURABLE.
HELEN KELLER

TALKING

HELEN AND ANNE USED A VARIETY OF HAND AND FINGER POSITIONS TO SPELL LETTERS INTO EACH OTHER'S HAND. THESE DRAWINGS SHOW THE BASIC POSITIONS FOR EACH LETTER IN AMERICAN SIGN LANGUAGE.

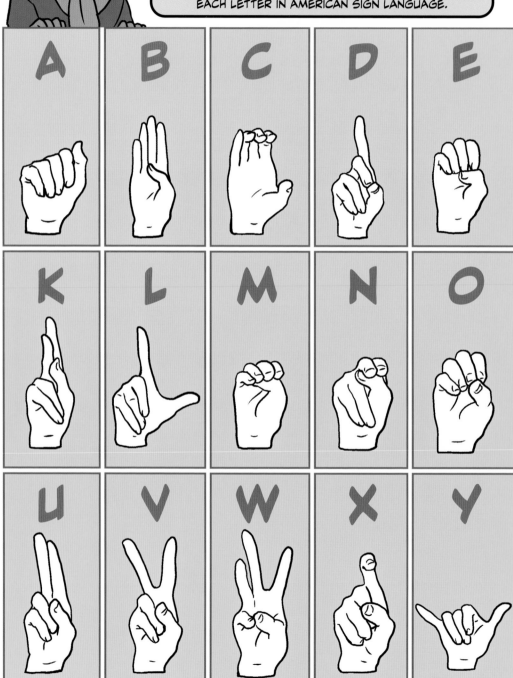

WITH HELEN

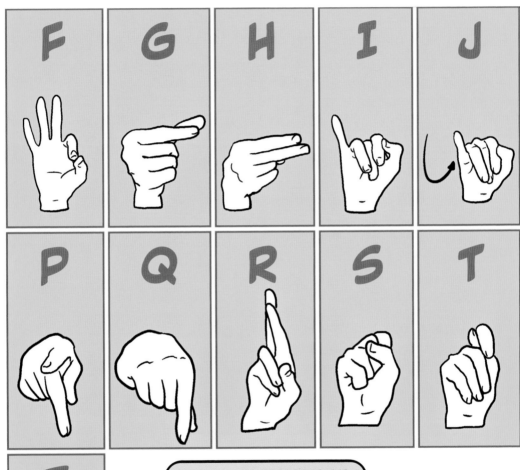

F G H I J

P Q R S T

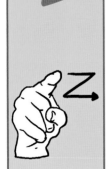

Z

SEE IF YOU CAN PRACTICE THEM WITH A FRIEND. CAN YOU MAKE YOURSELF UNDERSTOOD?

TRY IT WITH YOUR EYES CLOSED AFTER A WHILE. IMAGINE THAT THIS WAS THE ONLY WAY YOU COULD COMMUNICATE OR BE UNDERSTOOD.

HELEN AND ANNE WERE TRULY AMAZING!

OTHER HEROES OF DISABILITY RIGHTS

ADAPT (American Disabled for Accessible Public Transit) led the fight for buses, trains, and city streets to be made safer and better for people in wheelchairs and with other mobility problems. Their campaigns in many cities led to new laws against such discrimination.

JUDY HEUMANN (1947-) helped create the first Center for Independent Living (CIL) in Berkeley, California. She later served in several U.S. government posts that advocated for disability rights.

After her child was born with Down syndrome, **KAY MCGEE (1920-2012)** created the National Association for Down Syndrome in 1963, the first major organization dedicated to helping people with that genetic disease.

ED ROBERTS (1939-1995) had polio when he was 14. Because he became paralyzed from the neck down, he lived the rest of his life in an iron lung. Nevertheless, he earned two degrees from University of California, Berkeley. While there, he helped create the first CIL, a movement that spread around the United States. He later helped found the World Institute on Disability.

EUNICE SHRIVER (1921-2009) helped create and promote the Special Olympics. Now an international organization, the group puts on sports, games, and competitions for people with developmental disabilities.

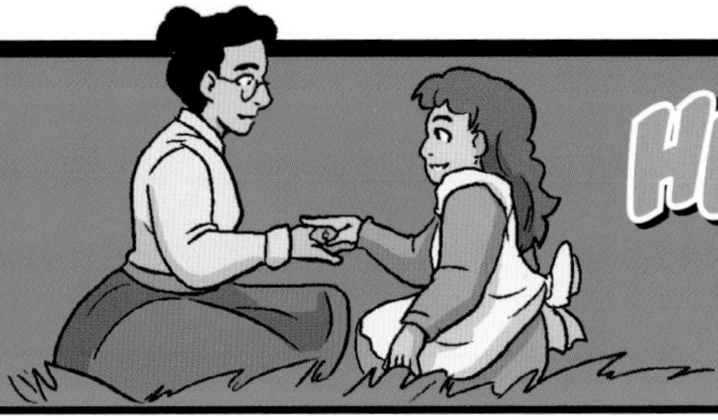

HELEN KELLER TIMELINE

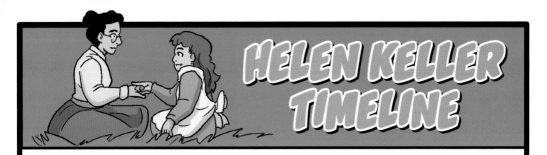

1880 Helen is born on June 27 in Alabama.

1882 After being struck with an illness, loses sight and hearing.

1887 Meets teacher Anne Sullivan of Perkins School for first time; Sullivan begins to teach Helen a form of sign language.

1891 Helen removed from Perkins School after "copying" a story and presenting it as her own.

1894 Begins studies at a school in New York City.

1900 Enters Radcliffe College.

1903 Publishes first book, *The Story of My Life.*

1904 Graduates from Radcliffe -- the first deaf-blind person to do so.

1908 Publishes *The World I Live In*.

1919 Goes on tour with Sullivan to do vaudeville, as well as give speeches.

1924 Takes job as spokesperson for American Foundation for the Blind.

1937 Visits Japan to promote disabled rights there.

1946 Begins a 35-nation world tour that she completes over the course of 11 years.

1955 Wins an honorary Oscar for her work on a documentary about her life.

1956 *The Miracle Worker*, a play about her and Sullivan, opens on Broadway.

1962 A film version of *The Miracle Worker* opens.

1964 Awarded Presidential Medal of Freedom.

1968 Dies at the age of 88.

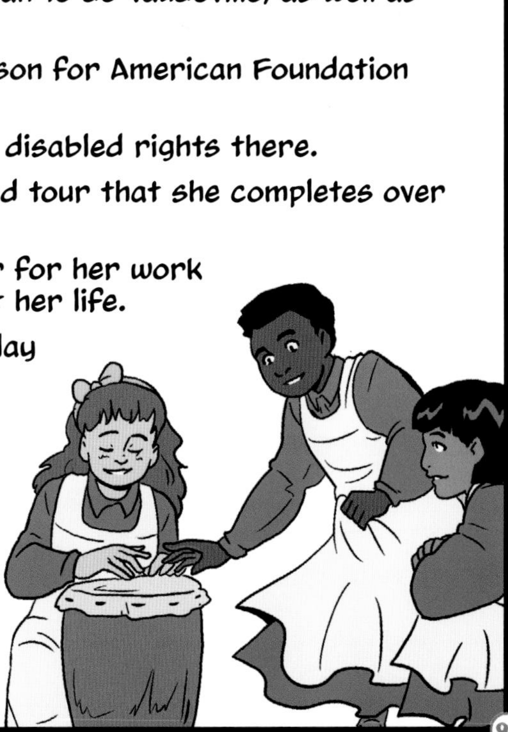

GLOSSARY

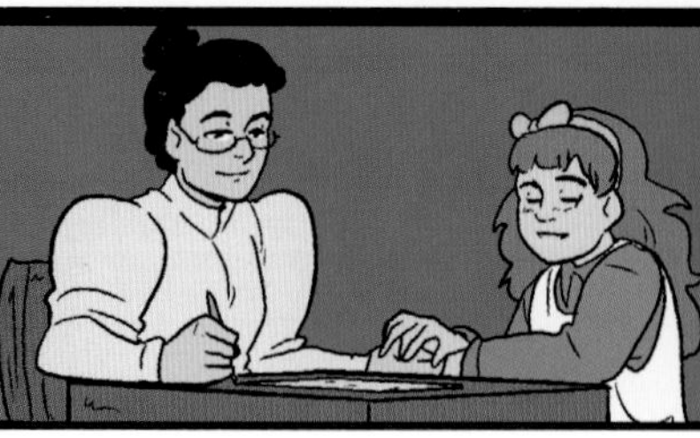

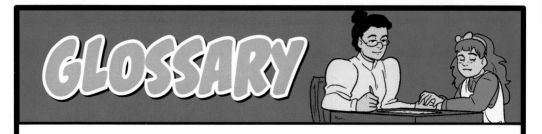

CIRCUMVENT: Find a way around something.

EARNESTLY: With great eagerness and enthusiasm.

FORESHADOWING: In literature, information that peeks ahead to later events.

GUARDIAN: A person legally responsible for another person.

HEARSAY: Words reported as being spoken by someone else, usually implying that they are not true.

INCALCULABLE: Describing an enormous amount, so large it can't be counted.

INDEFATIGABLE: Unable to become tired; resilient.

ISOLATION: The experience of being all alone.

MISCHIEF: Light-hearted troublemaking.

MUTE: Unable to speak.

PLAGIARISM: Copying the work of someone else and presenting it as your own.

REPROACH: Express disapproval.

SOLDIERED: Carried on in spite of obstacles.

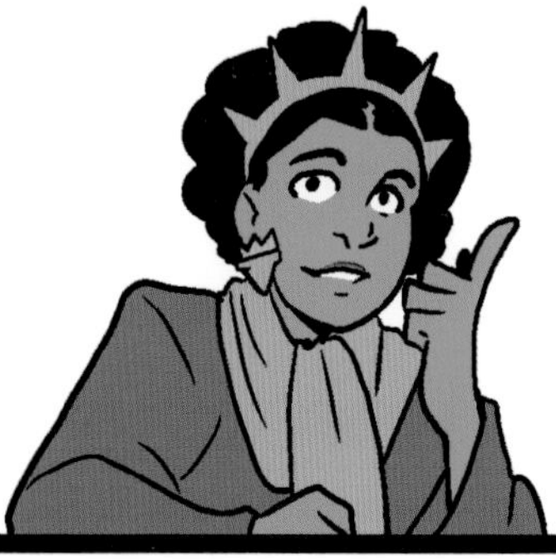

SPECULATORS: People who invest money, often on risky investments, with an eye to make more money.

VAUDEVILLE: A type of live entertainment that is made up of many small, short acts on a stage.

FIND OUT MORE

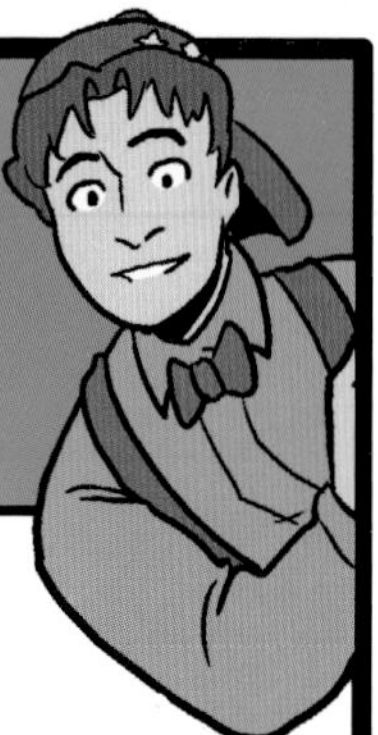

BOOKS

Davidson, Margaret. *Helen Keller*. Scholastic Biography series. New York: Scholastic, 1969.

Herrmann, Dorothy. *Helen Keller: A Life.* Chicago: University of Chicago Press, 2007.

Keller, Helen. *The Story of My Life.* New York: Dover Edition, 1996. (Originally published in 1903.)

Keller, Helen. *The World I Live In.* Public Domain.

Romero, Libby. *Helen Keller.* DK Life Stories series. New York: DK Publishing, 2019.

Thompson, Gare. *Who Was Helen Keller?* Who Was? series. New York: Penguin Group, 2003.

WEBSITES

American Foundation for the Blind: Helen Keller
www.afb.org/about-afb/history/helen-keller

National Center on Deaf-Blindness
www.nationaldb.org

Perkins School for the Blind: Helen Keller
www.perkins.org/history/people/helen-keller

VIDEOS

Hamilton, Nancy. *The Unconquered: Helen Keller in Her Story.* Albert Margolies Co., 1955.

Penn, Arthur. *The Miracle Worker.* Los Angeles: United Artists, 1962.

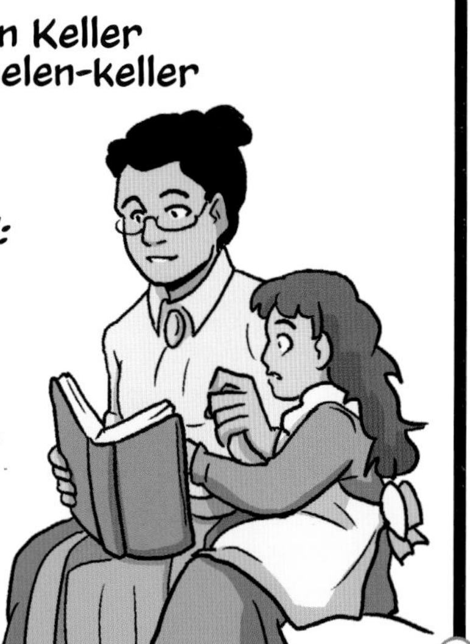

SHOW ME HISTORY!

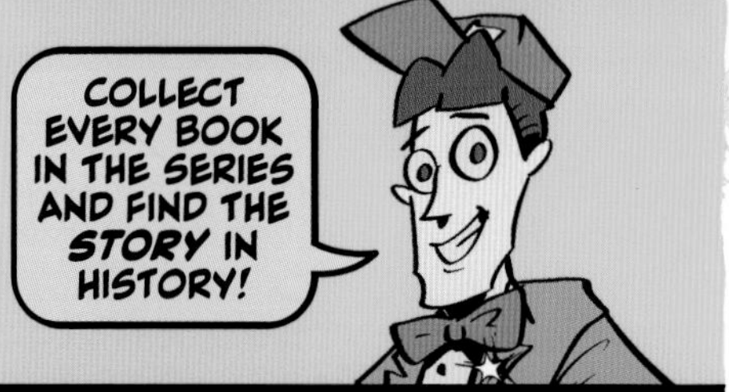
COLLECT EVERY BOOK IN THE SERIES AND FIND THE *STORY* IN HISTORY!

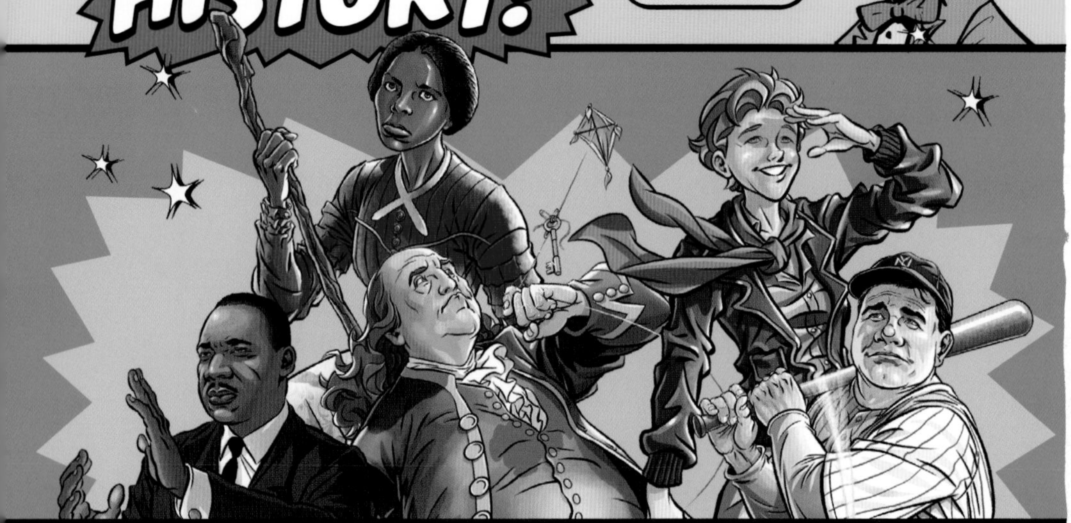

ABRAHAM LINCOLN
DEFENDER OF THE UNION!

ALBERT EINSTEIN
GENIUS OF SPACE AND TIME!

ALEXANDER HAMILTON
THE FIGHTING FOUNDING FATHER!

AMELIA EARHART
PIONEER OF THE SKY!

BABE RUTH
BASEBALL'S ALL-TIME BEST!

BENJAMIN FRANKLIN
INVENTOR OF THE NATION!

GEORGE WASHINGTON
SOLDIER AND STATESMAN!

HARRIET TUBMAN
FIGHTER FOR FREEDOM!

HELEN KELLER
INSPIRATION TO EVERYONE!

JESUS
MESSENGER OF PEACE!

MARTIN LUTHER KING JR.
VOICE FOR EQUALITY!

MUHAMMAD ALI
THE GREATEST OF ALL TIME!

SACAGAWEA
COURAGEOUS TRAILBLAZER!

SUSAN B. ANTHONY
CHAMPION FOR VOTING RIGHTS!

WALT DISNEY
THE MAGICAL INNOVATOR!

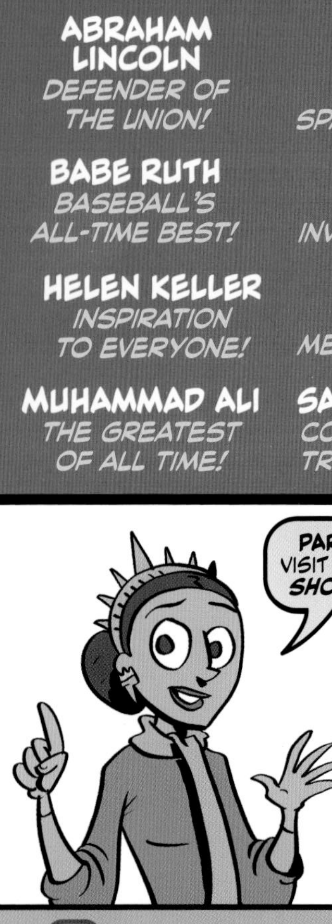

PARENTS AND TEACHERS: VISIT OUR WEBSITE FOR MORE *SHOW ME HISTORY!* FUN...

SHOWMEHISTORY.COM

... WHERE YOU CAN LEARN MORE ABOUT THE AUTHORS, SIGN UP FOR OUR EMAIL NEWSLETTER, AND DOWNLOAD OUR READING GUIDES!

ALSO FOLLOW US ON **SOCIAL MEDIA!**

@showmehistorybooks | www.facebook.com/portablepress | www.pinterest.com/portablepress | @portablepress

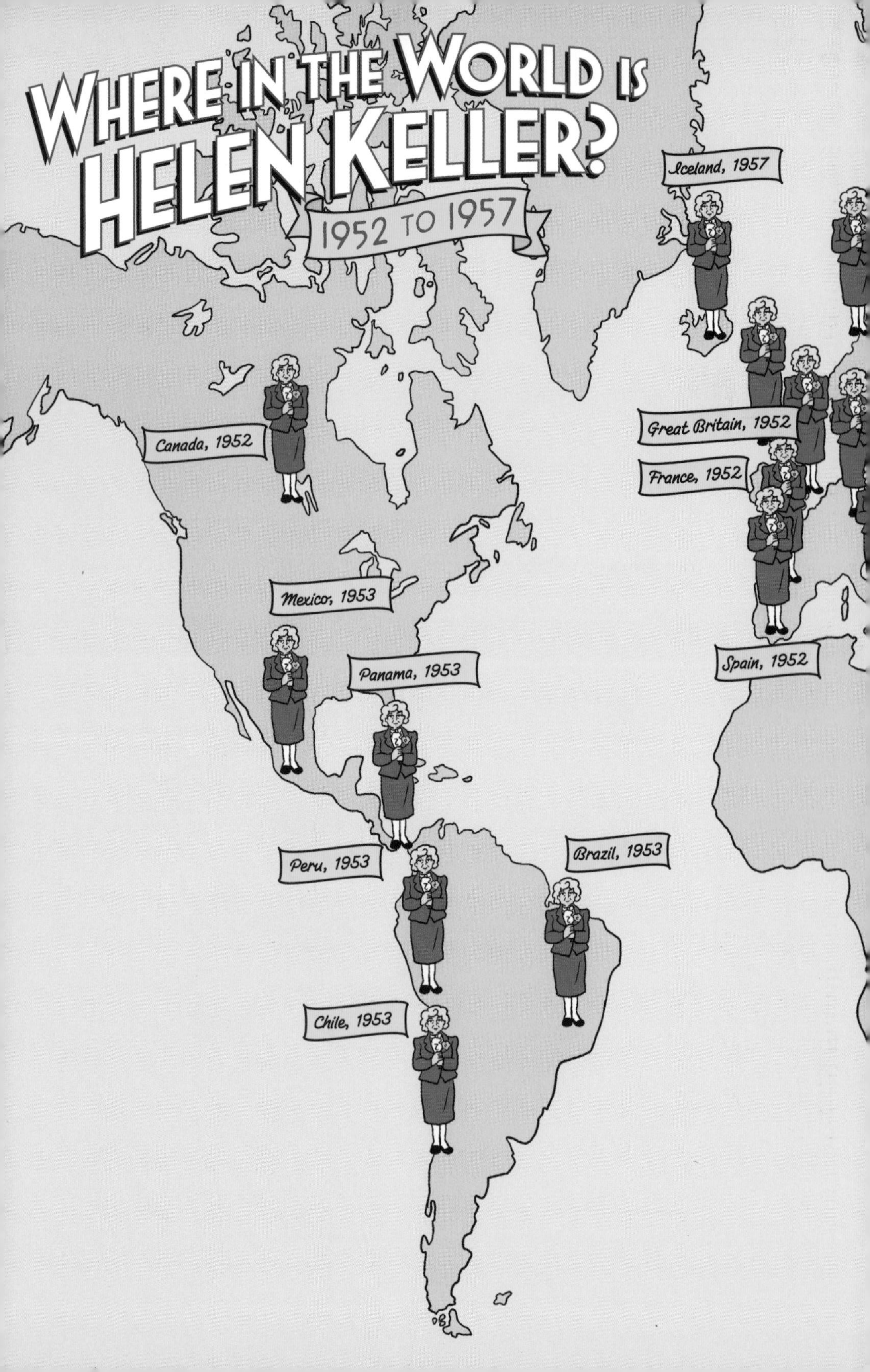
WHERE IN THE WORLD IS HELEN KELLER?
1952 TO 1957
Iceland, 1957
Canada, 1952
Great Britain, 1952
France, 1952
Mexico, 1953
Panama, 1953
Spain, 1952
Peru, 1953
Brazil, 1953
Chile, 1953